LET'S TALK ABOUT CATS

Conversations On Feline Behaviour

Anita Kelsey

KiZa

Contents

Introduction

Let's Talk About Cats is an extension of my thirst for knowledge of all things feline, and my desire to share that knowledge with other people who are passionate about the personality, beauty and spirit of cats. Initially, as a person who works with cats every day either grooming them or working on feline behaviour issues, I was interested in the light other experts could shed on various subject matters close to my heart. What else could I learn from their approach and philosophy?

This led me to delve deeper into the special and unique relationships that people have with cats, which is what fascinates me. Life with my two lovely Norwegian Forest beauties, Kiki and Zaza, has been a rollercoaster of emotions. They hold up a mirror to my failings as well as my successes, as I try to give them the very best life. I continue to be challenged in certain areas and excel in others, but their affection never lessens.

All cat lovers can say, with hands on hearts, that we've had our lives changed by cats. Cats are masters at weaving their way into the very core of our souls without changing many of their own distinct characteristics, which in itself is astonishing. With one weakness shown, the cat can detect it and manipulate us to perfection. The cat experts who have contributed to this book help take you on a journey that ends with a deeper love for these beautiful and noble creatures.

My love of cats started as a young child. My first cat was called Sooty. He was a large free-roaming black-and-white moggie that was a bundle of affection. I didn't understand cat psychology then and cringe at the memories of me teasing Sooty. I would place him on top of the wardrobe and find it funny as he tried to work out ways to get down. I would poke him annoyingly as he tried to sleep because I wanted his attention and because – though I was too young to think about it in this way – I felt like he existed for our pleasure only. He was a great example of the stoic tolerance of animals towards human ignorance.

As a family, we showed him love through food and fed him our leftovers resulting in Sooty becoming obese. It's easy to fail the animals we love because we don't understand them. When Sooty became ill with kidney disease, it was a heartbreaking downward spiral.

We clung to the notion that the vets could save him with various medications and injections, when in truth we were all just prolonging his pain. We, as naïve cat owners who didn't want our cat to die, went along with the endless treatment, until one day Sooty decided to take matters into his own hands. He rattled and choked as he went into a fit and was finally rushed to the vets to be put to sleep. Now, as a professional, it pains me to think back to those years. End-of-life care for cats is practised in a completely different way, and I'm now happy to see vets, such as Dr. Amy Bergs, offer mobile special palliative guidance for cat owners to help them not only to manage the last months or weeks of their pet's life, but also to advise when it's time to say goodbye.

My work with cats started ten years ago when I experienced the death of a close friend. I had never felt grief before: I had been shielded from its menacing grip. When I learned that my friend had taken their own life, my legs crumpled and I howled like an animal caught in a trap. The pain was piercing, as if someone had scratched my heart from the inside with a razor. At the time, I was working in the music industry, but from then on I struggled to sing or to enter the recording studio to work. Something profound had changed within me. I cried on and off for two years, feeling guilt, pain and sorrow.

The truth is that cats saved me.

I decided to change career. I started a successful cat-care company and began formal training in feline grooming and behaviour. After five years, I received a first-class honours degree from Middlesex University. I began to write a blog on feline issues, and over time started to add interviews with various people from the cat world who inspired me. That was in 2013. The blog satisfied my own curiosity whilst helping cat owners and cat lovers to make their own informed decisions.

After my first book, *Claws: Confessions Of A Professional Cat Groomer*, was published, I sought to find another idea for a second book. I could have written a sequel to *Claws*, but I wanted to get my teeth into something different.

The idea of combining excerpts of conversations with cat professionals on various subjects kept coming into my mind. The professionals, who were gracious enough to give their time, shared their knowledge and personal insight to make this the best book it can possibly be. I feel gratitude to each and every one of them for sharing with me, and ultimately with us all.

Many of them are authors in their own right and were kind enough to give me permission to use excerpts from their books. I've highlighted this in the chapters where they have been used. A recommended reading section can be found at the back of this book, which lists all of the participants' excellent written work as well as other resources for the information-hungry cat lover.

The book itself is not only about cats but also our relationship with them. I hope within its pages the reader will discover a variety of perspectives and approaches that will help them find something new in the relationships they enjoy with their darling mogs.

I owe this book to Sooty. He would be proud of me. I know a lot about cats now.

The journey continues ...

CHAPTER ONE
How Can I Bond With My Cat?

'As anyone who has ever been around a cat for any length of time well knows, cats have enormous patience with the limitations of the human kind.'

Cleveland Amory

CHAPTER ONE

In this chapter:

- Learn about the history of the cat.
- Understand what it means to bond with a cat – in conversation with Jackson Galaxy.
- Read a true behaviour case study on rehoming to get the right environment for Dicey the Ragdoll.

To understand how to connect with your cat, you may first want to understand the natural behaviours of the feline species and then understand the inner working of your own specific pet. In other words, every cat has a unique personality and – alongside basic evolutionary behaviours – reacts to situations in their own special way.

On my journey as a cat behaviourist, I have often come across cat carers who cannot understand why their cat isn't like their previous one (now sadly passed away), or who want their cat to be a certain way as 'naturally, all cats like to be stroked and cuddled'. As with everything, to understand the present we must first understand and appreciate the past, and this is also true of the ancestral journey of our cats.

Cats have a complicated history, which countless books cover in great depth, but briefly, our domestic cat's origins can be traced back to the wild cat in Africa, tamed and cross-bred to get the domestic moggie we have today. Talking about the variety of domestic cats would be another book altogether! The cat has played many roles since it first linked up with humans, which could be as far back as 4,000 years ago with the advent of ancient Egyptian agriculture[1], although a further discovery has been made in Cyprus of a cat buried with its human that dates back 9,000 years.

Cats, introduced to Europe and various continents via merchant-trading vessels, were at first seen not so much as pets but as working animals. They were given the job of catching rats, especially after the black rat (the carrier of the bubonic plague) ravaged the Mediterranean region during the 1st century[2]. It was probably also cats' special ability to catch vermin that earned them such high esteem in ancient Egypt, especially on land where corn was growing. With the personality of the cat being mysterious and aloof, this gradually turned into adoration and worship[3]. This extended to China, Rome and Greece, who also welcomed cats for their ability to catch vermin.

Working mills around the world were known to use cats to kill rats and mice hiding within the corn sacks. One of the mills with a record of keeping working cats was Briggate Mill in Norfolk[4] and others include Embreeville Mill, Pennsylvania and Cooper Mill, Washington[5].

Cats were also used on ships for rodent control dating back to ancient times. This kind of work would be essential on a ship, due to rats and mice eating the food stored for the crew, chewing through ropes and carrying the plague, the 'Black Death' being a major disaster, believed to have been caused by rats carrying the disease on to a ship[6].

Many other working establishments, such as storehouses, factories, government offices, museums and train stations used cats for rodent control. One cat called Towser even got into the *Guinness Book of Records* for killing an estimated 28,899 mice during its working life at Scotland's oldest distillery from 1963 to 1987[7].

When Emperor Theodosius declared Christianity a state religion around 400 AD and all other religions, such as the worship of pagan gods and goddesses, died off, cats saw a downturn in their fortunes, and soon entered the darkest period of their history with the burning of witches (nearly always women) and their cats, which were seen as 'The Devil's Helper' during the medieval period[8,9]. The cat's biology, the glowing light-reflected eyes and the blood-curdling howl of the female cat as the male withdraws after sexual penetration, were misunderstood and, although these factors were seen in a positive light during Egyptian times, these natural biological reactions came to be seen as demonic and things to be vilified[10]. Thankfully, cats' fortunes have since revived, and now they are acknowledged as being the wonderful pets we share our lives with today.

You now know a brief history of our cats' past and that, not only are we dealing with little hunters, but with animals that have their own personality traits too. A 'double whammy' to consider when working towards that special connection.

There are no benefits to seeing cats through our own emotions. This is what we call anthropomorphism and is the foundation of many cat–human relationship misinterpretations leading to prolonged anxieties on both sides. Sometimes it takes time and patience before the true character and personality of a cat rises to the surface. This is certainly true of cats who come from a rescue situation and who may not shine as brightly as they can on the start of a new journey with their prospective owner. This is why animal rescue centres place the most emphasis on volunteers spending time with the shyest or most aggressive cats, because these cats need the most help and are the most overlooked. In countries where 'kill shelters' are the norm, first impressions can be a matter of life and death. Most of us who work with cats know that they react very differently in rescue centres than in their final adoption homes. Removing a cat from a stressful or fearful situation can help them to find their way back to a normal relaxed state, which is why cat fosterers, who work closely with a cat over months in their own homes in order to gain their trust, are worth their weight in gold.

The only person I felt who could enhance this chapter in the way it deserves was US cat behaviour and wellness expert Jackson Galaxy, who was transformed into a TV star after hosting *My Cat From Hell* on Animal Planet. Jackson is a warm, approachable and deeply insightful person who has made it his mission in life to educate us all on why our cats do the things they do, so that we can develop a deeper understanding of them and their needs. From the early success of his TV show to the writing of his first book, *Cat Daddy*, his *'Catification'* book series and the latest book *Total Cat Mojo*, it seemed that Jackson was always set to take over the cat world and become king of the cats. Jackson recognised very early on in his career that all cats have unique personalities, coining the term 'cat mojo' in the process. This means a confident, relaxed, happy state and feeling on top of the world. We all say that we need to 'find one's mojo' when we have perhaps lost our way.

But how many people realise that cats can lose or find their mojo too?

Speaking on the phone from LA, Jackson talked openly with warmth and humour, giving his own personal take on cat–human relations. I first asked him to explain the philosophy behind *Total Cat Mojo* and how it can help humans connect to their cat:

> The inspiration for writing *Total Cat Mojo* was to finally have one definitive resource for people to go to who have been asking me the same questions about cats for years and years. There's a reason I didn't write it before, and that was because I felt it was disingenuous for me to put out a manual about cats and how to fix things, because I thought that was a disservice to the cat. In the same way I think that we, as humans, would probably be upset if somebody wrote *Humans for Dummies*. We want to respect the individual and not think there is a paint-by-numbers solution for everything. What finally really motivated me to move forward with it was a desire to dig beneath the surface to try and fix problems and just help people cultivate a better life with cats.
>
> In the book, I educate people about their cats, and about all cats, and the journey that cats took over millions of years to wind up on our laps. It was about the evolution of our relationship with them and where we are today. Moreover, the book aims to impress that you don't just have a cat. You have a relationship and it happens to be with a cat. As it goes with any relationship, you have an obligation to invest in that relationship if you want it to continue, which means you have to make yourself available and vulnerable to whoever is on the other side. That's a tall order, I believe, for humans: to elevate their animal relationships to a point of equanimity. But that was my goal, and it has been my goal throughout. Whether it's the TV shows or the books or anything else in between, it's to value cats possibly more than we already do.

In Conversation With Jackson Galaxy

What do you feel is the biggest misconception people have about keeping cats?

The biggest misconception, I think – and this is for people who tend to edge more towards dogs than cats – is that they're not an active part of your family. They're more like furniture, and it's part of my goal to debunk that. They're not aloof animals, they just express love in a different way. They're not so attached to the outcome of that love as dogs or humans are, so it's just a matter of learning how they express themselves that I think is really one of the keys. I do think that the biggest misconception is that they're not socially needy, that they're so independent that they don't care about you.

For years, experts have classified the cat as a species that's solitary in nature but I knew Jackson felt differently about this. Of course, it very much depends on the cat's personality and territory but Jackson, having nine cats himself, feels very strongly that it's just another misconception that needs stamping out. As Jackson states:

> It's a shallow idea that they are solitary animals. There are very few animals that are solitary. Community defines us as animals most of the time. Cats will hunt in a solitary way, for the most part, but they are part of a community. Anyone who has ever seen a colony of feral cats would never question that. They operate in a very communal way. There's a ton of stereotypes about cats and it's our job to bust those myths.

Whilst I had Jackson on the phone, I thought I'd ask him about the age-old problem of cats and dogs sharing space together. His series *Dogs vs. Cats* with Zoe Sander, highlights common issues people come across whilst introducing both species to one another in the home.

> Again it's about understanding the two species' natural behaviours, which are polar opposites. Cats will always see a dog as a threat and a dog will see a cat as prey to chase or become very interested in, even if the dog

was brought up with different cats in the past.

I think respecting them as being a different species, although that sounds really elementary, is primary. We tend to forget that their needs are totally different, and that their ways of associating and communicating and forming community are absolutely different. It's like saying I should be able to introduce a buffalo and an aardvark to be OK together. It's a completely different world.

The other thing I think people tend to do is not work on the training aspect of their dog enough. If you want to bring a cat into a home with an existing dog, don't do it until you have a firm grip on your dog's behaviour – that you can have them do a 'down, stay' no matter what's going on. That's the best way to have them meet. If you can't control your dog, you can't control their prey drive based on their breed, so don't bring a cat into the house. If you just haven't worked your training enough or haven't gone to class, do that before you bring the cat home. You only get that one chance to make a good first impression and you don't want to waste it. If you bring them into the same room together and the dog lunges after or chases the cat, then you're going to have a rough time after that. Being able to trust them in the same room together is really important.

Connecting with your cat also means separating your own needs and wants from the realities of what your cat can give you on its own terms. By that I mean looking at the void in one's own life that needs to be filled and the reasons behind getting a cat in the first place. What pressures do we unknowingly place on our cats by putting our own expectations ahead of their true nature?

Each episode of *My Cat From Hell* starts with a promise that you haven't met a cat you cannot help. In my work, I have come across several very difficult cases that have stumped me and which I continue to try to understand. Do you get cases like this?

It's a tough question. I try to look at it from a different angle. What I try to do is think about it in these terms: am I leaving a happier animal than when I first met him or her? In that respect, I don't think I've ever failed.

It's also about asking whether a cat wants to be in a particular situation, and if they perhaps don't, I have that conversation with the guardians. I'm working on one of these right now. We have tried everything and there comes a point where you're trying to put a round peg in a square hole: a round cat in a square house. Sometimes it's not meant to be, and in the worst-case scenario, the most loving thing to do is to find a home that a cat does want to be in, and for guardians to try to switch their mindset from being the parent to the foster parent. It's a very hard thing to do but it's a loving thing to do. That, at the end of the day, I think, is the most important thing.

Do you feel there's something far deeper going on – on a spiritual level – between a guardian and their cat?

Yeah, I think there's a relational spiritual subtext that's always permeating. I think that's part of our job. A lot of the time, cat parents don't want to hear it. I think that one of the most unfortunate things that people like you and I have to deal with is coming into a home, not to be a therapist, but to fix something that's broken and that's an un-winnable situation. I spend a lot more of my time these days setting that up. The stage show that I do right now, and the book that I just wrote, *Total Cat Mojo*... they concentrate on the heart of those things: the relationship, what you do in the relationship and the things that you do that make you feel uncomfortable in the relationship. Being vulnerable to one another is one of those things; being vulnerable to the outcome and not letting your ego dictate how things turn out. It's interesting, because I think that after all these years, that has become a more comfortable place for me to be.

Some UK organisations and behaviourists do not 'get' Jackson's way of doing things, especially his famous meetings with cats where they maul his hands in front of the rolling cameras, and his 'slightly uncomfortable to watch' cat-to-cat meetings, where he has to visually see how they respond to one another and whether any distractions can be managed so that the best way forward is determined. I work the same way. How else can we see at what stage we are at, so we can implement changes? I think Jackson has done more for bridging the gap of understanding about our way of sharing everyday life with domestic cats than practically anyone else on the planet! His unique way of doing things has prevented thousands of cats from being euthanised, and that deserves great praise.

Jackson's views regarding round cats and square houses really resonates with me too, and so I'd like to share one of my behaviour cases with you, in the following Cat Chat. It is about one such 'round' cat called Dicey, who tried to live in a square house with disastrous consequences. Luckily, with everyone on board and agreeing that Dicey needed a different environment, eventually it all worked out just fine. His family finally 'connected' with Dicey and understood life from his viewpoint, tapping into his unique set of needs.

 **A CATTY SUM UP**

1. Connect with your cat by having no expectations of how a pet should act or comparisons with a past pet.

2. Seek to understand and work with your cat's unique personality.

3. Understand the evolutionary natural behaviours of the feline species and try to see life from your cat's viewpoint.

CAT CHAT

The Cat–Human Relationship: Starring Dicey Doos

The case of Dicey, named after his owners' favourite pub – Dicey Reilly's in Ballyshannon – or Dicey Doos as he came to be known, had us all on an emotional rollercoaster. There was frustration one minute, euphoria the next; total confidence in my advice, followed by anxious soul-searching and doubt. On a few occasions I was reduced to tears as I questioned what was best for Dicey, a fluffy,

cheeky male Ragdoll, the Bart Simpson of the cat world.

Ragdolls are known for their placid temperament and are famed for a tendency to turn limp in the arms of their beloved humans. Ann Baker, a breeder in Riverside, California, developed them in the 1960s. Ann bred Josephine, a domestic longhaired female found running loose in her neighbourhood, with other toms she owned or adopted. By carefully selecting offspring with a unique look and loving temperament, Ann created this much-loved breed[1].

The Ragdoll is often portrayed as being ideal for indoor living and good with kids[1], so my client, Leanne, contacted a reputable breeder, who introduced her to a 12-week-old ball of fluff with the largest blue eyes. Leanne instantly lost her heart to the kitten she named Dicey, and adopted him into her family.

Although Dicey had been described as loving, playful and affectionate, it soon became clear he had a cheeky side. He enjoyed nibbling and biting hands, legs and feet. Leanne and her husband Paul did their best to discourage such behaviour, but Dicey's antics only escalated to full-blown predatory body attacks, and he began to intimidate Leanne's three-and-a-half-year-old son, Ted, who became fearful of the unpredictable family pet. As time went on, Dicey became more and more territorial. He would growl or cry if anyone tried to sit on the sofa or bed if he was there first.

It's little wonder that Leanne's initial email sounded so desperate. She signed off with a few sentences that I know must have been difficult to write: 'We are starting to think that if this continues we cannot continue to be Dicey's family, as it's too risky. We love him, so want to make it work though'.

With this cry for help, the pressure was well and truly on. Ted's safety was my top priority, so I quickly arranged a home visit. I was intrigued to find out how an 11-month-old Ragdoll could be controlling a whole family. What went wrong? What was causing such reactions? Although Leanne had filled in the extensive feline-behaviour questionnaire I request from clients before a home visit, the remaining pieces of the jigsaw would only fall into place when I saw the home environment and observed how Dicey's owners were interacting with him.

For the first consultation, I arranged to meet Leanne and Dicey together, so that the house would be quiet and she could talk freely without being disturbed. Leanne certainly looked relieved to see me and was extremely friendly and down-to-earth. While we were chatting in the living room, Dicey appeared and sniffed me briefly before climbing into a small cat tower with platforms that looked a tad small for such a cat.

When Leanne left me with Dicey to make a much-needed coffee, he showed lots of curiosity towards my bag of goodies, especially anything resembling things he could kill in the wild: mice, other rodents and birds. In the end he settled down to enjoy playing with a battery-operated hunting toy called Undercover Mouse. I realised that although Leanne was concerned about Dicey being territorially aggressive, he hadn't hissed or tried to stalk me, as you might expect.

Leaving Dicey to play, I joined Leanne in the kitchen and noticed then just how small the London flat was. City dwellers are used to living in small flats, and perhaps this blinds them to the space a companion animal needs, especially one kept exclusively indoors. Each of the rooms, accessed off a tiny central hallway, were cramped and cluttered. Taking my coffee outside, I realised that the garden was similarly tiny and mostly taken up with kids' outdoor toys.

I knew then what the problem was. Dicey had never been outside, and being cooped up left him more and more frustrated. Clearly Dicey's family loved him very much, and although I would advise them on how best to combat his aggressive behaviour, I knew space was going to be a problem. In fact, it would have a detrimental impact on Dicey's progress no matter what. My diagnosis was that Dicey suffered worsening predatory/play aggression due to frustration and boredom.

Predatory and play aggression is very common in cats, especially those with a high predatory drive who are kept indoors. Predation is a natural behaviour that's hardwired into cats. It usually starts during kittenhood, when owners play rough with their harmless new pet, but inadvertently encourage biting. As the kitten grows, the need to attack things results in the human and their ankles and feet becoming targets.

Naturally, a bored cat who has nothing to do all day will be more hyper when the owners are present. Focused play with appropriate toys can help correct such behaviour, which runs the risk of becoming a game if left unaddressed. If a bored cat lashes out at an ankle, the more its human victim flails around, the more a cat will bite. I could tell the family's response to Dicey was problematic because they were essentially 'feeding' his predatory nature by being fearful and on edge. With so much nervous energy in the home and everything being interpreted – sometimes rightly but often wrongly – as Dicey about to attack, he became reactionary. Much of the time that Dicey spent with his owners, he was wide-eyed and wired. It was a vicious circle.

Leanne followed my advice and bought lots of larger climbing platforms for Dicey to play on, as well as hunting toys and a harness and lead, to see if he would enjoy going for a walk outside. I made sure Leanne and her husband knew to be confident and relaxed around Dicey, even when he was playing up. They installed baby gates in the hallway to stop Dicey rushing for the front door, and also to protect Ted. It was like a military operation, and I knew they were trying to do what was best for Dicey.

Something that was always going to be difficult to change was Ted's reaction to the darting and unpredictable cat. I always ask clients to video what's going on, and on one occasion I was sent a video of Dicey jumping on the sofa behind Ted. Poor Ted thought he was being attacked and screamed for his mummy, but really Dicey wasn't doing much besides claiming a comfy spot on the sofa. Ted was frightened, and that was a problem.

One night, Leanne and her husband were really down about Dicey's erratic progress and arranged a late-night Skype conference. Dicey was lounging on his climber while we chatted, but eventually jumped down, and for the first time I got to see him in attack mode. He lunged at Leanne's body, jumping higher and higher, crying and yowling. Dicey was totally aroused, and indulging in full predatory play. With her husband filming, Leanne tried to get away until I told them both to exit the room, leaving Dicey contained on his own.

'I really needed to see that,' I said. 'This isn't going to work. I can't tell you Ted will remain safe, not now that I've seen this'.

Naturally, I had a heavy heart, but it was the right thing for Dicey.

'We can't change the space and Dicey isn't coping living alongside you in such a tiny environment,' I added. While everyone was devastated, Leanne and her husband were fully on board with my decision. Dicey wasn't happy and the family was constantly on edge. Things couldn't continue as they were.

Now that the decision to rehome Dicey was final, I got into battle mode and made it my priority to help find him a loving new family with a more suitable environment via my social media contacts. Leanne and I turned down a few enquiries and then a friend of mine saw a photo of Dicey on my Facebook page and messaged me. I knew then that the search was over. This was just two days after the decision to rehome had been made.

Donna is a single mum with two lovely daughters who lives in the rolling English countryside. After recently losing one of their cats to ill health, they decided to offer Dicey a home.

The excitement I felt was enormous. I gave Donna all the facts about Dicey in a 10-page behaviour report. This 'warts and all' approach was essential. It's important new owners know everything about a challenging pet before committing to taking them on. Donna was amazing. Being a teacher and well used to 'stroppy teenagers', she was determined to assist in providing Dicey with a home he could thrive in.

While Leanne and her family spent as much time with Dicey as they could, they sent lots of pictures of him being pampered and fussed over. These precious moments before the handover were extremely moving, and I found myself asking whether I had done enough. Seeing me in tears, my husband had to console me. 'Of course you did,' was his answer, and I hoped he was right.

When Donna arrived to collect Dicey, the belongings he had amassed astounded her.

'That's actually my fault,' I admitted. 'I was trying so hard to make it work'.

Somehow Donna made all of Dicey's things fit into her car alongside her kids and of course, Dicey, in his carrier. Understandably, Leanne was devastated. It took bravery, love, understanding and trust to see the rehoming through. Some behaviourists suggest rehoming and expect the owners to make a clean break from their pet. They arrange for the cat to be taken to a rescue centre and there is no contact between the previous owners and the new ones. I think very differently about this and positively encourage new owners to keep everyone in the loop about how things are progressing. Rehoming is painful enough, but handing over your much-loved cat knowing that you'll never know how they're getting on is a step too far in my opinion.

Weeks after Dicey was rehomed, I asked Leanne about her thoughts on the matter. 'I would have been more heartbroken if I hadn't received or been allowed any updates from Dicey's new owners', Leanne said. 'I would also have been worried about how that might appear to Ted, like we had just got rid of our much-loved pet and that was that. This way I think he learns about the right, responsible thing to do. We would also have worried that if Dicey was aggressive again, he could end up being put down, so knowing that's not the case makes him leaving easier'.

From the moment Donna got Dicey home, she updated both me and Leanne's family using Facebook private messages, appropriately titled 'Dicey's Progress'. Photos trickled through showing Dicey becoming progressively settled, even with the resident cat Arya to contend with. The icing on the cake came when, three weeks after he arrived at his new home, Donna videoed Dicey playing in his large secure garden. He was chasing flies, jumping high in the air with excitement. The old Dicey was gone; he was a relaxed, happy-go-lucky cat being lavished with the same love he received from his original family. The crucial difference now was that he had room to breathe.

Donna's home is now full of Dicey's large climbers and scratch posts, which he shares with his new feline friend. While her once uncluttered living room now looks more like a cattery, Donna shrugs it off. She was determined for Dicey's rehoming to be a success. In taking him on she made a firm promise to Leanne, which she kept. Seeing Dicey happy and stress-free is a joy.

I take my hat off to all cat owners who put their needs last and their cat's needs and wellbeing first. Sometimes the best will in the world cannot change circumstances and you can't fit a 'round cat in a square house'. It takes strength, courage and the greatest love to admit to yourself that your cat might be happier in another home. I have the greatest respect for Leanne, Paul and Ted. They connected with their cat and said a very difficult goodbye. Everyone will be eternally grateful to Donna and her children. Rehoming Dicey was an emotional rollercoaster that at times left us all feeling deflated, but in the end he got the happy ending he deserves.

Dicey with new family at the front and previous guardians at the back

CHAPTER TWO

How Similar Is My Cat's Behaviour To A Wild Cat's?

'The reason why I so much enjoy being friends with cats
is that they have two different characters, a wild side and
a domestic side. This is what makes them interesting.
A cat's a wild animal, and I like that.'

Léonard Tsuguharu Foujita

CHAPTER TWO

In this chapter:

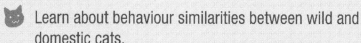 Learn about behaviour similarities between wild and domestic cats.

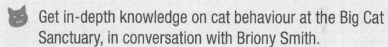 Get in-depth knowledge on cat behaviour at the Big Cat Sanctuary, in conversation with Briony Smith.

Understand the importance of play to the feline species.

To improve the environment of any species, one has to understand their basic evolutionary behaviour and needs, and this is no different when we consider sharing our homes with a cat. It isn't as simple as obtaining a cat and expecting them to fit in with our daily schedule because 'they are easy to look after and don't require much maintenance'. In Chapter One we learned about the past history of the feline species and how humans saw the advantage of taming cats and keeping them close by, mainly as workers because of their built-in predatory drive to hunt and kill. It's easy to forget that 'Fluffy', our indoor furry companion, who is waited on hand and foot and whose every whim is catered for, would tear a mouse or bird limb from limb given half the chance. On our journey to better understanding the cat, it's now time to compare our domestic cats to the big cats in the wild. Only then can our eyes be opened to a new approach to sharing life with a cat.

Wanting to extend my knowledge regarding comparisons of the different species I paid a visit to Briony Smith, head keeper of the Big Cat Sanctuary in Kent,[1] who gave me an unforgettable tour and answered my questions along the way. What struck me most on the walk around the sanctuary was the breathtaking beauty of the rarer cat species. There were clouded leopards, Pallas's cats, north Chinese leopards and rusty-spotted cats. I have a dislike of zoos, or seeing wild animals confined in any way, but reading the sanctuary's mission statement – 'to assist in the conservation of the world's endangered big cats, to preserve breeding integrity and to assist the return of big cats to the wild wherever possible' – helped me understand how important its work is.

I was intrigued to know more about the cats in this sanctuary compared to the cats I see on a daily basis in my behaviour practice. One recent client said 'domestic cats cannot be compared to wild cats. They are totally different in every way!' Are they?

In Conversation With Briony Smith

What are the chief similarities and differences between wild and domestic cats?

The biggest behavioural difference is very simply that the animals we have in the sanctuary are not domestic. Although held in a captive environment, they are wild animals and as such, it can be expected that natural instincts, including aggression, are displayed more readily. They haven't gone through thousands or more generations of domestication. Just as in other zoos, the animals here are used to living around humans, but it doesn't go as far back in their natural history as with domestic cats. They are also not bred for good temperament, as might happen with domestic breeding programmes. For example, with domestic cats, breeding for temperament has meant that breeds will generally become more affectionate towards humans. With wild species, because temperament is irrelevant, the more aggressive cats may produce aggressive offspring as cubs may learn to behave this way from their parents.

In general, our big cats' behaviour is very similar to domestic cats in play, hunting and also socially. Almost all species of cat are solitary, but this is not necessarily represented in domestics because owners will quite often have more than one.

Being a strong advocate for environmental enrichment for cats, especially those kept exclusively indoors, I was interested to know whether the stimulation provided in the sanctuary was similar to that recommended for domestic cats. It's one of the core areas that make a huge difference when working to change a cat's unwanted behaviour. What are the methods and different approaches and do they differ for each species?

Can you tell us more about environmental enrichment?

The purpose of enrichment is to try to encourage natural behaviours and give captive animals the opportunity to spend their time as closely as possible to how they would in the wild. This can include things like adding scents into their enclosures to encourage smelling, the Flehmen breathing response[2] and marking. Many of the enrichments we provide for the cats in our care are similar to those given to domestic cats, in many cases just on a bigger scale. Toys like balls obviously need to be a lot bigger and tougher for a lion than a house cat, but the big cats enjoy chasing them just as much. Scents such as perfumes put into the enclosures can include things like catnip, commonly used by owners of domestic moggies.

Tying food up encourages them to use their muscles and weight to bring it down; just as many species would with prey. Their enclosures are also designed around natural behaviours. Leopards, for example, which are mostly arboreal and shy, prefer to have high walkways and areas where they feel hidden. Therefore enclosure design varies, depending on the species. For example, in a leopard enclosure we are far more likely to have little tree-houses, which they can spend their time in. Even in their dens they have elevated boxes in which to rest, as feeling enclosed is more comfortable for them. Lions, on the other hand, will enjoy using a big elevated platform so they can survey their territory but, as predators right at the top of the food chain, they are much more comfortable being exposed. In the wild, not a lot will bother a lion, and so they have the confidence to be out in the open. Lions also like to bask in the sun, so any hard surface that heats up will be popular. In some zoos, this may be heated rocks or even in our case, the tarmac that runs through their paddock. The lions can often be seen lying on the warm tarmac rather than out on the grass.

When it comes to habitat, lions need a lot of ground space. In other words, if an enclosure were to be extended for a lion, it would be extended outwards. Leopards, on the other hand, are fantastic climbers, and are enriched by the opportunity to climb that's provided by extending their enclosures vertically and by aerial walkways.

Other enrichment methods include scattering feeds and hiding food, which are great for encouraging animals to search for and smell out their meal. Toys are also added to enclosures. One of our pumas really enjoys footballs, which she can hit and chase, sometimes for half an hour at a time. This desire to chase is an important part of natural behaviour in predators. Hessian sacks filled with straw or cardboard boxes are popular too, because the cats can get their teeth and claws into them. This need for destruction mimics their behaviour with prey, but it also just seems to be fantastic fun.

By far the best enrichment our cats appear to get is from the native wildlife living around the sanctuary, mostly rabbits and birds. Legally, we aren't allowed to provide our animals with live prey in this country, but if they enter the enclosures themselves, there isn't a lot we can do about it. The cats, however, love it.

What about training?

Training is a fantastic way of mentally stimulating the cats, and at the same time, it helps with husbandry. Zoo animals around the world are being trained to accept things like vaccines without anaesthetic, and to open their mouths to allow keepers and vets to look at their teeth. The cheetahs at the Big Cat Sanctuary are trained to accept their annual vaccine via a needle injected under the skin, as are some of our lions. Many of our cats are also crate-trained, meaning they will walk into a transport crate if, for example, we want to move them across site from one enclosure to another. This avoids the need for them to be anaesthetised. One of our tigers is being trained to open his mouth so we can inspect his teeth and to lie against the mesh so that we can start injection training. If we can inject the animals, we are also able to take blood samples, administer anaesthetics without the need for a dart and administer some medications; all in a calm, consensual and stress-free environment for the animals.

Our lions and tigers share a space and can sometimes stalk each other, especially the young animals. To counteract this, we simulate each stage of stalking by encouraging sniffing, searching and – finally – jumping or chasing, by tying food up. We could attach food to a rope and pull it through the bars, but we wouldn't want to encourage the habit of grabbing things in this way. The big cats are also so strong that the keepers could risk being hurt if pulled against the mesh.

Is it possible to simulate hunting with toys such as feathers on a rod, like we do with our moggies at home?

It's easier with the small cats and we do use almost exactly the same concept as a feather on a rod, except ours is food tied to a rope on a stick. This is fabulous for some of the small cat species such as servals and lynx. We do have to be careful because these cats are still strong and potentially dangerous and it requires us to be in the enclosure with them.

I come across a wide range of behavioural issues and wondered whether some, such as pica[3] or over-grooming, are mainly the preserve of domestic cats – or do you see similar symptoms with the big cats?

Any cases I've known have happened with our small cat species; not so much the big cats. That said, leopards are quite worrisome animals, and if they have a wound, they have been known to over-groom and show other signs of stress. The only other case of over-grooming I have known is with our male clouded leopard, Ben. We have to separate him from the female for feeding to prevent him from eating all the food and becoming very overweight, but if we separate them for too long he sometimes shows signs of stress and over-grooms his tail. We manage this by making sure we put them back together as soon as we can.

Pica has only been seen here in one of the small cats. The proposed cause was that if she was fed just one meal, too early in the day, her metabolism would speed up causing her to be hungry again, and the lack of a second meal would result in her eating non-food items within her enclosure (wooden bark chippings for example). Small cats are often designed to eat small meals regularly so we have altered her feeding patterns, feeding her multiple times per day, and we no longer see her exhibit this behaviour.

We have a tigress with some behavioural issues stemming from a bad experience with people when she was young. She used to be so nervous of visitors and keepers that she would either charge at the wire mesh or run away and hide, and would always refuse to go into the house where we keep the cats while cleaning their enclosures. We tried everything to encourage her to relax, including enrichment and a milk protein, which supposedly has a calming effect. It wasn't until we moved her to a different enclosure that she relaxed a bit, and after having cubs she transformed into a different cat. I expect she was scared, then when she had the cubs, perhaps there was a hormonal change that led to the behaviour change, because now she will very happily wait in the house.

I have to say that some of the most fascinating things I've seen here are natural behaviours, not things that are out of the ordinary. It's incredible to watch the social interactions of the lion pride: especially mothers with young cubs that are being introduced to the rest of the group. How the mothers encourage their young and control the interactions between them and the father at the beginning is complex and fascinating to see.

It was interesting to hear that the sanctuary, on one occasion, had used a domestic-cat behaviourist for an issue with one of the big cats. Is this common?

Although each cat species does have behavioural and physiological differences, for the most part they are still extremely similar to domestic cats. We have had a domestic-cat behaviourist visit twice to talk about our cats. Her knowledge of house-cat behaviour, together with the keepers' knowledge of the subtle differences between each species, is the perfect combination to come up with new ideas about how to manage certain cats, but also for information and ideas to be exchanged and for us to all learn from each other.

What meat are the cats fed and how does it compare to what they would eat if they weren't in captivity?

In the wild, big cats have a varied diet centred around deer and antelope, and in many cases wild pig. We feed our big cats mostly horse and calf meat. There seem to be a few myths surrounding what meat should or shouldn't be fed to big cats, and I know that different zoos have different policies. Some won't feed horsemeat because the levels of phosphorus are high and supposedly you would not be able to add enough calcium for it to create the correct calcium-phosphorus ratio. The ratio is important in renal health and also in bone development, particularly in youngsters, as the two minerals combine to form bone. Too much phosphorus in the diet can lead to calcium being drawn from the cats' bones to bring the ratio back to normal levels. This can cause weaknesses and breaks in the cats' bones. In captivity we keep the ratio in balance by choosing foods lower in phosphorus, adding a supplement to the cats' meals that's high in calcium, and encouraging them to eat more bone by feeding them cuts with smaller, softer bones that they are more likely to ingest.

Red meat is important because of the levels of iron, and of the essential amino acid, taurine. A deficiency of taurine can cause blindness, reproductive issues and abnormal heart function, so it's imperative that cats receive enough in their diet. Iron, as for humans, is essential for the development of red blood cells, and without enough a cat can become anaemic.

It sounds disgusting, but in the wild, the prey's guts and organs can provide great nutrition. Our small cats are given a variety of quails, rats, mice, fish, chicks and chickens, which they receive whole, including the organs, fur, feather, bone and everything else the cat would receive if hunting in the wild.

With the big cats this isn't possible, as the meat we provide for them is in meal-sized chunks, always with bone but often not with anything else. So many nutrients can be obtained through the organs and guts that the big-cat meals require supplements to ensure that all of their nutritional needs are met.

Some vets and food manufacturers say kibble is beneficial to the health of domestic cats' teeth because it keeps them clean and removes plaque. Do you believe this is true and do any of your cats eat dry food?

We provide food that has bone in it and this is what keeps the cats' teeth clean while also providing calcium and nutritious marrow. Essentially, the cats need to be chewing on something hard and crunchy in order to keep their teeth clean. It's the same principle as giving a dog a dentastick. We have experimented with domestic-cat biscuits for our small cats, but as enrichment; not part of their diet. So far, they have not been too popular as the cats don't seem to recognise them as food and certainly don't like them compared to what they usually eat, which is meat.

Lastly, my domestic-cat-grooming clients have asked me more than once why cats' coats don't get matted in the wild. Have you any thoughts on this?

Domestic cats that are most prone to matting are the longhaired species, such as Turkish Vans. I would suggest that by ratio, most wildcat species don't have hair as long as these domestic cats. Some wild species, such as the Pallas's cat, do have very long fur, but this is not common in the wild. Male lions obviously have long manes, but they also have a family group to help groom them. Here at the sanctuary, manes have been known to get matted if seeds or burrs get tangled in them, but they just get groomed out in time. It's my personal belief that wild cats have longer barbs on their tongue by ratio of size than domestic cats, and are therefore able to comb their coat more thoroughly. After all, parasites like fleas appear to be very rare in captive wild cats and I believe they are removed by the cats' tongues. Some collections treat their wild cats for fleas but we don't, as it's so incredibly rare for them to have them.

With my brain in overdrive and feet frozen to the core due to the typically British cold weather, I bade farewell to Briony and the stunning cats in her attentive care. What a fantastic experience. It showed me that domesticated moggies and their big-cat cousins have very similar patterns of behaviour that have hardly changed over thousands of years. I always knew that studying big cats and their behaviour in captivity would help us to understand our pets' actions and needs and hopefully you, dear reader, will hear the penny drop too. Only by seeing cats as animals first and pets second will we truly be able to give our cats the best lives possible, with every conceivable home comfort and welcome moments of wild spontaneous excitement.

It was fascinating hearing how Briony invented games for her big cats to engage them in play activities. So, why is play so important for the physical and psychological wellbeing of our feline friends, and what types of toys can bring that hunting instinct to the fore and turn your house mog into the wild cat of their ancestors? These are questions I will go on to explore in our next Cat Chat.

 A CATTY SUM UP

1.   The behaviour of wild cats is very similar to that of our domestic moggies in terms of grooming, predation, food, nutrition and play.

2.   Wild cats can suffer from the same behavioural and psychological issues as our domesticated cats should the environment not be right, or if they are anxious about something else; thus behaviours change to outwardly show us there is a problem that needs addressing.

3.   Environmental enrichment is just as vital for wild cats born in captivity as it is for domestic cats.

CAT CHAT

Wild At Heart: The Importance Of Play

Play is an important part of growing and learning for any cat, be they lion cubs or domestic kittens. When domestic cats play, they are exercising instinctive behaviour that helps them to socialise, hunt and survive just like their wild ancestors. Surprisingly, though, according to a 1979 paper entitled 'Relations Between Kitten Behavior And Adult Predation', there has been no proven research to connect play in domestic kittens with an adult cat's ability to hunt. This may explain why some of our little tinkers are quite rubbish at it. But I digress…

In her excellent book, *The Cat: Its Behavior, Nutrition And Health*, Linda P. Case talks in depth about three types of play that start in kittenhood[1]: social play, exploratory play and object play. The big-cat cubs also participate in these various activities. The ages may vary between domestic and wild cats, but with domestic cats, exploratory play starts to show at approximately seven weeks of age and is an important activity in developing agility in the adult cat. This type of play revolves around climbing, jumping and balancing, which hones the kitten's muscle tone and motor skills, so that they go on to develop physical strength and coordination.

Social play is directed at other kittens in the litter and is usually seen from three weeks of age, helping cats to socialise and build a bond with one another, although social play is directed at humans later down the line. As a kitten, this type of play involves actions such as pouncing, standing over another kitten or lying on the floor with the belly exposed, and can involve pawing and biting each other in a playful manner. Social play can appear rough at times but it's usually nothing to be concerned about. Kittens learn from rough play and will be 'told' by their playmate should they feel pain.

Object play develops when kittens can manipulate small objects and seems to overlap with social play, increasing in frequency from seven to eight weeks. Although object play has been associated with feline predatory behaviour, the movements are more post-predatory, such as what we cat owners may experience when our cats bring in live prey. The cat will prod, poke and tease the unfortunate prey with some level of curiosity and excitement. Object play is also stimulating for the brain.

Once cats, domestic or wild, reach adulthood, they will have well-honed motor skills, streamlined agility and a playful but predatory nature that needs an outlet. The feline species thrives on stimulation, curiosity and investigation, and all of these actions are tied into the skills of hunting and stalking. Therefore play should focus on toys that mimic the ability to explore, stalk, hunt and kill, all of which are stimulating. This is highlighted by Briony in her examples of the numerous ways that she engages with the big cats using items to mimic natural behaviour through play.

Playing with our cats is also highly beneficial for humans too. It helps lighten our mood and enables us to step outside of ourselves and engage with another species, a communication that often involves fun and laughter. Who doesn't smile watching kittens playing, or doesn't laugh out loud watching a cat squeezing into the smallest box, or experiencing that pre-pounce wiggle of the bum of an engaged cat as it prepares to jump? We all find these actions endearing, even though the reality of the overall meaning of the pounce is one of death and destruction!

Playing also has a nurturing aspect for us, which makes us feel good. Animal lovers – especially women – nurture their pets like they would their children, satisfying a biological need. Play is in the moment and it allows us to experience the joy of living in the moment too. So, start playing with your cat and they will feel on top of the world and, just as importantly, so will you.

Some of the best playthings for cats are of the hunting toy variety. These toys are made to look and feel like prey a cat would hunt in the wild, such as birds and mice. The toys come as attachments and are fastened to a rod or wire so that their movements can look realistic to the cat. Some of the toys are made from real fur or feathers. One company I can recommend is called Purrs In Our Hearts who ethically source their feathers and fur attachments. Placing hunting toys under newspaper or a rug can really help to engage a cat who then becomes excited at the thought of its prey hiding underneath.

For special-needs cats the toys need to be altered to match their disability. For blind cats, toys that have a strong scent, such as catnip or valerian, are great as are toys with sounds, such as a bell attached to a toy mouse. Partially sighted cats may be able to see some bright light so toys that light up and have sound are perfect.

For timid cats, who may be frightened of rod-type toys, try the softer approach with pipe cleaners, sponge balls, furry solo mice, string or ribbon.

In all of my years working with cats I have never come across a cat who doesn't engage in some form of play once the correct toys are found to match the individual cat's personality.

Believe me, playing with cats is a real stress-buster – and who doesn't need that in this day and age!

CHAPTER THREE

Do Cats Like Music?

'There are two means of refuge from the miseries of life: music and cats.'

Albert Schweitzer

CHAPTER THREE

In this chapter:

- Learn the reasons why music is considered to be important to cats.
- Get in-depth knowledge behind the research for *Music For Cats*, in conversation with David Teie.
- Understand how our actions can affect our cats' demeanour.

It's an exciting prospect to be able to communicate with animals through music, especially for people who work in animal rescue, veterinary practices and grooming parlours, as well as the millions of cat owners around the world. Reassurance and calm 'vibes' can help enormously with how an animal perceives what's happening to them at any given moment. If the music is also having a calming effect on the human handlers, then it's a win–win situation. Of course, music cannot work miracles! A feral cat will not suddenly lie down and light a menthol cigarette as soon as the vet hits play on their iPod, but anything that helps to calm a situation down and create mellow vibes can only help in the long run. This is why many rescue centres play soothing classical music in their cat and dog enclosures.

As a groomer of cats, some of whom do not welcome me with open paws, I have come to rely on a CD called *Music For Cats*, written and performed by classical music composer David Teie after he aided extensive research by scientist Dr. Charles T. Snowdon (a professor of psychology who ran a colony of cotton-top tamarins in Madison, at the University of Wisconsin) and Dr. Megan Savage. The research focused on the emotional changes that occur in animals from various pitches and other soothing sound formations with the hypothesis being 'that in order for music to be effective with other species, it must be in the frequency range and with similar tempos to those used in natural communication by each species'. The science behind the research paper 'Cat's Prefer Species-Appropriate Music' was published in the journal *Applied Animal Behaviour Science*[1]. It makes for a fascinating read.

A *New York Times* interview by Eleanor Stanford highlighted important factors of the research[2]:

> Dr. Snowdon sent David Teie recordings of tamarin calls that demonstrated fear and calm. The fear-based calls 'showed evidence of tritones and minor seconds,' Snowdon says, and the calming calls had 'long slow notes with some nice harmonic structure'.
>
> Teie wrote four pieces for cello and voice based on the tamarin vocalisations, two 'threat-based' and two 'affiliative'. So that the tamarins could hear the compositions on their own terms, he sped them up three octaves. Even at human tempo, the threat-based music sounds martial and alien. Teie also chose four pieces originally designed for human listeners and played them to the tamarins for comparison, including bits of Barber's 'Adagio for Strings' and Metallica's 'Of Wolf And Man'. Over two months, seven pairs of adult tamarins heard all eight pieces of music. Monkeys 'really don't care much for human music,' Snowdon says, and they showed very little response to it, with the weird exception of excerpts from Metallica and 'The Grudge,' by Tool, both of which soothed the monkeys slightly.
>
> The monkeys responded more profoundly to Teie's music. The threat-based pieces led to 'tongue-flicking, head-cocking, scratching,' and other signs of anxiety, Snowdon says. The calming music 'increased foraging behaviour, eating and drinking'. As he composed, Teie was careful not to replicate any of the tamarins' natural vocalisations; otherwise the animals might simply respond to what they already knew. Snowdon and Teie published their results online in September in the journal *Biology Letters*[3].

Eleanor Stanford went on to describe *Music For Cats* as follows:

> In some tracks, sounds similar to the chirps of birds are overlaid with hurried streams of staccato for an energising effect; in others, crescendos of purring and suckling sounds are designed to relax. To a human ear, the sounds are otherworldly and at times soporific.

As intriguing as the music sounded, I wanted to chat to David to find out more about *Music For Cats* and what role sound plays with our furry companions.

In Conversation With David Teie

How did the idea initially come about? After all, music for cats is not a general idea that would pop into most people's minds.

It began as a test of the validity of my theory of how music affects the emotions. If the theory is correct, it should be possible to compose music that's effective for another species. The first test was in fact on monkeys.

What started you on the journey of discovery regarding music and emotions in the first place – to the depth of study that you took it to? That's quite a leap from general interest to studying monkeys and music.

I was initially working on a series of lectures on how performers could enhance the listener's appreciation for the structures of music. I realised firstly that every aspect of our music is calibrated to the human scale and secondly that each thread in the fabric of music was adopted at a given time in history, i.e. the major third that makes up the major chord first appeared in an English round in the Middle Ages. At one point I decided to take music apart and separate it into as many indivisible parts as possible, for example, melody. Then I began asking the question of each element: why would this be recognisable to us? Why would this be emotionally salient for humans? Once I was into this type of research, I was so encouraged by the answers that presented themselves that I just kept going until I had something of a complete theory.

Why were cats chosen to be the subject of such a project?

I chose cats because they are very consistent across the breeds. My interest was in creating music for a species that was popular and connected to people. Dogs and cats were the obvious choices and cats won out because there were fewer complications with the different breeds. It began as a test of the validity of my theory of how music affects the emotions. If the theory is correct, it should be possible to compose music that's effective for another species. The first test was, as I've mentioned, on monkeys. [It was found that tamarins were unresponsive to human music, a point also made by McDermott and Hauser in 2007 who concluded that tamarins disliked music overall, but tested tamarins only with human music.[3]]

How did you meet the scientist, Charles T. Snowdon, who assisted with this project?

When I decided to test my theory I thought I would start at the top: contacting the most eminent scientists. As they refused me, I would work my way down the list, thereby finding the most qualified scientist who was willing to do a study of the effects of species-specific music on animals. As it happens, I didn't need to go any further than the first name on the list. I sent Dr. Snowdon, a psychology professor who ran a colony of cotton-top tamarins in Madison at the University of Wisconsin, my ideas and he was interested but not inclined to spend grant money on the project at first. At one point he sent me two newly discovered calls from his colony of cotton-top tamarin monkeys. I was able to identify the general meaning of the calls and their contexts without having been told by him. He was impressed that a musical analysis could, in general terms, identify emotional valence and agreed to perform the study.

I noticed your research was mainly focused on indoor-only cats, 36 out of 47 to be precise, with only two cats totally free roaming. Is there a particular reason why?

This surely was a result of the testing procedures, whereby they wanted to do the testing in the home environment of each cat and needed a controlled space to put the music for cats on the one side and the control music for humans on the other.

The research was conducted on cats in a calm state. Do you feel this music can help towards calming a cat already in a heightened state of fight or flight? This would certainly help vets and groomers.

Before the study I had assumed that the music could be appreciated by a cat in a normal state but that a cat in an anxious state would not respond. The feedback that I have received, however, indicates that the music may be very helpful in calming anxious cats. There is a study going on right now at Louisiana State University veterinary school on clinical applications of the music. The person conducting the study had enough preliminary data to go ahead with the study and informed me that she had heard from many owners about how calm their cats were when returning from the study.

Can you explain the procedure of the study?

In the cat's own home environment, we placed two speakers either side of a computer and played cat-specific music through one set and human music through the other at different times. The cats were left to act naturally before the music began and the behaviours were recorded during the music sessions to determine which speaker they gravitated to and which behaviours indicated the most pleasing or calm responses.

What was the main conclusion of the study?

The cats responded more positively to the speakers playing the music designed for cats (the frequency range and tempos appropriate for that species). These included the rhythm of purrs (but not actual purrs), frequencies one octave above human vocal ranges, and the rhythm of kittens sucking milk from their mother's teat (but not actual suckling). We can say from our studies that appropriate audio can be used for feline enrichment in conjunction with environmental enrichment and play, and that audio can play an important role when working on and with the behaviours of domestic cats.

Apart from the cats themselves, who do you feel can benefit the most from *Music For Cats*?

I have designed the music in such a way as to include music that should be calming for humans as well as cats. The music in the lower register is below the vocal range of the cat and, therefore, does not carry information that's emotionally salient for cats. Music in the lower range is basically traffic noise to the cats. In this register I have blended in music for humans. In the testing done on the tamarin monkeys, the researchers found both types of monkey music to be irritating. I realised that if the cat's music was irritating to the cat owners they would not put it on. This way the music can be shared by both cat, and cat person. We love our pets. Most pet owners think of their pet as a member of the family. I have long thought of music as love in sonic form. Love being the ultimate connecting force; sound and expression form that connection. I truly believe that when this music is shared it can enhance the bond between people and their cats.

To support the research of Dr. Snowdon et al, *The Journal Of Feline Medicine And Surgery* (JFMS) conduced their own studies around cats and music in a veterinary setting. The paper was called 'Effects Of Music On Behavior And Physiological Stress Response Of Domestic Cats In A Veterinary Clinic'[4]. To quote:

> ... the cats were exposed to three different audio states: silence, classical music and cat-specific music during three physical examinations two weeks apart. The results showed lower cat-stress scores and mean handling scores whilst listening to the cat-specific music composed by David.

Since being sent a copy of the album, I can vouch for the compositions bringing a lovely calming effect into the room when I'm grooming. The clients love the music and the humans seem to relax, passing on calm positive energy to the cats I'm handling. Sadly, some cats still do not like grooming and no amount of music will help to change their minds but, overall, the album is working wonders.

My cats, starting out already in a peaceful frame of mind, doze off to the album and seem to love the tones and rhythms mixed in with simulated catty purring. And on the first day of listening to disc one, my husband fell into a deep sleep whilst my cats just sat there staring at him. That made me chuckle.

David's research highlights an important area of debate with regards to animals and whether they have emotions or feelings. Many researchers believe that an animal's emotions and feelings are merely projections from us in what they term as anthropomorphising. Anthropomorphising means projecting our own human thoughts and feelings on to an animal. An example of this is when a cat's owner thinks they are being personally punished after a night out, with the cat refusing to use its litter tray upon their return. However, although the emotions and feelings of an animal might not be the same as how we experience them, we should recognise that animals can feel fear and pain and certainly respond to the energy a human emanates.

Sarah Hartwell, on her extensive feline website **messybeasts.com**, delves into the question of whether cats have emotions, and after studying research for and against, she concludes:

> Cats and other animals have feelings. However, their feelings must be interpreted in the context of their own physical needs and their own environment. They have a more limited range of feelings than humans and their reaction to environmental stimuli is different to humans, but they show many responses indicative of emotions.

I believe that David's research has proven that animals respond emotionally to music, that they have emotions and therefore must be sentient beings.

The following Cat Chat looks more deeply into whether cats pick up on the 'subtle' energy of humans around them, using examples from my work with them on the grooming table.

 **A CATTY SUM UP**

1. Cats can respond in a positive way to various frequencies and sounds, especially if the sound is also helping to calm us.

2. A cat's response to sound is an emotional one, thus proving that cats do have a form of emotions.

3. Sound is important to cats' perception of what's happening around them in the moment.

CAT CHAT

Do Cats Absorb Human Energy?

Working with cats, I learned very early on that our energy could contribute to their reactions. They pick up on the tone of our voices and body language when we are feeling emotions such as nervousness or fear. In other words, what we project outwards is interpreted by sight, sound and touch rather than smell. Cats, as with all animals, cannot smell fear, but rather pick up on our energy, which dictates our movements.

A good example of this is my body language around horses. Unfortunately, despite the fact that I adore them, I'm also afraid. I always tense up when I'm on a country walk if they come trotting over to say hello. I jump if they move their face towards me and I move my hands in an unpredictable way when trying to stroke them, edging back if they express an interest in me. My voice breaks out in a squeal, being unsure how to react. In reality, all they are doing is seeing if there is food in my hand. My perception is that they are going to bite me and so I react. It's not that they smell my fear but that I start acting differently from another person who is calm around them. This can make them feel nervous.

It's the same with timid cats. Some cats perceive a rising hand from a person intending to stroke them as one that's going to hit or confine them. It's why I always advise not to move your hand over a cat's head when stroking them but to allow the cat to smell your hand first. Usually the cat responds with a headbutt, which most times you can take as a green light to gently touch them.

In my first book, *Claws: Confessions Of A Professional Cat Groomer*, I wrote about a cat-grooming client who was so anxious that her cat started to wonder why she was acting so jittery, which in turn made the cat restless on my grooming table. My client's voice was loud and, when talking on the phone, was grating to hear, like an argument was in flow. However, her vocal tone was just shrill to the ear. It was only when I politely asked her to leave the room that her cat was able to relax, enabling me to finish the job.

In a 2015 study entitled 'Social Referencing And Cat–Human Communication'[1], it was shown that cats change their behaviour in line with an emotional message (either vocal or facial) given out by their owner. In one experiment, the emotional message was based on the facial expressions of the cat's owner towards an object that was unfamiliar. This was to see if the emotional message provided by the cat's owner changed the behaviour of the cat. According to the study, 79% exhibited referential looking between the owner and the object, and also to some extent changed their behaviour in line with the emotional message given by the owner.

This study shows that our cats are not as aloof as we may assume.

A cat picking up on the energy we give out is linked to survival. If we are angry, our voices get louder and our bodies become tense, which changes our posture and all that we do from then on. This can cause a cat to fear for their safety. They will respond by running away, cowering from us or hissing and growling as a way to keep us at a safe distance. Some will attack if cornered, which they consider to be the ultimate threat. A fearful cat, backed into a corner, will attack if you move nearer to them because there is no escape route. These are the most dangerous situations and the reason why one should never approach a fearful cat directly from the front.

Whilst working on a recent behaviour case, I came across a classic example of a cat perceiving danger and reacting to the energy of their humans. The cat was elderly and was in the process of grieving for a past owner, as well as getting used to a new home. The male owner was frustrated by the cat's inappropriate toileting, and in moments of frustration he would smash something in the home or cause an argument with his partner over the cat. This led to the cat hissing at him whenever he tried to spend quality time with them. Cats live in the moment, but they also remember past negative experiences, which determine how they respond to various situations if they arise again. The cat was never personally reprimanded, but they continue to hiss at the male owner to this day, despite all of his efforts to be kind.

On the dreaded fireworks night, when all pet owners fear for the mental stability of their animals, my cats, Kiki and Zaza, take solace in how my husband and I respond to the loud bangs. They listen to our voices talking softly to them and respond to our calm relaxed movements. They instinctively know there is nothing to worry about because we do not appear worried ourselves. Kiki always looks at her sister Zaza to see how she is responding. It's very interesting to watch. If Zaza is calm then Kiki relaxes too. If Zaza sits up on high alert then Kiki's eyes widen and you see panic rising within her. But despite humans remaining calm during difficult times for cats, such as fireworks night, there are times when an animal's fear will be immune to our attempts to reassure them.

When working with a cat, we should try to imagine how our emotional state is being perceived. We may be excited, speaking to the cat in loud high-pitched tones, saying nice things about the cat, only to receive a growl in return. What does our voice and tone really sound like to the cat? What atmosphere are we creating? When we change, our cats' responses change. This is advice I repeat often to my behaviour and grooming clients.

Whilst I was writing this chapter, another study was published, in February 2019[2], exploring the idea that cats share parallels with their owners' personalities. The study 'provides the best evidence to date of the relationship between owner personality and cat behaviour, welfare and lifestyle parameters, showing for the first time clear parallels with the parent-child relationship and the associated wellbeing outcomes for children'. In other words, our personalities can be mirrored back in our cats' behaviour.

Dr. Lauren Finka, in an interview with Eric Dolan of PsyPost[3], goes on to state that:

> Neurotic owners were more likely to report that their cats had ongoing medical conditions, were overweight or very overweight, displayed more frequent stress-

linked sickness behaviours, had behavioural problems, and had aggressive or anxious/fearful behavioural styles. More agreeable owners were more likely to indicate that their cats had a normal weight and displayed less aggressive and aloof/avoidant behaviours. Owners higher in openness and conscientiousness were also less likely to report aloof/avoidant behaviours in their cats. In addition, owners higher in extroversion, openness, and conscientiousness were more likely to report their cats as being more sociable.

Our neurotic cats, it seems, have only us to blame!

CHAPTER FOUR

Why Does My Cat Scratch Furniture?

'Mankind's true moral test, its fundamental test (which
lies deeply buried from view), consists of its attitude
towards those who are at its mercy: animals. And in this
respect mankind has suffered a fundamental debacle, a
debacle so fundamental that all others stem from it.'

Milan Kundera

CHAPTER FOUR

In this chapter:

- Understand why cats scratch and the main use for their claws.

- Get in-depth knowledge on the declawing process and why alternatives should be sought, in conversation with Dr. Jennifer Conrad.

- Get expert advice on alternatives to help furniture-scratching issues.

Scratching is a natural behaviour for cats and if suitable cat scratchers are not provided, then watch out. Your sofa sides, bed legs, dining table legs and carpets are going to get your cat super excited and ready for some serious scratching action. It's surprising to see many cat carers with little in their homes to provide this natural outlet, or the scratcher they have is so tiny that their large feline just looks at it in exasperation and wanders off to find the nearest chair leg again!

To begin, here are some catty toe facts from Linda P. Case, an Adjunct Assistant Professor at the University of Illinois, College of Veterinary Medicine, taken from her excellent book *The Cat: Its Behavior, Nutrition And Health*:[1]

> A cat's feet are digigrade meaning that it walks on its toes. The front paw has five claws and the back paw four. The claws are protractile meaning that the claws are sheathed in the resting positive (already out)... They do not retract. When a cat's claws are fully retracted the tendons lock the two final phalange bones together, holding the joint in a rigid position, thus keeping the claws unsheathed.

That's the paw anatomy out of the way, but what about the behaviour? Cats use their claws for a variety of functions. The obvious one is defence. The claws are powerful tools against predators, or when attacking prey for food. One of the main reasons many cats don't like their claws to be trimmed is because they have little understanding of why you would be taking away their natural 'defence', as well as the paw being a sensitive area. Cats also use their claws for climbing and marking territory. When your cat is scratching in the home, they're marking territory, leaving visual marks from their claws and depositing scent from their paws. Visual and scent markers are two important ways a cat communicates.

Did you know, then, that in certain countries around the world, removing a cat's claws surgically is legal and could be for minor reasons like protection of furniture? In the UK declawing was banned by the Animal Welfare Act of 2006 by explicitly prohibiting 'interference with the sensitive tissues or bone structure of the animal, other than for the purposes of its medical treatment'. Almost all vets in the UK consider the practice cruel and it's rare for anyone over here to ask for the procedure to be done.

Dr. Jennifer Conrad founded an organisation called The Paw Project, highlighting this unnecessary practice with an ongoing campaign for it to be banned outright. A documentary film followed with the same name.

The first time I sat down to watch *The Paw Project*, I lasted about 15 minutes before feeling a pain in my heart. With tears rolling down my cheeks, I switched off the film, remaining miserable for the rest of the day, recalling images I couldn't erase from my memory. A friend convinced me to watch the rest of it and so I returned to my TV the next day. I'm glad I did. Although the beginning was hard to watch, with images of various wild and domestic cats suffering from (at times, crippling) movement-related issues as a direct result of being declawed, the suffering endured by these animals was made palpable and I found myself cheering for Jennifer and her supporters every step of the way. The film was deeply inspiring and left me filled not only with a sense of outrage, but also with a sense of injustice for these sentient beings with whom we share the planet. I felt the same fighting spirit that spurred Jennifer on. I vowed I would spread the word in any way I could. The message: that declawing is inhumane, barbaric and needs to be banned outright.

As the founder of The Paw Project (both the film and the charity), I wanted Dr. Jennifer Conrad to be a part of this book.

In Conversation With Dr. Jennifer Conrad

Can you give us some insight into what first prompted you to take action?

I encountered a lot of declawed big cats while I was working as the veterinary medical director of a large sanctuary in the Los Angeles area. A disturbing number of them were crippled. That was in 1999. I researched the problem and found that the lameness was directly attributable to the declawing. I worked with others, particularly Kirk Wendelburg, DVM, to develop a surgical technique to improve the lives of these cats. The technique was published in a paper in 2002 in the Proceedings of the American Association of Zoo Veterinarians[2].

'There were a number of local exotic-animal vets who made a significant income declawing cats for the entertainment industry; one even wrote that his vet clinic had declawed 40,000 big cats and that he himself had declawed 8,000. A trainer told me that this vet declawed 12 white tigers in his kitchen one afternoon. At the time, most of the trainers thought that declawing was just a normal and necessary step to prepare the cats for their work. Many knew that lameness was inevitable but felt that the skill of the surgeon made the difference. I began to educate the trainers. When I showed them that it was the declawing that caused the problem, a great many of these trainers became convinced and stopped declawing their animals. One trainer told me that I was now his vet because I was the only one who refused to declaw his big cats.

Can you talk us through the humble beginnings of your campaign? It's now a powerful movement, but how did you get the ball rolling at the beginning and what opposition, as well as support, did you encounter?

I began repairing the feet of declawed big cats. It was through a conversation with Hernan Molina, the deputy to the Mayor of West Hollywood, California, that the movement to end declawing through legislation began. He watched me work with a declawed lioness and I asked him if we could just ban declawing in West Hollywood. Little did I know... We have a lot of support from the animal-protection community but the opposition is primarily professional veterinary trade associations, such as the American Veterinary Medical Association (AVMA), although some groups that benefit from the concept that animals are property, such as breeders, also oppose our legislative efforts. I'd like to note that as we gather more and more data proving that declawing truly is harmful and unnecessary, the opposition's ability to rationalise its position is weakening.

What did the trainers feel about your campaign to stop declawing cats, as surely they would see this as making their job more difficult?

Some trainers were early converts. Others resisted at first and opposed our efforts. I actually lost a lot of business in my private practice, but I was convinced that I was doing the right thing for the cats. In 2006, federal-government regulations prohibited the declawing of animals 'owned' by government-licensed 'trainers' and other 'owners'. In 2018, a federal court ruled that declawing wild and exotic cats was a violation of the Endangered Species Act. This provided protection to these cats across the USA.

Could you explain what declawing entails, in layman's terms?

Declawing is a surgical procedure, also called onychectomy, in which the animal's toe bones are amputated at the last joint. Most people do not realise that all or at least some of the bone – not only the claw – is removed. Declaw surgery is usually performed when the animal is a cub. While some felines will have immediate complications from the procedure, it may be many months or years before the damaging effects of declawing become obvious. Declawing may result in permanent lameness, arthritis and other long-term complications. Cats normally walk with their toes bearing the weight of their bodies; each step is cushioned by the digital pad under the toe. Declawed cats can experience extreme pain supporting their body weight when standing or walking if the tendon attached to the retained segment of the third toe bone pulls that bit of bone under the foot. The displaced bone fragment produces a painful 'pebble-in-the-shoe' sensation when they stand or try to walk. Also, bone fragments may contain remnants of claw-forming tissue that may continue to grow deep within the foot, causing infection. The pad is often displaced backwards, toward the rear of the foot, causing the weight of the cat's body to push the end of the second toe bone through the thinned tissue on the underside of the foot. These complications may occur in combination, resulting in great pain for the animal to stand or walk. In more severe and particularly heartbreaking cases, the mutilation from declaw surgery may cause so much tenderness or pain that the animal can move only by walking on its 'wrists'[3].

Big cats are declawed by their owners with the intention of making the animals less dangerous to handle. Typically, the owners are private collectors who are trying to make a household 'pet' out of a felid that's, by nature, not a suitable pet. It's rare for public zoos to have declawed cats. Unfortunately, the tiger or cougar that was cute and playful as a cub can be dangerous as an adult, whether or not it has claws. A 'pet' that weighs several hundred kilos and eats 5–10 kilos of meat a day may no longer seem like such a good idea. These cats, victims of human ignorance or arrogance, are sometimes killed. The luckier ones find themselves abandoned or confiscated by authorities and become residents of animal refuges. There are over a hundred such sanctuaries in the US alone, housing thousands of declawed big cats.

When it comes to the long-term effects of declawing and procedures for reversing the process, can the paw ever be completely repaired?
No… we may be able to improve the cat, but because the parts of the paw that are amputated and removed cannot be replaced, we cannot 'fix' them by returning them to their normal state.

In 2013 you managed to convince the American Veterinary Medical Association to ban declawing of wild and exotic cats. How was this done and why not for domestic cats also? What's the difference?
The AVMA does not 'ban' declawing, but they did publish guidelines that 'opposed' and later 'condemned' the declawing of wild and exotic cats.

They do not explain why a procedure known to cripple wild cats and worthy of 'condemning' is acceptable, in their opinion, for domestic cats.

What's the argument used against not banning declawing and what are your thoughts on this argument? I'm astounded that two polar-opposite views exist amongst the vets that still approve of and perform this procedure and those that believe it's cruel.

You can read about the AVMA position on declawing on their website[4] but it's worth noting that this is an unenforceable guideline. We reject any non-therapeutic reason for declawing and believe we have good and compelling evidence that declawing is harmful, inhumane and neither guarantees cats their homes nor protects human health.

How is it possible that declawing is legal in the US when it's banned in so many other countries?

Declawing is illegal in many countries. In many other countries, declawing is not illegal, but the veterinary profession considers it unacceptable, so it's just not done. I believe that was the case in the UK until 2006, when the Animal Welfare Act was passed. Before that, the Royal College of Veterinary Surgeons said that declawing was 'mutilation' and stated that declawing for the 'prevention of furniture or carpet damage is unacceptable'.

On the other hand, declawing is performed on approximately 25% of American cats. It's often offered as a part of a 'kitten package'. Many Americans aren't aware of what declawing entails and many believe their vets would never offer anything that wasn't good for their cats. I've had vets tell me that declawing is their 'bread and butter'. We are working to overturn this deep cultural ignorance.

Is declawing standard practice for domestic cats in the US when an owner may go to their vet and complain about scratched furniture, or do many vets now refuse to do this surgery even in states where it's still legal?

Some vets do it and some don't. Based on available surveys, we think most vets in the US will perform declaw procedures, but the criteria they use for declawing varies tremendously. Many vets are fearful that if they don't declaw, they will lose their clients. We have found the opposite. Vets who don't declaw are very happy with that decision. They are considered heroes in the community and clients know that they are champions of the cats' welfare and wellbeing. In 2016, I had the honour of meeting Daniel Joffe, DVM, head of VCA Canada. We discussed ending declawing. In 2018, VCA Canada, with over 100 hospitals in 5 provinces, elected to stop declawing. Dr. Joffe says he was prepared for a backlash but instead received nothing but love and admiration for this ethical policy.

Lastly, how close are we to seeing the end of declawing? Which states/countries are left to convince?
I think the tide is turning and that we will see an end to declawing in many areas of North America in my lifetime. As of 2019, nine US cities and four Canadian provinces have banned declawing. That's a population of around 12 million people. We have bills in several states. Eventually we will prevail. Declawing is wrong. There's no question about that.

I find it difficult to comprehend that, with so much evidence proving how cruel declawing is, there is still a long way to go before every state in the US and every country around the world makes this practice illegal[5]. Educating cat owners is vital if people are going to be dissuaded from declawing when furniture is getting torn to bits. It's down to the practising vet to simply say the word 'no' and offer an alternative solution to this natural feline behaviour. This does not have to be an expensive process. As The Paw Project rightly points out on their Frequently Answered Questions page:

> it can be far more expensive to deal with a declawed cat who from then on has trouble using the litter tray, making it more likely that they toilet elsewhere in the home.

All great causes have many people connected to them but, like many great causes, it took someone of courage and nerves of steel to put their head above the parapet knowing that to do so would bring the huge mountain waiting to be climbed firmly into view. As Marc Bekoff, author of *The Emotional Lives Of Animals*, rightly points out, 'Silence is the enemy of social change'.

Thousands of cats should know the name of Dr. Jennifer Conrad. If only they could read!

Note: since this chapter was written New York City stepped up to become the first state in the US to ban declawing[6].

A CATTY SUM UP

1. Cats not only scratch to keep their claws in shape but also to leave their scent and visual markings.

2. Scratching is a natural hardwired behaviour that's part of having a cat.

3. Understanding a cat's natural behaviour should help the cat carer provide the necessary outlets.

CAT CHAT

Cat Claw Covers And Other Alternatives

A recent UK news article caught my attention and started a friendly worldwide debate amongst cat groomers regarding the use of claw covers such as Soft Paws™. The article was about a domestic cat called Christina[1]. Christina was taken to the vets after showing signs of distress and pain from red claw covers of an unknown brand. The caps were stuck firmly on the claws, and it had not been determined in the report how long they had been there. The decision to remove them under anaesthetic was taken by the vets at Battersea Cats and Dogs Home, with the story covered in UK newspapers such as the *Telegraph* and the *Vet Times*.

The specific details of what happened did not appear in the reports but I can only assume that the nail caps were not fitted by a professional groomer or were left on for too long, causing the extreme outcome they did.

This 'growing fad' has actually been a staple service of cat groomers for a long period of time, more so in the US than in the UK. The companies selling nail caps state, 'If applied correctly and removed within the time frame stated, the nail caps should cause no physical pain', although there is never any mention of the anxiety this may cause a cat whilst restricting them from their natural behaviour and about which they have no say.

Before I go any further I would like to point out where I stand on this subject. I have always seen animals as sentient beings we share this planet with and feel that we have a great duty of responsibility to ensure any animal we take as a pet is not forced to change their natural behaviours to fit in with our lives, likes and dislikes. 'They are not commodities or fashion accessories', quite rightly pointed out by Battersea's head of catteries Lindsey Quinlan. But whilst discussing the cat-claw covers with my US grooming colleagues, a worrying trend started to rear its ugly head and highlighted the serious consequences of banning claw covers outright over there. Many US cat groomers feel that claw covers are better than the worst option some cat owners would consider – declawing their cats or, worse still, taking their cat back to a shelter which may well result in euthanasia.

Bonnie V. Beaver, in her book *Feline Behaviour: A Guide for Veterinarians*, reported in a US study that between 24.4% and 52.3% of cats are declawed, with 86% of cat owners stating the reason was down to household damage. Of this percentage half of said cat owners would have chosen to get rid of their cat if declawing was not an option. This is where claw covers can save lives in the US. But what does it say for humans? Sadly, not much!

In the UK, declawing was outlawed by the Animal Welfare Act 2006. Even before the 2006 Act, however, declawing was extremely uncommon, to the extent that most people had never seen a declawed cat. The procedure was considered cruel by almost all British vets, who refused to perform it except on medical grounds. The *Guide to Professional Conduct* of the Royal College of Veterinary Surgeons stated that declawing was:

> only acceptable where, in the opinion of the veterinary surgeon, injury to the animal is likely to occur during normal activity. It is not acceptable if carried out for the convenience of the owner ... the removal of claws, particularly those which are weight bearing, to preclude damage to furnishings is not acceptable.

It's no surprise then that a US vet designed vinyl claw caps in 1990 – probably as a solution to thwart declawing.

It's appalling that in the 21st century such a cruel practice of amputating an animal's claws from their body still exists in a first-world country. I'm further appalled that people would consider declawing or dumping their cat back in a shelter rather than educate themselves on why cats do the things they do so that environmental changes can be implemented.

I do understand that in some circumstances claw covers may help in a dire situation and that every case should be looked at closely and, if needs be, claw covers considered as a last option. An example of this was when I was asked to give advice on a cat who was seriously self-harming. Their claws were long and the cat had an issue with scratching themself, causing open wounds on the body. All avenues were investigated, including medical causes plus behavioural causes as well as advising on trimming the claws. I then advised that if all else failed then claw covers, like the brand Soft Paws, would have to be professionally applied, as a temporary measure, to try and stop the wounds getting any worse. I very rarely suggest such measures but know that in the UK declawing or killing an otherwise healthy pet would not happen. I was lucky in that I had room to try different options out. However, cultures and attitudes differ across the world.

I checked the website of my favourite US cat behaviourist Jackson Galaxy to see what he felt about claw covers. I wasn't surprised to see that he mentions them as an option at the end of a blog piece on how to stop a cat scratching furniture. I have no doubt that this is due to declawing still being legal in many areas of the US as well as animal shelters being overrun with unwanted pets. Thus, he knows claw covers could save the life of a cat and are far better than amputation of the claws. How a cat owner would ever consider declawing their cat to save the furniture is beyond me.

All claw-cover brand websites, in their FAQs, state that their products are completely safe and humane and that they're an excellent alternative to declawing. I have no doubt they are safe and, somewhat humane (depending on how you define humane) for indoor cats, but is this the right way of looking at it? It reminds me of when a cat client asked me to shave her domestic shorthair cat under sedation because it left fur around the home. Yes, it's a cat and they have fur. I could have given the popular 'lion cut', a cut that removes all of the hair from a cat, leaving the paws, feet, tail and mane, but this would have felt wrong to me. I can hear readers shouting at me 'but they probably had asthma'. No, they didn't! It's lazy cat parenting.

SCRATCH FACTS

According to Bonnie V. Beaver, 15% of cat behaviour complaints are down to cats scratching furniture. So, let's first examine the main reasons why cats scratch:

1. Marking territory by leaving scent from the scent glands in the paws.
2. Leaving scratch marks as a visual marker for other cats.
3. Scratching rough surfaces such as furniture removes the outer dead layer of claw, exposing a fresh sharp new claw underneath.
4. Stretching the muscles in the paw, which is a necessary action for cats.
5. Stretching out other parts of the body when reaching up to scratch a vertical post.
6. Conditioning the claws. The old claw sheath falls off to reveal a fresh sharp one underneath.
7. Grooming using the claws.

Thus claw covers, although not usually harmful physically, can stop a cat's natural everyday activities that are important to it.

GIVING A CAT ALTERNATIVES

Let's now look at environmental options to guide a cat to the correct places to scratch. (What about cats scratching frail old ladies with thin skin?, I can hear you ask. I will cover scratching humans later!)

I have seen many clients with the wrong sized scratch posts for their cats, or designer furniture their cat doesn't use, so it's good to try to understand what your cat prefers from the start. For example, many cats prefer to stretch upwards for a good scratch so a small vertical kitten post for an adult cat is unsuitable. Other cats prefer to scratch on a horizontal surface, but again ensure the right size is bought. Look for large, chunky, solid vertical posts such as the ones sold by Kalvin Scratchers, or large, horizontal scratchers such as the lovely Pet Fusion cat loungers. Sprinkle the scratching furniture with catnip and place your scratchers in areas your cat likes to hang out in, or close to their bedding for when they wake up and want a good scratch and a stretch. Deter unwanted scratching areas by using double-sided sticky tape or a motion-sensor air deterrent placed close by.

Other great scratching options are wall posts or sofa corners. Posts don't have to be expensive. There are many DIY articles, for example on the Purina website, on how to make scratch posts in an economical way.

Cat owners should strive to understand a cat's basic needs and behaviour, rather than putting their furniture first. If an animal is not suited to a home or lifestyle then perhaps another pet that is, should be considered?

Finally, we come to elderly or medically vulnerable cat owners. A vet, cat groomer or an experienced cat-loving friend can help keep a cat's claws sufficiently trimmed, should an elderly cat owner be worried about getting accidentally scratched by their pet. If a cat is aggressive, then steps should be taken to understand their behaviour to keep the cat owner safe. Steps can include hiring a cat behaviourist or speaking with a vet to see if any aggressive reactions have an underlying medical cause.

CHAPTER FIVE

I've Lost My Cat: What Should I Do?

'My relationships with my cats has saved me from a deadly, pervasive ignorance.'

William S. Burroughs

CHAPTER FIVE

In this chapter:

- Learn about the job of a cat detective.
- Get expert 'lost cat' advice, in conversation with Kim Freeman.
- Guidance on what to do if a cat is found.
- Step-by-step instructions on letting your cat out for the first time.

In central London, missing-cat posters adorn many lampposts on a weekly basis. Some offer rewards, some appeal to people's consciences by mentioning how much their children are missing their cat and need them home (almost as if the cat had been deliberately taken or held captive) and some just give a basic contact number under a photo of two large eyes peering out from the page. Often, the pictures are soggy from rain or of a very poor quality and it's hard to make out the colour of the puss in question, let alone any distinct markings.

It's a cat owner's worst nightmare when their cat goes missing. Panic sets in and we feel that our little fur babies will just curl up and die without us. Well, the first thing you should be reassured by is that cats go into survival mode if lost. They will hunt or scavenge for food and most will find a warm place to hunker down in. They may be hungry and dirty when found and slimmer than when you last saw them, but most healthy young cats will not be starving, or on the verge of death.

I wrote about a lost cat in my previous book, *Claws*. Lucky, a timid indoor cat had managed to escape from a cat carrier on the underground as she and her owner returned home from a visit in the country. Terrified by the rush-hour mayhem, Lucky jumped on to the train tracks running into the darkness of the tunnel. A search ensued over days, and guess what Lucky was doing when a Transport For London worker stumbled upon the poor dirty, bedraggled cat one early morning whilst doing some repair work before the stations opened? Lucky was eating a mouse.

There are multiple things to consider when our mogs 'go walkies'. Are they street savvy? Do they know the area? Are they male or female, spayed or neutered? Are they friendly or very nervous? All of these things carry significance and determine how our lost cats will act. Sometimes a cat isn't lost. They have just gone exploring in their territory. This can happen particularly when a cat has moved into a new area and is finally let outside. Other cats are confident and friendly and may have several homes they go to for food and attention, so always ask neighbours and local businesses. It's surprising what people assume when they find a cat who isn't wearing a collar. The cat may be crying for food or attention, as if it's going to be their last diary entry before they starve to death! Little does the recipient know they could be the fifth person the cat has tried their sob story on.

We are a nation of cat lovers on the verge of a nervous breakdown every time we see our cats' back legs disappear through the cat-flap door. The silence deafens us as we watch the clock's hands slowly creak round and round. When will they be home? What are they doing? Are they safe?

Incidentally, a friend of mine had been watching the slow hands of that 'lost cat' clock for two years when out of the blue she received a phone call from a veterinary practice, a 40-minute drive from her home, stating that their elderly cat had been found.

Morrissey was a streetwise longhaired cat and knew his area well. Perhaps he climbed into a removal van or another mode of transport, which carried him unbeknownst outside of his territory. Two years later, Morrissey was found in the countryside all skin and bones, matted fur and in extremely poor health. He had obviously survived as a hunter but without regular grooming, care, warmth and attention, this elderly chappy was dangerously underweight and too matted to be able to move comfortably. It was only when I had rushed to my friend's home to help try and de-mat Morrissey that we found a tumour near to his bottom, previously obscured by matted fur. Heartbreakingly, Morrissey, having found his way back home, had to be put to sleep.

Whilst reading the wonderful book, *Lost Cat* by Caroline Paul, I became intrigued by cat-cams and cat-navigation systems. Researching gadgets on the internet, I came across various pet detectives, and the one that caught my attention was renowned US cat detective Kim Freeman, author of a book called *How To Find Your Lost Cat*.

Kim's work involves tracking down missing cats. Being on call night and day to find our pesky critters, she certainly has her work well and truly cut out for her.

Whilst doing a Google search, heaps of lost-kitty advice comes to the fore and this made me intrigued as to what Kim, the ultimate cat detective, thought. Does she roll her eyes at some of the suggestions?

> Well, a boyfriend at the time said (about my missing male neutered cat), 'He's just out looking for a girlfriend, he'll be back'. That should have told me something about that particular boyfriend! And there's always the standard comment in Texas, 'Oh, ya know there's coyotes round here'. I still can't believe people say that to someone in crisis mode. Would they say that if a toddler were missing? Or a puppy? The cat experts' advice ranged from putting food and used kitty litter outside (I still see this awful advice passed around on Facebook), to walking around calling, shaking a bag of treats, which can quickly turn into a Pied Piper disaster that attracts all the local cats in the area.
>
> When a cat is missing, people think like humans. They generally approach the search as if it were a missing dog. Instead, they need to think like a cat: throw logic out, bring the litter and food in and read up on feline-focused methods, which may seem counter-intuitive at first, to recover a missing cat.

In Conversation With Kim Freeman

You tell cat owners to think like a cat. Would you say that understanding the natural behaviour of a cat is at the forefront of being a cat detective?

Yes, absolutely. Most people approach a lost-cat search from a linear, human perspective. They need to understand and factor in how a cat's instincts are key to proper search methods and a successful recovery.

Being a cat detective is a fascinating job steeped in mystery. Could you please expand on the training aspect involved?

The basics of the training came from the world of 'missing persons' procedures and investigative questioning. This means profiling the subject, learning their habits, personality and preferences, then assessing the location based on probability theory and using tracking and clues to find the direction of travel. I've also had additional training in mammal tracking and bird language (which helps determine the location and movement of cats). Another key element is learning to use a variety of high-tech equipment, such as sound-amplification devices, night-vision cameras, thermal scopes, borescopes and humane trapping techniques.

Regarding the general behaviour of cats versus the behaviour of lost cats: do the two act very differently in terms of natural behaviour? For instance: if a lost cat's personality or typical behaviour changes, can you rely on the fact that they will remain consistent; and therefore are you still able to use information about their normal character/personality to find them?

Yes; it does change when they are lost or displaced into new territory. For example, even cats who always meow or reply to the owner's calls at home will go silent when in a new place. It's cat instinct; they stay silent in order to be invisible to potential predators. Owners who go out calling them think that they'll come bounding out of hiding, then assume the cat is not there, when, actually, they may hear the call but not respond. This is one reason I tell people not to call their cat unless in a closed environment such as a neighbour's garage. There is also the chance that calls outdoors all around the neighbourhood will draw the cat away from home. This is another example of the importance of knowing how cats think in order to get them recovered.

What does your success rate of finding a lost pet depend on?

A lot depends on the owner's willingness to follow my advice and whether the cat is indoor-only or has outdoor access. In terms of an indoor-only who has managed to get out, many owners might think their cat wouldn't manage to survive, being left to fend for itself.

Is it true that most indoor cats can easily revert to being semi-feral in order to survive? Also, please explain how you change your approach when dealing with indoor versus outdoor cats?

When an indoor cat escapes, the question to ask is, 'Where is the cat hiding?' When an outdoor-access cat does not return home as usual, the investigative mystery to solve is, 'What happened to the cat?' Even the most pampered indoor cat will have decent survival skills if displaced outdoors. People worry that their indolent, indoor-only kitty will starve or wander into the road, but cats have strong instincts that keep them alive.

Are you ever told about any behavioural issues after a cat has been missing for a long time and then found?

Yes, especially in multi-cat households. There is often hissing and scuffles between cats when a long-lost cat returns home. It's almost as though you are bringing a new cat into the home. This might be a situation where I should refer them to you! Recently recovered cats can also tend to either hide or become very clingy and be prone to food gorging. Owners need to be aware of re-feeding syndrome if a cat has been in starvation mode. People want to give them all they can eat, but that's actually a bad idea. After starvation, cats need to be fed small amounts frequently and have their liver and kidney values checked with a veterinarian.

After reading the book *Lost Cat* by Caroline Paul, I picked up on two things: the fact that neighbourly relations can be important if your

cat goes missing, and that people sometimes assume that their cat won't know how to survive, which causes them to panic. What's your experience of the role of neighbours and cats' ability to survive?

Yes, people do assume the cat is not going to be able to survive and give them up for dead, often within a week. Cats are amazing survivors! And yes, talking to neighbours is key not only to persuade them to allow a search but also to know what their cat's territory was prior to going missing. Most GPS cameras are only useful if they've been used to track a cat's daily rounds before they were lost.

Does it matter where a person lives in terms of following set advice? For instance, would you advise a different search approach depending on city or country living?

Yes, but the search radius is still roughly the same. Cats who live in the country are also more likely to come into contact with a predator, at least here in the States. Most altered cats stay within 250 feet of home with occasional excursions out of that zone. When an indoor-only cat escapes they are more likely to be hiding nearby than an outdoor-access cat who roams daily.

Yes, true. Someone said to me that the search methods would be different for cat owners who have lost a cat here in the UK but I'm convinced it's roughly the same. What do you think?

I might look more closely at the terrain in a country setting, in case a cat regularly visits other homes or special hunting grounds, but in general, my search methods would remain the same. I would certainly have less stress without the worry of finding fur or bones as evidence of an unfortunate encounter from a coyote. On a side note, cat owners should keep in mind that domestic dogs go into a pack mentality in groups of two or more, and probably kill more cats in the US than coyotes do.

You mention the personality of cats in your book. Does the sex of a lost cat make a difference to your search methods?

No, the personality is more important than the gender, but whether the cat is intact or spayed/neutered does make a difference. Some male cats are friendly and will approach strangers, while some are extremely skittish. The same goes for females, so the search technique depends primarily on personality and circumstances. Cats who have not been altered tend to roam further in search of mates.

Last but not least, what immediate advice can you give to a desperate cat owner whose cat hasn't returned home for 24 hours?

Start searching and take action right away. Do not 'wait and see'. Do not leave food or kitty litter outside as it can create complications, luring other cats and dogs in, and sabotage your recovery efforts.

As you can see, it's quite a scientific approach to finding cats. It must be a very fulfilling job when ringing a client to tell them that their little one has been found. I remember a friend of mine who had lost a cat that he was caring for whilst the owners were away on holiday. The cat was an indoor-only cat who had darted unexpectedly out of the front door when he returned home from work. This is where profiling comes in handy. The cat was indoor-only and therefore not street savvy. Her personality was timid. Thus, she would certainly have been scared suddenly finding herself outside in unfamiliar territory.

Therefore, this cat went into survival mode and hunkered down in thick bushes close by. No doubt she hunted for food when no one was around or maybe scavenged from a local bin. Four days later, she was found when I advised my friend to go out calling when the streets would be at their quietest, around 4 to 5 a.m. It remains a mystery why this indoor-only cat ran outside in the first place, as the owners stated their cat never went by the front door or showed any interest in going outside previously. Perhaps she wanted to understand where it was?

Another friend's cat disappeared for two days. Her cat was very friendly and was a free-roaming cat so, as well as having street smarts; they also had no fear of people. In fact, quite the opposite. Her cat was found peering out of a neighbour's window across the busy street, having wandered into the home a few days previously. As the cat settled down for the night and wasn't wearing a collar, the neighbour felt very relaxed feeding this wandering feline. In fact, it turns out this cheeky chops was a regular in their home and treated it like a hotel.

This is what Kim means when speaking about personality types changing the way a search is conducted. It's a simple thing but perhaps not one that people think of straight away.

Although there's a lot of advice online (not all of which is helpful) to assist people through the initial panic that rises as each hour moves past your cat's usual dinner time, hiring your own personal cat detective would not only save time, but would also be the coolest thing. Plus, your cat would love the fact money was spent on the best cat tracker even if they were close by, watching with a wee, sly catty smirk! The next Cat Chat will guide you through letting your cat out for the first time. Don't panic. Help is at hand.

A CATTY SUM UP

1. Male cats tend to roam further than female cats.

2. Your cat's personality and whether they are indoor or street savvy can help determine how they are likely to act and whether they will be close to home or further afield.

3. Never give up hope. Cats are strong survivors and prolific hunters.

CAT CHAT

Letting Your Cat Out For The First Time

So, you have decided to allow your cat out. That's great news! Obviously, circumstances will dictate if this is right, such as where your home is situated, the density of cats in the area (which your cat may find stressful), or what breed of cat you have (some cat carers are worried about their cat being stolen if an expensive breed), but this chapter should help ease you into taking those first tentative steps.

I know people are fearful of letting their cats roam. I know and I understand that feeling too well, having two indoor Norwegian Forest Cats that are lead-trained. However, an interesting study by Jessica Wilson and colleagues at the University of Bristol[1] on the risks of letting cats out came up with some unexpected findings. A low percentage of 3.9% were reported to have been involved in a road-traffic accident within the first year of being let outside. Cats living in rural areas were at a higher risk, probably due to drivers speeding and the unpredictability of traffic making it difficult for cats to learn any road lessons.

Whilst writing this, I'm reminded of a stunning male Bengal cat called Benji, whose behaviour I was trying to assist with. Benji lived with his single male owner in an urban street. The home had a large garden, which slotted nicely in with neighbouring gardens either side. Benji's owner worked long hours and Benji would spend his days looking out at the garden, howling. His behaviour became destructive and his moods turned to aggression towards his owner. It all came down to Benji wanting to go outside. He was bored and frustrated at home, with little else to do but look out on to a lovely garden he couldn't use. Eventually, Benji's owner took my advice and, after introducing his cat to the outside world on a lead, took a leap of faith and started to let him roam freely via a cat flap. Cat-proofing his garden wasn't an option at that stage although the reasons why fail my memory now. What I do remember is that Benji's behaviour changed dramatically. He became a happy cat and loved being outside. No one stole him, he didn't become lost, he didn't get beaten up by other cats and he wasn't run over by a car. He just enjoyed being a cat and lived a long and happy life doing what cats do when they go outside. I'm not saying that the unfortunate things I have listed do not happen, but in this case Benji's life was transformed by letting go of the worst case scenarios, the 'what if's' and taking a leap of faith. This was the best option for this cat in this set of circumstances.

I'm all for cats being allowed out and will champion this but I agree that circumstances must dictate and I would never advise a cat be let outside if the home is on a busy main road or near to other dangers. Having said this, there are always different options to look at, which we can discuss later. I can only speak for cat owners based in the UK, before you all start tweeting me about coyotes!

Here are some steps that can make the 'letting out' process easier and give you peace of mind when considering whether and how to introduce your cat to the big wide world:

Microchip: Make sure your cat is microchipped and also wears a collar with your details on. If your cat starts meowing at a neighbour's kitchen window, they will know straight away that they are not a stray. The chip protects you even further: in the event that someone tries to claim your cat as their own, by including your address in the information it will show up the moment they're taken to a vet and scanned. The chip is as small as a grain of rice and is put within the loose skin at the back of the cat's neck. This procedure is painless. Your cat might feel a tiny pinprick but it's over in seconds. My cat Zaza didn't even know when the process was complete, and my other cat Kiki just gave a barely audible meow when the chip entered the skin.

The Collar: Get your kitten used to wearing a collar early on. The collar should have your contact details on and not be too loose around the neck or it could get caught on something. An easy-release collar is the most advisable one. Feel around the neck to make sure that the collar is not too tight either. A good rule of thumb is to stick two fingers between the collar and the neck. Remember that when your cat is still growing, you will need to re-adjust the collar as their neck expands! I know one client who didn't think about adjusting it the older or heavier the cat got, not until I told her it was too tight. Extra things to think about: a little bell on the collar could alert any bird that your cat tries to catch.

Neutered/Spayed: If you do not want your cat to get pregnant, or your tomcat to impregnate all of the un-spayed females in the area, it's wise to get them spayed or neutered at your vet's clinic before allowing them outside. Un-neutered male toms will go far and wide seeking females, will howl at night outside any homes where they suspect a female cat resides, and will also mark everywhere around your home with a pungent smell. It's also responsible cat parenting to ensure that your cat is not contributing to creating lots of kittens that may well end up in rescue centres.

Age: You can gradually start introducing your cat to going outside at around the age of six months, once they have been neutered/spayed and had all of their injections. Obviously at this age they are still going to be getting into trouble so it's really important to make sure they are supervised until you feel confident to allow them to roam further.

Up-To-Date Injections: The Blue Cross advises that kittens should not be allowed outside until at least a week after finishing their first course of vaccinations. Please ask your vet for detailed advice. Vaccinations should be once a year, although cats that are never going to be in direct contact with other cats may not need all of the recommended vaccinations. My cats are 12, are lead trained, never have direct contact with other cats and have not been vaccinated since being kittens. They are still extremely healthy and have never been ill but everyone's cat will encounter a different set of circumstances, so best check what your vet's stance is on this.

Recall: It's really important to make sure your cat comes back when they're called or when you make a noise, like the shaking of their favourite treats. Start working on this before you introduce them to the garden. My cats come running when I shake a tube of their favourite treats, and when they come to me they get rewarded. Once your recall has been established, you are set to open those doors.

Early Days: Start taking your cat out a little at a time. You can either do this with or without a harness. Your cat will be curious and nervous at the same time, so 15–20 minutes of outside time should whet their appetite. They need to get used to the garden – its smells, its borders – and also the route back in again. At this early stage, don't introduce the cat flap. Open the door and take your cat out and then bring them back again when you feel they have had enough time. This could be 10–15 minutes, although your cat may wish for longer to explore. You could also just sit outside the open door and call your cat until they walk out under their own steam. Play with them outside and make it a fun time. Keep doing that every day. Take the treats with you and try to call them to make sure that they come back when needed. You will know when it's time to show them the cat flap. Don't force your cat out if they really don't want to go outside. The whole process should be gentle and go at the cat's pace, not your own.

Cat Flaps: There are lots of cat flaps to choose from. Some open once they are programmed with your cat's microchip number, some work with special magnet collars, and they all come in different sizes to accommodate the shape of your cat. The best ones to go for are the ones that do not allow other cats to come into your home, so I would personally go for the microchip-operated ones. It's fairly easy to get your cat used to using the cat flap. Have one person stand on one side, with you on the other, and keep passing the cat through until they understand. Then try to coax them through with their favourite treat waiting for them at the other side, holding the flap open and then letting go slightly once their body is halfway through. Within five or ten minutes they should be clambering through it. Other ways to get your cat used to the flap are to either have the flap tied open with string, gradually lowering the flap over time until they are passing through, or to have the flap tied open and a clear thin sheet in its place, so the cat gets used to going 'through' something to get out. You could also train your cat to walk through the flap before it's fixed into place. If you have a multi-cat household I would advise two entry and exit points to relieve any tensions around a major resource.

The First 'Wander': The first time your cat ventures outside you will feel worried. It's only natural. Your cat will wander further afield because they naturally want to explore and establish their territory and home range. They will also make themselves known to neighbouring cats. Don't worry. Cats have a great sense of direction and can find their way around. You can go outside and use your recall technique (like shaking a treat packet) and see them come running through the bushes. Make sure that you don't do this every minute or your cat will never get to see anything! Males have a much wider range than females, who will stay close to the house, possibly only venturing a garden or two away.

Other Cats: Your cat will need to establish their territory and do what all cats have to do: learn to share space. There may be stand-offs, but this is totally natural and hopefully your cat will come out of the 'meeting all the neighbourhood cats' experience with no lasting trauma and learn when and where to go! If you have another cat entering your garden and trying to assert itself over your cat or your cat's territory and your cat is not sending them packing, then go outside and deter the intruder with a squirt from a water pistol. It's fine if your neighbour's cat is just being friendly, as long as your cat is fine with it, but if any of your neighbours' cats think that your garden is their territory too, then watery dissuasion is the answer – oh, and get your cat some boxing lessons!

Wildlife: To help the local wildlife, you should always raise any bird feeders high off the ground and in a place your cat cannot get to. A bell on your cat's collar may help in warning prey that danger is near. Keeping a cat in at night can help with reducing their hunting escapades.

Cat-Proofing Your Garden: Some people may want to consider securing their garden, as you would if you built a large aviary. This option should be considered if you are too worried about your cat being free-roaming, but don't want them to be an exclusively indoor cat. It's a simple solution that can easily be done using wire mesh, garden poles and some advice from a landscape gardener or a handy friend! Get some ideas from websites like the cat enclosures section of Cats Of Australia[2]. There are plenty of other sites too. Google *cat runs, cat enclosures* and *garden aviaries* and you'll have plenty of good ideas to consider.

One company that has come up with a rather unique idea is based in the UK and is called Katzecure. They have invented a simple wooden roller that attaches to any garden fence. The roller does not allow the cat to get a stable footing on it and therefore keeps the cat safe in the garden. Their designs also blend well into a garden landscape. Another company I highly recommend is called ProtectAPet. They use thin mesh and brackets to ensure a completely safe and secure garden border.

Night Time: Cats are not nocturnal but 'crepuscular', meaning that they would naturally hunt for their prey at dusk and dawn. However, some cats love going out at night due to the fact that it's quieter, with fewer people. Though cats go out and hunt for prey at night, some people do not feel comfortable leaving their cat flap open at this time out of fear for their cats' safety. They worry about potential dangers like foxes, other neighbouring cats and traffic. In the early stages and to give peace of mind, I would recommend shutting the cat flap at night whilst your cat gets used to their new freedom. It may be confusing for your cat, but they will soon understand the routine. Everyone feels differently and you should do what makes you feel comfortable, especially at the beginning of your cat's outdoor life.

GPS Tracking Devices: The market has exploded with some very good GPS tracking devices for cats with improvements on weight, bulkiness and precision being the goal of most pet-tracking companies. Four companies to check out are: Pawtrack, Tabcat, Pawtrax and Pawfit. Your cat will always be on your radar if they don't mind the collar, so it's definitely worth checking out what's on offer[3].

It's not uncommon for a cat to go missing for several days at the beginning of their outdoor adventures, only to saunter back to you without a care in the world. This is largely due to the cat seeing what's outside and exploring their home range. A paper entitled 'Search Methods Used To Locate Missing Cats And Locations Where Missing Cats Are Found'[4] reported on data gathered from an online questionnaire that asked questions regarding search methods used to locate missing cats and locations where missing cats were found. Firstly, the most important finding from this retrospective case series was that approximately one-third of cats were recovered within seven days. Secondly, a physical search increased the chances of finding cats alive, and 75% of cats were found within a 500-metre radius of their point of escape. Thirdly, those cats who were indoor-outdoor and allowed outside unsupervised, travelled longer distances compared with indoor cats who were never allowed outside. Lastly, cats considered to be highly curious in nature were more likely to be found inside someone else's house compared to other personality types. These findings suggest that a physical search within the first week of a cat going missing could be a useful strategy. The study shows clearly that personality and lifestyle are the most important factors when deciding how to find your cat.

WHAT TO DO IF A CAT IS FOUND THAT SEEMS LOST

After reading the story of a kitten[5] who was found by a family who then wanted to keep the kitten, despite them being microchipped and belonging to another family, I thought I would conclude this Cat Chat with a few tips.

Cats can stay close to home but some can also wander far and wide, especially if checking out a new territory. Males roam further than females, who tend to stay closer to their home range. Some cats, for whatever reason, may find themselves lost. When you find a cat who looks dirty, a bit thin or disorientated, who may be in your garden, in your garage, by the bins or outside of your home crying in a distressed way, you should offer this cat some warmth and food. (Caution: some cats are thin because they are old or have hyperthyroidism.) This doesn't mean you should be feeding every cat who visits your home! We will get into that later, but I think we can safely say that a lost cat tends to have that look of being lost (can't quite put my finger on it!) and will appear thin, gaunt or dirty. A lost cat may also vocalise more and in a distressed way. However, bringing a cat into the home doesn't mean that's the end of it and the cat is now yours. There's always a story behind a lost cat and nine times out of ten there's a heartbroken human desperate to find out what has happened to their pet. Here are some steps you can follow having found a cat you feel is lost:

- Ask neighbours if they know of anyone with a cat of that description, or if they have seen the cat around the area before.
- Call the local vets in the area to see if the description fits one of their clients' cats, who may have reported the cat missing to them, and take the cat into the nearest vet to see if it has a microchip that can be scanned.
- Use social media to post a photo of the cat for people to share – many local groups set up on Facebook to share information.
- Join and post on the website 'Next Door', which is for local communities to share information.
- Post a photo of the cat plus details of where it was found on websites such as Animal Search or The National Pet Register.
- Post flyers with a photo of the cat giving your details.
- Ask for vet information or proof of ownership of the cat before handing it over.

FEEDING LOCAL CATS IN GENERAL

Cats are curious by nature and confident, friendly cats will visit lots of local homes to have a nose if a window is left open or they know they will get some attention and treats. People assume a crying cat by their window, without a collar, is starving and lost. Don't be fooled. Your home is probably the fifth house the cat has visited using the same old trick! Many cats become obese this way because everyone locally gives it a treat. The main differences between a local cat who loves visiting other homes and a lost cat is that usually the former has a healthy, clean coat, looks a normal weight, goes away if doesn't get attention, has a collar (but many times not), and has a streetwise, relaxed look about them. Things to consider when a local cat keeps visiting the home:

- The cat could be on medication or a special diet which doesn't include titbits and treats.
- The owners may find it upsetting that their cat is staying away from home longer.
- The cat could become obese.
- It encourages food begging.
- It isn't nice for any resident cats if another cat is encouraged to visit the premises.

The above isn't saying you shouldn't give your neighbour's cat a stroke. It's merely pointing out that a neighbour's cat shouldn't be given treats and encouraged to stay in the home, unless of course you have checked with the owner that it's OK for their cat to enter your home to hang out and to give it the occasional treat.

CATS AND THE LAW: WHO OWNS THE CAT ONCE FOUND?

The original owners who have documentation via a microchip, vet visits, photographs or email proof own the cat. Anyone who finds a lost cat must do all they can to find the original owners before deciding whether to offer the cat a new home. If you feel suspicious about the original owners or the background the cat has come from then contact the RSPCA (UK) or your local rescue. However, most lost cats have simply wandered a bit too far after possibly getting a fright, or from other unforeseen circumstances, leading to disorientation. Only after trying all steps to locate the home of the cat can steps be taken to adopt. This could include getting the cat microchipped with your own details. Extensive information for cat owners wishing to know how the law might apply to certain situations can be found online at **www.thecatgroup.org.uk/pdfs/Cats-law-web.pdf**.

CHAPTER SIX

Can Our Cats Talk To Us?

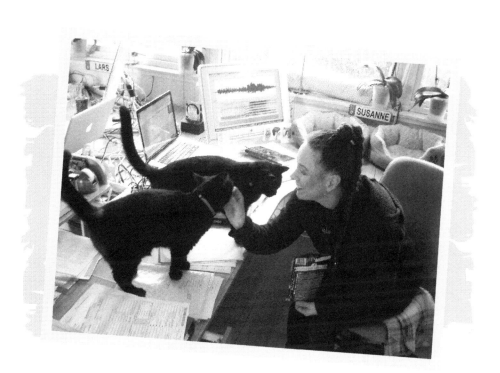

'Cats have it all – admiration, an endless sleep, and
company only when they want it.'

Rod McKuen

CHAPTER SIX

In this chapter:

- Understand the language of cats.
- Hear insider knowledge on the research to date on cat talk, in conversation with Dr. Susanne Schötz.
- Learn how else cats communicate with us.

Every cat lover I know has conversations with their cat(s), including me. Every cat lover I know is also convinced that they know what their cat is saying back to them, including me. We enjoy putting words into our cats' mouths when we speak back to ourselves in cat-reply, never thinking that we might be wrong in our interpretations. We speak to them as we would to a baby, and when cat lovers get together, we speak way more about our cats than any other subject!

Cats have many ways they communicate with us, which I will go through in detail in this chapter's Cat Chat: *How Else Do Cats Communicate?* But when it comes to language, no one is quite sure what our little tykes can or can't understand, or if their meows mean anything in human-language terms when they do answer us back. A recent study entitled 'Domestic Cats Discriminate Their Names From Other Words'[1] suggested that cats can recognise their individual names in the midst of other words, although I'm convinced this is probably more to do with the 'tone' of how we say the name rather than them understanding it's their name. Their response may also have something to do with usual expectations of attention or food. One of the researchers, Dr. Saito, further commented: 'Cats understand human cues better than many people think, but that did not mean they would respond as their owners might hope!'

When I read a review, in *Your Cat* magazine, of a book entitled *The Secret Language Of Cats,* and realised that the author, an associate professor of phonetics, was halfway through a five-year research project on feline language at Lund University in Sweden, I knew I had to track her down for a quick Cat Chat for this chapter.

Dr. Susanne Schötz aims to apply her knowledge of linguistics to the enigmatic world of verbal feline communications, which every cat-loving guardian is desperate to understand. Can our cats talk to us? Let's find out more.

In Conversation With Dr. Susanne Schötz

What was the catalyst for wishing to study the language of cats?

At a phonetics conference in 2010 I listened to a talk by Dr. Robert Eklund, who described his studies comparing the purring of a house cat to the purring of a cheetah. He had discovered a great number of phonetic similarities. His talk made me realise for the first time that maybe I could also contribute something to the research on cat sounds. Once I got home again, I got out my old video camera and recorded the purring of my cat Vincent. From then on I also began listening much more carefully to cat vocalisations, and quickly discovered that they have a very wide vocal repertoire. I started to regularly record my own cats and other cats that I met, and began studying their vocalisations with phonetic methods.

It must have been hugely exciting to study the language of your own cats. Please tell us a bit about them?

My cats have very distinct personalities and also different personal voices. I quickly learned to tell them apart by just listening to their voices. When you share your home with five cat individuals and communicate with them every day, you realise how much cats are able to vary their voices and still retain their personal voice quality. My females Donna and Vimsan both have high-pitched voices, but my biggest male Kompis can meow with an even higher voice. My other two males Rocky and Turbo have more low-pitched voices, but Turbo uses a more raspy and hoarse voice, while Rocky's voice is softer and more breathy.

Could you tell us more about your research project, Melody in Human–Cat Communication?

The purpose of this five-year project, which started in 2016 and is funded by The Marcus and Amalia Wallenberg Foundation, is to study the communication between humans and domestic cats. Specifically, we will investigate how prosody, including voice, melody (intonation) and speaking style – in human speech as well as in cat vocalisations – influences vocal communication. The research team is Robert Eklund, Joost Van De Weijer and me. We also have a team of consultants on hand, from clinical veterinarians and zoologists/biologists, to experts on animal communication and felid vocalisations.

In the first study, we will investigate how cats vary their melody (intonation) in human-directed and cat-directed vocalisations. How is cat prosody varied in different contexts or situations? How do human listeners perceive this intonational variation? We will develop a prosodic typology of cat vocalisations and present our results on a popular scientific website.

In the second study, we will apply new methods to examine how cats perceive different prosodic cues in human speech. Do they distinguish between different voices (familiar–unfamiliar, adults–children) and speaking styles (pet-directed, adult-directed), and do they prefer certain intonation patterns?

The project primarily concerns basic research and represents pioneering work within human–cat communication. Our results may lead to an improved quality of life for cats and potentially for other companion animals (pets) as well. Understanding the vocal strategies used by humans and cats in human–cat communication will have profound implications for our understanding of how we communicate with our pets in general, and has the potential to improve the relationship between animals and humans in several fields, including animal therapy, veterinary medicine and animal sheltering[2].

You say in your book *The Secret Language Of Cats* that cats may speak in dialects or accents, depending on their guardians. Have you managed to find any scientific evidence for this idea and could you talk us through your findings?

We are currently categorising and analysing our data (from the 70 cats mentioned above), and one of the questions we will look into is whether cats living in different parts of Sweden (South, East-Central) adjust their vocalisations to the different dialects or accents that their owners or human caretakers are speaking. [Research update (June 2020) concludes that cats living in Sweden have not developed any significant dialectal variation.]

Do you personally think the data will show they can?

I honestly can't say yet. However, we have much anecdotal evidence of cats trying to imitate the voice quality and pitch of their owners, and now we are excited to find out if cats also imitate the dialectal intonation of their owners.

We know that, primarily, a cat's vocalisations are directed at humans. Do you know if cats from the same household can understand what their fellow cats are trying to communicate to us?

I would think so. They are probably able to interpret the mental and emotional state of their fellow cats when they communicate with their human caretakers or owners with sounds. For example, my cats all come running if one of them meows at me to solicit a treat.

Are they running to you because they understand what the cat said, or are they responding to a cue, like the sound of the treat jar?

I don't know. It would be interesting to do a more systematic study to find that out.

A cat's meow can mean a variety of things, but do you feel the meaning we give to different meows depends on the human interpreting it? Or do you feel that we all, as humans, roughly interpret different meow sounds the same?

I think that the meaning of a meow is strongly related to the context or situation and also to the mental and emotional state of the cat. It's up to us humans to learn to listen more carefully and also to observe the context in which the vocalisations take place.

How do you hear vowel sounds in the vocalisations of cats, as I cannot hear the vowels myself?

I have played back numerous cat sounds to trained linguists, and they can all hear different vowels in many of the meowing, howling (yowling) and snarling (crying) vocalisations. For instance, some meows may contain e vowels (the mew), some contain a vowels (the squeak, the snarl, the chirp), some o and u vowels (the moan), and some will contain several vowels like eou (the meow) or oi (the howl or yowl). Some sounds, however, like purring, trilling and hissing do not contain any vowels.

Cats have learned how to use a voice to communicate with us, proving they are aware we are a species that responds well to sound. Do you feel cats are aware that they have the ability, using sound, to manipulate us as well as ask for what they want?

I don't think that cats deliberately try to manipulate us. They know that we react to sounds, and use vocalisations to communicate their needs, desires and intentions.

But doesn't that 'manipulation' get louder and louder until we give in?

Yes, you are quite right! I believe that cats learn to adjust their voices so that they can better manipulate us. But it's also up to us if we give in and allow ourselves to be manipulated.

Do you feel we will ever evolve to directly link meow sounds to actual words, or is it more the case that we can only assume what the meow sound means depending on what's happening at that time?

No, I don't think that we will ever be able to link a meow directly to a word in English or other human language, as cat vocalisations – as mentioned earlier – are so strongly related to the context and the mental state of the cat. Different cats also use slightly different nuances (in the voice quality, melody, etc).

I was thinking about the context of when meows are given. Differences between every cat, every owner and every situation mean that there are many possible interpretations. Could this be another reason why cat language can never be interpreted into human words?

Yes, I think that every cat has learned a slightly different way to communicate their special needs and wishes to us. But I also think that most cats use many sound categories and types. It's, for instance, not difficult to understand that hissing and growling are warning signals. However, it's difficult to translate them into English words, as the context and mental state also play a role here. Sometimes a hiss can mean 'Hey, enough now! Get lost', and sometimes a very similar hiss can mean, 'Oh, I didn't hear you coming. You scared me'.

We know cats use sound mainly in antagonistic responses to other cats (fighting/warnings) or in a sexual way (calling). Why do you feel that cats don't communicate with other cats in the same way they do with us?

Cat mothers and their kittens also communicate with sounds: trilling for greeting, chirruping to ask the others to follow them, mewing when a kitten has gone astray and can't find its way back to the nest, hissing and growling when the kittens play too violently, and purring when nursing. Many befriended cats communicate with friendly sounds like trilling, chirruping and purring, so in many ways, cats communicate with us in the same way that they communicate with other cats. One exception is the meow, which adult cats seem to use mainly with us humans to get our attention and when they want to tell us what they need, want or are about to do.

Is cat communication taught or instinctive? For example, does a kitten learn from its mother the art of 'speaking' to us through meows? Does the mother teach the kitten or do both do this instinctively?

I think both. Some vocalisations are innate, others are learned. For instance, mother cats seem to teach their kittens different 'words' for different prey animals (using different sounds for small and big prey), and cats also seem to learn to adapt their vocalisations to us. By trying different sound variants, they learn which ones get our attention and produce the quickest results (for instance when their food bowls are empty).

What has been your biggest discovery in your studies to date?

That cats seem to have a very complex and varied vocal repertoire, and that they seem to vary the voice quality and melody depending on context, their intentions and their emotional state. I have learned that if you only listen carefully you will be able to interpret your cat's vocalisations a lot better.

If we tried to mirror the meow of a cat do you think they would understand us?

I think that depends on what you are trying to communicate. If you just want the attention of your cat, meowing could do the trick. But if you want to tell him about the movie you saw last night, he probably won't understand, no matter how much you meow.

Do you think cats change their meow sounds for a different human – someone other than their usual guardian – or do meows remain the same? In other words, do they use the same pitch, vibration frequency and/or tone for their specific guardian's ears as they would for an unfamiliar person?

Yes and no, I think. Some variants would be the same, others won't. For instance, I have heard cats calling for their caretaker when she was away with a particular type of meowing that they would normally never use when the caretaker is nearby.

Do you feel cats would have developed such a variety of sound communications if they hadn't been domesticated?

I think that cats have a fairly wide range of sounds used in cat–cat communication. However, I also think that cats living with people are able to widen their sound repertoire to communicate better with their owners or caretakers.

Do cats in the wild have the same ranges of sound communication as our domestic cats, excluding the purr?

Most sounds are used in cat–cat communication, but I think that cats have developed some meow variants which are used mainly with humans.

What are the main emotions you have linked so far to cat vocalisations? For example, is there a meow equivalent of frustration?

Cats sometimes convey their emotions in their vocal communication. A kitten in distress mews, stressed and anxious cats often moan, happy and content cats may trill, purr or chirrup, while cats who are discontent can warn other cats (or humans) by growling, howling (yowling), hissing, spitting and snarling. Moreover, the melody (or intonation) also seems to vary depending on the emotional state of the cats.

I know it's evolutionary that cats hide and become quiet when they are in pain or suffering so that predators do not easily spot them, as they would do in the wild, were they not to adopt that strategy. But they have learned to get many desired actions by using sound with us, so why have they not learned to tell us more clearly when they are suffering long-term pain?

I don't know, but perhaps the instinct is still very strong. However, sometimes your cat will tell you when he or she is in pain. If you happen to step on your cat's tail by mistake, she will scream, and if you touch your cat's paw when he has injured it, he will hiss or growl at you.

Do you know if the way we talk to our cats influences the sounds that they make back to us?

Hopefully we will start recording in 2019. I think that cats know when we address them, as opposed to when we address another adult, as we tend to use a higher pitch and a larger tonal range when we talk to our cats. And there seems to be some evidence of cats that imitate the voices of their owners. An Australian study [by Burnham, Kitamura and Vollmer-Conna (2002) *Science*, Vol. 296] showed that there are differences between infant-directed speech and pet-directed speech. Although the fundamental frequency (pitch) was higher in both adult- and pet-directed speech compared to adult-directed speech, the measures of affect and vowel hyper articulation were lower in pet-directed speech than in infant-directed speech. However, the fact that many humans use a different speaking style with their pets than with adult people still may suggest that we tend to treat pets more like infants than adult humans. Perhaps we may also try to sound more like our cats by elevating the pitch in our voices. Similarly, there seems to be some evidence of cats that imitate the voices of their owners.

We still don't know for sure if cats prefer to be spoken to with a pet-directed speaking style or if they would rather we used an adult-directed speaking style when addressing them. And although this (as far as I know) has not been proven yet, we will address this question in our next study.

Cats seem to be doing pretty well in getting exactly what they want even though they speak a language we have yet to properly master. I have a feeling when we do master our understanding of our own little fluffballs' verbal communications, we will eternally seal the fate of our slavery. How else do our feline taskmasters communicate with us? Read on to the following Cat Chat to find out.

A CATTY SUM UP

1. The meaning of a meow is strongly related to the context or situation, and also to the mental and emotional state of the cat.

2. Cats have learned which different sound variations get our attention and produce the quickest results.

3. We will probably never be able to link a meow directly to a word in human language.

CAT CHAT

Interpreting Cat Language: How Else Do Cats Communicate?

Cats communicate with us and other cats in a variety of ways, some very subtle and only noticed by a trained eye that's looking out for such signs. Other than vocal clues, cats use their body posture, ear and tail positioning, eyes and pupils, scent markers (pheromones) from face and paws (including urine and faeces scent communications) and whisker positioning to communicate their daily emotional states. I have listed below a brief outline of some of these communications, starting with the most common. Of course, these separate communications go hand-in-hand with each other, depending on what's being communicated, and can mean different things depending on the different combinations of states and emotions. All explanations rely on context. For example: a relaxed cat could be found low to the ground lying in the middle of a room, and we can see from other parts of their body that they are confident and content. Another cat in a low position may be a submissive, fearful cat. We may find this cat flat to the floor at the back of a cage in a rescue centre, with their tail completely under their body and large pupils, meaning that the cat is very fearful and is trying to be submissive, making themself as small and invisible as possible. Another example of a low-to-the-ground cat is a cat walking very close to the ground trying to be undetected and cautious of strangers nearby. They are trying to tiptoe out of view. Three different explanations of low-to-the-ground cats whereby the context and other communications let us know exactly how this cat is feeling.

LET'S START WITH THE TAIL...

A cat's tail is used for balance, but it's also an important visual communicator to humans and other cats. A normal happy cat will greet us with an upright tail and sometimes with the tip curled at the top. The fur on an upright tail of a happy, relaxed cat is normal. Sometimes you will see it quiver and this usually means excitement and arousal. A cat sometimes does the quivery tail when they are excited to see us, rubbing around our legs too. However, an upright tail doesn't always mean a positive communication, and this depends on the fur. If the upright tail's fur goes brushy and prickly looking, like the cartoon cats who've had a sudden fright, his means the cat is suddenly angry, startled, fearful or acting in a defensive manner, so watch out! The term for a brushy prickly tail is piloerected.

We may also see a piloerected tail on a scared cat. We know they are scared because the tail will be lowered. The tail will be completely tucked between the legs and under the body of a very frightened, nervous, submissive or apprehensive cat. There are some cats that have no tail but the Manx cat is the only tailless cat specifically bred to keep this mutation going. Manx cats are born with shortened stub-like tails and are the result of a genetic mutation that was then intensified by the cats' remote location on the Isle of Man. The cats are thought to date to 1750 or later, but whether a tailless cat was born there or arrived on a ship and then spread its genes throughout the island's cat population is unknown. The island became known for tailless cats, and that's how the breed got its name of Manx[1].

A CAT'S EYES AND PUPILS

A cat's primary sense in how they perceive their environment is not visual like ours but a combination of visual, olfactory and auditory. The eyes are designed specifically for hunting and are said to have dichromatic colour vision, meaning that apart from seeing colours within the spectrum of blues and greens our mogs are colourblind. It's assumed our cats are more concerned with movement than colour[2]. We can tell a lot about how our cats are emotionally feeling from the shape of their pupils. Usually big, wide pupils are a sign of a cat either feeling fearful or excited. Watch your cat's pupils when you play with them. In the moment of excitement or pre-pounce, the pupils will be wide, making it look like your cat's whole eye is jet black. On my grooming table some cats are very scared and the cat is communicating this to me with widened pupils. When your cat's pupils narrow like a tiny spear it means your cat is in serious concentration mode or they are aroused. The arousal could be pre-fight mode when the cat is both highly focused and fired up for combat. Normal-sized pupils indicate your cat is relaxed and content.

EYE KIT TIP

A cat blinking to another cat means the cat is not a threat and is a signal of acceptance and friendship. This is why experts tell cat guardians to blink to their cats to communicate they are not a threat. A cat who blinks back is saying yes, it accepts you as being friendly. Just as it is with some other animals, staring at a cat is a challenge and can be seen as threatening behaviour to a fearful cat. A staring cat, at another cat in the household or at a human, can also be a subtle sign of dominance and control.

A CAT'S EARS

A cat's hearing is far superior to ours, which makes them masters at finding the position of their prey. Their frequency range can be at least four times higher than that of humans. It explains why a cat may sit bolt upright in our company detecting a noise our ears cannot hear. Some people's imaginations go wild thinking their cat has detected a spirit in the house, when it's far more likely they have heard a fox or cat call from a distance, or even a nearby mouse!

The ears are great communicators to other cats and now we understand the messages behind their positioning too. When our cat's ears are in the normal upright position we have a friendly, relaxed and interested cat. We need to be cautious when the ears are in various other positions. Ears flat to the head and backwards facing indicates a frightened cat who may go on the defensive and attack if approached, or may become frozen to the spot and cower. Context and knowledge of the cat and their background is important in these situations. Ears that are upright and facing forward usually portrays a confident cat who is being offensive rather than defensive. This means they are likely to attack if approached, or ready to move forward and attack anyway. Again, context is necessary. When we see our cat's ears swivelling round it means they are alert and listening to sounds all around them. Watch your cat when they 'appear' to be asleep. Watch their ears. They may not be as unaware as you think.

BODY POSITIONING AND ACTIONS

Cats can also tell us and other cats of their emotional state by their body posture. Seeing a cat slink low to the ground indicates either a nervous, scared cat or one who's in stalking, predatory mode. The ears and eyes tell us which emotion it's likely to be. Flat to the ground is usually indicative of being a submissive or fearful cat, but can also be a pre-pounce hunting posture. A cat who makes themself bigger by puffing out their fur and moving slowly sideways is telling other cats they are confident and ready for attack. The puffing out of the fur makes the cat look bigger. The typical arched-back hair-on-end cartoon figure is a frightened, defensive cat.

And what about the cat lying on the floor exposing their belly? Many mixed signals around this one, which need to be understood. The belly is a sensitive area for cats and them exposing it to us doesn't give us a green light to stroke them there. For humans it's a sign of trust and contentment, but know your cat well before thinking it's an invitation for rubbing the belly. This position, ironically, is also the ultimate defensive mode when fighting another cat because the cat is using all of their weapons: the claws, the teeth and all four paws.

Other communication actions are kneading, which indicates a relaxed cat, affection and feelings of security. Some experts say that the kneading stems from when a kitten would knead around their mother's teat to stimulate milk flow. A cat who's face-rubbing or headbutting is marking us or furniture with their scent, and this is considered a friendly and affectionate action as well as a sign that the cat is indicating ownership. Sometimes facial rubbing can go to extremes, like a form of Obsessive Compulsive Disorder (OCD), which can be a sign of territorial anxiety.

WHISKERS

Even a cat's whiskers can communicate with us. Their function is to give the cat information as to what's close by and for protection of the body area. The main whiskers are found on the cheeks and above the eyes, but there is also another set of sensitive hairs, called carpal hairs, found on the back of the front wrists[3]. A normal sideways positioning of the whiskers means a cat is friendly and relaxed. However, if a cat is scared, angry or defensive, the whiskers will be flattened against the face. If the whiskers are pushed outwards and forward this shows us a cat is excited and alert, and often in offensive mode – meaning ready for attack!

TOP WHISKERS KIT TIP

A cat's whiskers are highly sensitive and are used for many functions, including judging the width of spaces, feeling and detecting objects close by, and for hunting prey too close for their eyesight to detect. For this reason, food bowls should be large and, if possible, open sided like a saucer or plate so that the whiskers are not bashing on to the sides of the bowl.

STRESS ACTIONS

Cats can suffer from anxiety connected to territory – perhaps too many cats sharing space – lack of stimulation and separation anxiety. Common signs of stress are over-grooming, cystitis and urinating around the home. Multiple licking of the lips is also a stress signal. When the normal routine or movement of your cat starts to be noticeably different it's a good idea to have them checked at your vet. Once any medical reasons have been ruled out, then it's more than likely a behavioural issue that would need a feline behaviour practitioner to explore further. There's no point double-guessing what the reasons are behind your cat's behaviour, as this wastes precious time.

A definitive diagnosis is what's needed, not listening to every cat owner's opinion online.

DISPLACEMENT ACTIONS

These are actions that are out of context to the situation, like licking of the paw or a yawn when a cat has, say, slipped from a jump in front of us. Just like we yawn or cough when we don't know quite what to do or we have tripped in the street in front of a full bus looking down at us, cats do the same! It's when a cat doesn't quite know what to do, and it's also an action that defuses an emotional feeling. Classic examples I see of this are from studying my own cats. Kiki always yawns when she doesn't know what to do and it's a half yawn that isn't necessary.

THE PURR

The sound we all love. Not all cats purr – the bigger cats in the wild can only roar – but when they do it's more than likely telling us that they are content and are enjoying whatever we are doing to them. Sometimes a cat's purr is hardly audible to us, but bend your ear towards your cat and you may be able to pick up the faintest purr, which is always a thrill to hear. The purr is also used by cats as a self-soothing tool, so when they are ill or afraid they may start to purr to comfort themself.

THE GRIMACE

When you see your cat standing still, pulling a strange face with an open mouth, like a type of human gurning, you can rest assured they are not having a stroke or turning into a devil cat. This is called Flehman, and what your cat is doing is using an organ called the vomeronasal, located behind the incisor teeth, to gather additional information from an odour[4].

These communications are a basic list to help you further understand the language of cats. A whole other book could be written about feline scent communications using urine or faeces. The issue of inappropriate elimination or urine and faeces marking can be complex, and can be related to a variety of issues such as litter-tray avoidance, dislike of the positioning of a tray or the litter used, territorial stress, marking or illness. What we can be sure of, though, is that our cat is letting us know something is wrong, a totally natural response for the species. Therefore any reprimanding is pointless and gives the cat no clue as to why they are being punished, thus causing added anxiety. When dealing with these complex types of communication, it's best to involve a professional feline behaviourist. Getting the diagnosis correct first time around means a definitive plan of action can be constructed, which will save time and money in the long run. Getting advice from countless people on the internet, or a vet not trained in specific feline behaviour, may only confuse the issue, with the cat guardian going round in circles, trying lots of unnecessary and ineffective things before having to start again from scratch. A list of accredited professional feline behaviourists registered in the UK can be found on the Canine and Feline Behaviour Association website (**https://cfba.uk/**).

Other ways that a cat can communicate to us include changes in their normal behaviour, such as sleeping too much, not eating as much or eating too much (obsessive with their food), vomiting (other than the odd fur-ball), hiding from us, being agitated in an abnormal way when being stroked, or staying away longer from home if free-roaming. If any behaviours seem out of character it's best to err on the side of caution and do a quick vet visit. Just as humans do, a cat will communicate when things are not right and this could be down to agitation due to anything from joint issues to excessive hunger due to worms!

Cat owners, when dealing with behaviour issues, should realise that their cat deals with stress and other issues it's unhappy about with responses natural to the species, which understandably don't sit well with humankind. An example of this is a cat dealing with stress by way of urinating outside of the litter tray, or lashing out because of anxiety to do with another cat in the neighbourhood. Any kind of reprimand is pointless, as your cat will have little idea about what you are saying to them or what you are responding to, and this may add more anxiety to an already stressful situation.

CHAPTER SEVEN

Do Cats Grieve?

*'All animals, including humans, have a right to lives of
dignity and respect, without forced intrusions.'*

Marc Bekoff

CHAPTER SEVEN

In this chapter:

- Explore the world of grief from a cat's perspective.
- Get insider knowledge on research into what emotions cats feel after experiencing loss, in conversation with Dr. Jessica Walker.
- Read a true-behaviour case study involving a cat called Toby who suffered from the loss of his close companion cat.

We are beginning to realise that we are not the only species that suffers or has an altered state from the loss of someone who once filled our lives. Research into animal grief started in the 19th century when a chimpanzee was shown to experience a different emotional state when its female companion died[1]. Interestingly, though, it was noted then that grief doesn't have a lasting effect on animals as when we experience it, but perhaps this is because we are only seeking out actions that mirror our own in such circumstances.

Marc Bekoff, a professor of ecology and evolutionary biology, has spent a lifetime studying the emotions of animals, and in particular grief. He found there was a state of emotional trauma after the death of a companion animal in elephants, wolves, sea lions, chimpanzees, geese and magpies, to name a few. This tells us that cats, like most animals, will show a change in their behaviour with a change in circumstances connected to other animals they have shared space with.

I have first-hand experience of grief in cats on a regular basis. One such cat was called Toby. When I met him, he was suffering from the sudden loss of his cat companion resulting in over-grooming by way of pulling his fur out. We would anthropomorphise and label this a broken heart, given the circumstances.

Other cats may cry for a few days afterwards with a meow the owners have not heard before but then become more affectionate and confident. I am dealing with a cat showing the very same actions right now. Her lifelong 'fur friend' died in a road-traffic accident. The friend was always the super affectionate one, leaving her in the shadows, quite reserved and always spending most of her time away from the humans in the home. When she became the sole cat she suddenly found there was room for her to grow and blossom. Now she is a totally different cat who enjoys being stroked and getting all of the attention. Another client's cat stayed away from an ill companion cat during the last days of their cancerous journey. On the day of euthanasia, which was performed in the living room at home, the healthy cat nose-kissed her friend, before departing again. Extraordinary, considering that she had stayed away before this. After the sad act was done and her companion buried in the garden soon after, defecating outside of the litter tray in the living room started.

In human terms the word 'grief' means extreme sadness but this ultimate state can be the umbrella under which many different emotions take cover. Scientists have much evidence now that animals go through a changed state that can be labelled as shock, fear, depression, anxiety, awareness of a void and of something not right, all of which humans can suffer too, under the grief umbrella. It is interesting to note the words of psychologist James Anderson of Stirling University, who has been studying chimp responses to the dying. He stated: 'pining or grieving for a dead relative or friend is possible without any knowledge of death.' This means, as Roger Di Silvestro of National Wildlife points out, that:

> ... even if long-lived creatures as intelligent as elephants and chimpanzees do recognise that the dead are gone for good, they may not recognise that death eventually will come for all, a knowledge that may be solely human[2].

There has been little research focused on feline grief so I was delighted when Dr. Jessica Walker, a New Zealand lecturer in applied animal welfare and scientific officer at the Society for the Prevention of Cruelty to Animals, agreed to contribute to this chapter.

In Conversation With Dr. Jessica Walker

As one of the researchers for the study entitled 'Owners' Perceptions Of Their Animal's Behavioural Response To The Loss Of An Animal Companion', what made you decide to research cat grief?

Initially I became interested in the impact of the loss of a cat on the owner. Having lost a number of cats myself over the years (to old age, traffic accidents, snake bites and other medical reasons) I was acutely aware of the intensity of the grief experience from the human perspective. Once I started looking into the topic, I discovered a plethora of research on the impact of animal loss on the human carers. This led me to question the grief experience from the perspective of the animal, and I discovered there had been very little work in this space. I then embarked on a PhD, which aimed to take an initial look at the existence and non-invasive measurement of grief in animals. One aspect of my work was to investigate owner-reported behavioural changes in their companion cats and dogs following the loss of an animal companion.

What was the process of the research?

My PhD supervision team and myself carried out a survey of cat and dog owners and asked them to report on behaviours they observed in their animal following the passing of another companion animal within the household. To find participants we distributed our survey via publications (magazines, newsletters, website adverts) produced by SPCA New Zealand and RSPCA Australia. We also sent the survey to a number of veterinary clinics within New Zealand so that clients could complete it.

What were the results?

We received responses relating to 152 cats. We found that the behaviour of cats changed in response to the loss of an animal companion. These behavioural changes suggest the loss had an impact on the remaining cat. Owners reported that most cats demanded more affection from them, some were described as becoming more clingy/needy and a small number were reported to seek less attention than they previously had done from their owner. The territorial behaviour of cats was also reported to change with cats reported to seek out the deceased animal's favourite spot, seeking higher ground, or displaying increased hiding behaviour. Vocalisations also increased both in frequency and duration and aggressive behaviour towards other animals in the household increased. These changes lasted anywhere up to six months.

What do you feel the grieving process is for a cat?

My research was not conclusive with regard to the underlying cause of the behaviour changes observed. For example, it's important to consider that the behaviour changes observed could be further complicated by changes in human behaviour (as part of their own grieving process), lack of competition for resources and/or changes in the hierarchical structure within the household, in addition to the experience of loss or grief. More research is needed to tease these factors apart to really understand what the grieving process for a cat looks like.

Do you feel cats understand the death of a companion animal or human?

Yes. Death is a naturally occurring phenomenon. Grief, however, is more complicated because it's really a human construct that relies heavily on an individual's ability to understand the loss in reference to past or anticipated future experiences. For example: when humans grieve they often do so based on their memories of the person or animal and for the loss of being able to have interactions or experiences with the deceased again in the near and far distant future. We have the ability of mental time travel with the anticipation of future events. This is fundamental for the grief process as we know it.

Do cats experience mental time travel?

They certainly seem to have memories but it is unknown whether they can anticipate events or experiences far into the future. So, although I am sure they understand the finality of death, I'm not sure whether they experience grief in the same way that humans do.

What do you feel about a cat being shown the body of its deceased companion animal?

We asked owners if they showed their animal's deceased body to their remaining cat: 42% of owners did, yet behavioural changes were observed regardless of whether the deceased's body was shown to the remaining animal. This might suggest that loss resulting from the removal of a companion animal from the household, for example the sale of one or rehoming, could have a similar impact on behaviour. However, further research is required to clarify this. It's not always possible for owners to show remaining animals the deceased body, but doing so may help provide closure for the owner and the animal. It would be useful to our understanding of the grieving process in cats to explore this further.

What other emotions do you think cats have?

I think cats experience a range of emotions from the more basic like joy to the more complex like jealousy. During my PhD work we surveyed 1,000 members of the public to investigate belief in the animal's ability to experience emotions: 96% of participants (954) indicated they believed animals could experience emotions. When subsequently asked if animals could experience specific emotions, 99% believed all animals experience fear, 96% happiness, 95% distress, 92% sadness, 86% anger, 85% love, 84% grief and 70% depression[3].

Do you have personal experience of a cat in the emotional state of grief?

No. Until now I have never had multiple animals at one time. I currently have three Burmese cats, who are strongly bonded to one another. When the day comes that we lose one, I have no doubt that the remaining two will respond in ways that suggest they too are experiencing some form of grief.

We have only just started to explore feline emotions and have much still to learn in terms of understanding how cats grieve and how subtly similar the process may be to our own human grieving process.

Whilst writing this chapter I was reminded of a video that went viral in 2010[4]. The video shows a street cat kneading a dead cat with whom it must have had a close relationship. The cat is seen kneading their 'friend' continuously and cuddling up to embrace the still lifeless body. Occasionally the cat lightly bites the neck of their dead friend. Passers-by are seen watching the cat uncomfortably, not knowing what to do about the sad encounter. We have no further information as to how long this behaviour went on for or how the living cat acted in the days that followed on from the loss of their companion, but we cannot deny that we are seeing a cat express some form of emotion, and the sad music placed on the video pulls at our heartstrings to label the emotion in the video as grief, because that is what we are feeling or would feel as humans.

Also on YouTube I decided to see if anyone had posted videos of their cats being shown the body of a deceased companion cat. The first one I came to showed reactions of two adult cats smelling the body of their dead brother, wrapped in a blanket[5]. The first cat cautiously smells his brother all over, appears confused, walks slowly away and then throws up. When the second cat comes to investigate they are hissed at by the agitated first cat, who returns to the brother to sniff all over again in a 'confused and deeply interested' manner.

Another video[6] shows a cat displaying similar actions to the street cat – lightly biting into the neck of their dead companion and, like the brothers, intensely smelling the body. However, in the latter video the cat's actions become more frantic as the minutes pass, when the body of their companion is still not moving or smelling right. Are we witnessing the exact moment of realisation that their companion is dead, or the knowledge of what death means? In the days that follow, time and time again, we see the cat lying in and exploring the exact same spot where his companion was lying, almost like he cannot leave the area.

I will never forget a video I saw of baby piglets being slaughtered in an abattoir. One of the pigs that was the next to follow into the slaughter room could hear and smell death all around. The video shows the pig writhing on the floor having a heart attack, as he watches the pigs before him squeal in pain and fear. It was one of the worst things I have seen. Did this pig know death was imminent and was the smell of death and fear linked to their heart failing?

I am convinced that cats, as do all animals, experience grief and are affected by the change that loss brings.

The next section is a behaviour case of mine about a grieving cat called Toby.

 # A CATTY SUM UP

1. Loss has an impact on the remaining cat.
2. Animals may not recognise that death eventually will come for all.
3. Behavioural changes were observed regardless of whether the deceased's body was shown.

CAT CHAT

Toby And His Broken Heart: The Hidden World Of Cat Grief

I often have to comfort cat owners. It's part of my job, and I know at first hand how deeply people feel for their cats. It's a special bond that only another pet owner can truly understand. Mine, for instance, are my fur babies. Yes, I know. Folks hate that expression: especially other animal behaviourists. But I know my clients appreciate that I feel the same way they do and we speak the same language. I have empathy that taps into exactly how they feel and that's why solving the issues they are having with their cats becomes very personal to me. I can step back and be professional and give advice, seeing the cat as an animal first, but I also see the owners as people who see their cats as their children, and that cannot be trampled upon or dismissed. That's why my heart hurt when a client broke down in front of me the moment she realised her precious cat Toby had been grieving for his lifelong companion, Oliver, and that certain things that the family did surrounding Oliver's death had unknowingly contributed to the state that Toby was in.

Toby was introduced to Oliver at two months old, and from that moment on they became lifelong companions, with Toby treating Oliver like his surrogate parent. A third cat also lived in the household, but Toby and Oliver were the pair that were always together, sleeping or wandering in the garden. Toby looked up to Oliver, who was the older and more dominant of the two. It was Oliver who defended the garden, always chasing away neighbouring cats. Oliver would also come running when the local bully cat cornered Toby, too timid to fight back. Their owner Dorian would always marvel at the closeness of the two, commenting that you couldn't fit a blade of grass between them. Toby would follow Oliver around like his shadow and so, years later, when Oliver became ill with an aggressive cancer and was taken away to be put to sleep at the vets, Toby's world fell apart.

Suddenly, without warning, his companion and protector had simply vanished.

The family missed Oliver terribly and the grieving began. However, Toby's feelings were overlooked. Animals pick up on emotions and energy given out by humans. With family members crying and depressed, Toby would have picked up on the change of human behaviour on top of his own confusion regarding the disappearance of Oliver. During tears and heartache, life carried on as normal with Oliver's food bowls, litter tray, toys, climbers and bed left in the home as if he was still around. The scent of Oliver was everywhere, and every day Toby spent hours walking around the home and garden searching for something. What came to my mind the first time that I heard this was that he was searching for Oliver.

One of a cat's main channels of communication is through scent: either depositing or smelling it. Sarah Hartwell (cat behaviour researcher and cat enthusiast), writing about grief in cats on her fantastic online blog Messy Beasts, points out that 'although cats probably do not mourn in the same manner as humans do, it's safe to assume there will be some behavioural changes as they adjust to the gap in their lives'[1]. Toby was aware that Oliver was no longer present, and may have searched for him or sat waiting for his return for some time. It's why, in my opinion, it may be better to show a resident cat the deceased companion's body, so that they stop looking for them. Sarah Hartwell, on the question of whether a cat should be shown the body of their deceased companion cat, says that:

> They may sniff around the body, lick him and maybe try to wake him up before concluding that their friend has gone. We cannot know what cats understand by death, but they probably have some awareness that a dead animal does not return to life. If there is no danger of infection and you believe that it will

help your other cats come to terms with the loss of a companion, then by all means allow them to see and smell the body.

I agree completely.

Naturally this might make us feel uncomfortable and may not sound like the most ethical thing to do, but some animals may cope better after recognising that an animal has died. This process might give them the opportunity to accept the death of a cherished companion. This is only the first stage, the second being the possibility of acceptance.

When you reflect on the passing of Oliver, from Toby's point of view – the sudden and unexplained disappearance of a constant presence – it's easy to understand how anxious this would have made Toby feel. He no longer had protection from Oliver's territorial defensive actions in the garden. On top of this, the other resident cat, the one Toby never bonded with, automatically became the top cat. He had lost his surrogate parent: the cat who groomed him and ran to defend him. His special friend had simply vanished. His owners, unknowingly, didn't pay special attention to Toby. He was merely overlooked within the usual hustles and bustles of everyday living.

So, why did Angela, Toby's mummy, contact me? Because poor Toby, having spent weeks acting out of character, seeking no-one-knew-what, started to over-groom and self-harm. When the self-harm became chronic and dangerous, I was contacted. By the time I was emailed, the condition had turned into Obsessive Compulsive Disorder (OCD), a habit-forming condition that's very hard to break. Over-grooming is a coping mechanism for many cats when stress or anxiety is felt. It's also seen as a displacement action. When a cat licks themselves, they are depositing their scent over their body, a familiar scent that comforts them. The trigger for most over-grooming cases is stress, although it can be caused by other triggers such as a skin condition. Their vet had already tested Toby's skin for parasites and allergies before the behaviour consultation took place, which is why I was certain that stress was the only cause of his behaviour.

On my visit, I spoke at great length, from Toby's perspective, about what I felt was going on with him around the time of Oliver's death. Tears flowed down Angela's cheeks. Her daughter, with tears filling her eyes, sat next to her. The penny had dropped with them both and it had dropped hard. Suddenly it all made sense.

I felt mortified seeing both of them so upset and held out my hand to comfort Angela. 'I'm so sorry to have upset you'.

'No,' Angela said, wiping her eyes. 'You are right. We totally ignored Toby after Oliver's death. Life got busy and we just got absorbed in our own grief'.

Toby sat on the kitchen counter, a handsome large tabby covered in bald patches from where he had been pulling out his fur. He had no idea everyone was so upset over him. He started intensively licking himself again, just five minutes after the last grooming session.

'But things can change now. We are going to make life better for Toby,' I said, as I got up from the kitchen table to give Toby a gentle pat on the head.

Whilst I was there, I helped Angela and her daughter collect all of Oliver's belongings to bag them up. They would be taken to a charity or local rescue centre. Then I sent Angela links to good-sized litter trays and cat trees. Toby was going to get a whole new array of cat furniture and other cat-related products that did not smell of Oliver or have any connection with him. Having understood that Toby was never played with (Angela assumed that he didn't need play sessions because he had a garden), I advised on buying a few good hunting toys. These would be used to help distract Toby from over-grooming. The garden was also worked on and 'cat-proofing' put up to stop the local bully cat from intimidating Toby. He never roamed far anyway, so this was a perfect solution.

The home quickly filled up with new things for Toby. He must have felt like it was Christmas.

Gradually, Toby's excessive grooming started to lessen. He really loved his play sessions and spent more time out in the garden now that the threat of other cats was not at the forefront of his mind. All reminders and smells of Oliver were removed as far as was possible. Angela gave Toby lots of attention and played with him every day, releasing any anxieties he may have been feeling. It took several months before I received a telephone call from Angela. She couldn't have been happier. Toby had lost weight and become more active, and he was spending far more time in the garden. Most important of all, he found his mojo again, and stopped over-grooming. His fur was getting back to normal. Even relations between him and the other resident cat had improved. I was so happy that day.

It was a team effort. We fixed Toby's heart. Now that's something worth being proud about.

CHAPTER EIGHT

Can Cats Communicate Telepathically?

'I have lived with several Zen masters – all of them cats.'

Eckhart Tolle

CHAPTER EIGHT

In this chapter:

- Explore the little-known world of animal telepathic communication, in conversation with Penelope Smith.
- Read expert hands-on experience and fascinating true cases.
- Explore what it means to be mindful when spending time with your cat.

I don't know any cat carer who wouldn't want to know what their cat was thinking. We would all jump at the chance to get inside our little tinkers' minds. What's going on when they give us that 'stink eye' look, or they turn their noses up at all the good brands of food we buy them? It's hard to trace the history of when humans first discovered they could communicate telepathically with animals, and even harder to find much in the way of scientific research, although I did come across an article written by Dr. Rupert Sheldrake, a biologist at Cambridge University, who conducted his own experiments after being inspired by naturalist William Long's study of wolves and telepathy in 1909. Knowing how cynical most of the scientific fraternity was, Dr. Sheldrake gathered information from 1,000 accounts of dogs and more than 600 of cats behaving in an unexplained way that could confirm telepathy and a pretty accurate sixth sense[1].

I'm fascinated with the concept of being able to communicate telepathically with animals and hoped that one such communicator, Penelope Smith, would enlighten me further with her expertise on the subject. For over 40 years, Penelope has been the founding pioneer of interspecies telepathic communication, the terminology and philosophy of which she invented. Author of the popular classic books *Animal Talk*, *When Animals Speak* and *Animals In Spirit*, many audio recordings and founding editor of *Species Link* magazine, Penelope has been one of the guiding forces of this growing world-wide community of animal communicators for decades. Penelope has a huge heart that comes across in her writing, and I am grateful she gave her time to speak with me for this chapter.

In Conversation With Penelope Smith

How does one study the art of communicating with animals? Is there formal training and what does this involve?

Yes, there is training in communicating with animals. It involves learning how to listen telepathically, being able to set aside your own thoughts and preconceptions and open yourself to the direct communication from animals; getting their true thoughts and feelings and being able to translate them. It also covers how they understand themselves and others, and takes into account their natural behaviours. I offer animal-training communication seminars and books on my website and many of my students have continued to develop their training programmes online. Other practitioners also have various training programmes online, teaching how to differentiate your own thoughts from those of the animals, and how not to push your agenda on to people and animals.

Can you remember your first cat client?

My first animal client was called Peaches[2], a small, black and white female cat that was left with me when her person could no longer care for her. She was definitely a 'scaredy-cat'. She would run and hide from people and was afraid of other cats in the neighbourhood.

A few weeks after her arrival, she came in with a bloody bite on her back, where another cat had attacked her. I cleaned it and put on ointment, expecting it to heal with no problem. Peaches, however, had other ideas. As soon as it would scab over, she'd scratch it open. Bandages and soothing preparations were to no avail as she was determined to get at the wound. The bloody area was no longer the original half-inch bite but now extended two or three inches, and the hair around the area was falling out. She looked gruesome, and my roommates were beginning to complain about doing something with 'that cat'.

So, I sat with Peaches across from me on a chair and decided to counsel her as I would a human being in trouble. I asked her specific questions about the physical trauma and her feelings, and she answered me telepathically. She relayed to me many mental pictures of other cats scaring and attacking her. By facing up to these frightening incidents, she released a lot of emotional charge and felt much better.

We continued with our counselling session, and she discovered that keeping the wound there and making it worse was actually a solution to the problem she felt of being afraid of people and other animals. She had figured that if she made her body very ugly, people and cats would stay away from her. It was working, though making her life miserable in the process. When she uncovered and fully brought to her awareness this subconscious decision, she visibly became very peaceful and purred happily.

The remarkable results of this session were that, by the next day, her wound had scabbed over, and in about one week the hair had grown back so you couldn't tell she had ever been hurt. Even more amazing was that Peaches was a changed individual. No longer did she run away when people entered the room, but instead she curled up on their laps and purred! The cats in the neighbourhood no longer singled her out for attacks.

I know you communicate with many different animals, but I'm particularly interested in your work with cats. Would you say that people in your field of expertise need to know about feline behaviour to really begin to communicate with them?

No. You don't need to know about anyone's behaviour. They will teach you. It's better to get information from the cat than people's opinions. People who study behaviour often generalise on behaviour and they might not necessarily get what's happening with that particular individual. A good cat behaviourist will be a good observer, and – if they're sensitive to animals – be able to drop into the telepathic mode more easily. People like that will be better able to really feel what the animal is feeling. I was not an expert. I have always loved cats and they have always been special to me. They have always been my companions so I have observed a lot of their behaviour, but really I talk to all kinds of animals. Species I've never been close to before have taught me about their feelings and how they look at the world, how they behave and why they behave as they do. So, it's really important that you communicate with the individual. You get much more information than if you generalise from a book.

I've read things in books; people who say 'this always means this' or 'a cat puts its tail this way and it always means this' but it doesn't always mean that. With one particular cat, it may generally mean something, but another cat may be signalling something else or may have something to communicate in addition to that particular behaviour, which may be an automatic flicking of the tail. Telepathic communication helps you to get the depth and the individuality; the exact why of what they are doing behind the observation of behaviour. Having said this, I would say that it helps to have knowledge of animal anatomy and behaviour to add to your understanding so that you can translate to humans what the animal has communicated. It can help other humans understand it and add clarity. However, it isn't necessary for me to understand behaviour.

I would say that telepathic communication underlies the communication of all species and gives you the most detail because you're getting the individual's point of view. However, they may not understand their own behaviour, as many humans don't, and so if you have a lot of experience with cats or dogs, for example, then you may be able to understand their behaviour purely by understanding other animals. So, it helps. The more information we have, the better. Telepathic communication really helps you to open worlds; to go into an animal's world in a way that's not available from observing them from the outside or looking at them as a thing or as something just to observe or to study behaviour. They are individuals. They are beings with feelings, depth, wisdom and understanding; you have to understand each of them individually, and in that moment of time get the particular communication that they want to give you.

It states on your website that your telepathic communication complements current scientific knowledge and traditional methods. Can you talk us through what the scientific knowledge entails and what are the traditional methods?

When I say scientific knowledge I'm talking about knowledge research that has been done scientifically on animal behaviour, their psychology and physical illnesses. So, a telepathic communication can add to that. An example of how an animal communicator can complement these traditional methods is if an animal is ill and a veterinarian is puzzled by what's going on. We could ask an animal where it hurts, how it feels, when the pain or illness started and how long it has been going on. Things that would help a veterinarian to zero in on the illness to find out what it is and also if the remedies and medicines that the vet is giving are working.

The same can apply with scientific research on behaviour. Often, scientists will research for years and years or observe, say, dolphins in the wild, and they will sometimes come up with conclusions based on observations for 10 or 20 years. With telepathic communication, however, you can find out directly and immediately what's going on with the animals. The animals can tell you about their history, where they are going, their migration, and why they are doing what they are doing. All these things you can find out in an instance or in a very short time (compared to 10 or 20 years of observations) and then from observation you may come up with the wrong conclusions if you don't have what the animal is thinking and their unique viewpoint.

I remember I did a consultation with a horse and a cowboy. The cowboy was a very perceptive-based person, knew his horse well, and had a great relationship with him. He asked me questions and I told him things about his horse and what was going on, and he said to me 'you just told me in a few minutes things that took me many many years to learn about my horse and you told me more'. So, that's how telepathic communication is complementary to any observational methods, whether scientific or from an individual guardian.

When I say traditional methods, I'm talking about things that have been known and used for a long time, like indigenous methods of healing with herbs, energy healing and shamanic healing. These are things that have gone on for thousands of years. Acupuncture, homeopathic, Ayurvedic medicine; these are things that are traditional rather than modern technological scientific-era methods and telepathic communication complements all of these too. Telepathic communication is an incredible tool to enhance any other knowledge that one has about animals.

What common things are our cats trying to tell us?

First of all, cats are individuals. They are spiritual beings just like everybody is, whether human, dog, cat, horse; it doesn't matter. Everyone is an animal and animal is derived from the Latin word anima, which means soul, spirit, breath, air or life[3]. Everyone is a spiritual being, and when you treat them that way – as spiritual beings who are in a particular form, having a particular experience in a particular species – then the results are quite amazing.

The changes in behaviour and healing begin when the animal feels respected and understood. So, common things that cats are trying to tell us are common to what all animals are trying to tell us. They want you to understand who they are and how they view the world, how they feel and what they think. They also may want to tell you how much they love you and how much the relationship means to them. With cats, it depends on how much is going on with them. If it's a litter-box problem, they can tell you why they are not going in the litter box; what needs to change. For example whether it needs to be a litter-box change – literally, a clean up – or whether it's something that's bothering them in the environment or the texture of the litter or something that's internally bothering them that they need to see a veterinarian about. Those are some of the common things cats will tell me about.

Litter tray and inappropriate elimination issues are very common reasons for cat guardians emailing me. Do you get that too?

Yes. I have often been called upon to help with cats who urinate or spray outside their litter box. Dixon was a three-year-old neutered male tabby who, when his family called me, had been spraying around the house for a few months. The family were at their wit's end, as the furniture and carpets were being destroyed. They were even considering putting down Dixon if the problem could not be solved.

Communicating at a distance, Dixon showed me images and explained to me that there was a strange, wild dog coming to the sliding glass doors when his family was away. Dixon sprayed in the house as a signal that this was his and his family's territory. It also relieved the tension and fear he felt upon seeing this predator.

His family confirmed that the neighbours had seen coyotes in their yard. Dixon showed me that the family dogs lived in a kennel attached to the house. Rather than barking to chase the coyote away, they seemed to be in canine collusion with him, just watching as the coyote stared into the house. Dixon was the only one guarding. He had tried to alert his people to the danger, but they weren't listening so he needed to spray to get their attention.

Well, it certainly did get their attention! Fortunately, they managed to understand his viewpoint before they decided to get rid of him. I suggested that they acknowledge Dixon's good intentions and his help in guarding home and family by patrolling for coyotes before they left home in the morning and when they returned home. I checked with Dixon to see if this would help, and he was greatly relieved. The people went around the house daily, assuring Dixon that there were no coyotes, and Dixon, now assured, stopped spraying in the house.

Another time a woman called me for help because her cat, Misha, repeatedly peed on the bed. This started after the woman broke up with her boyfriend and moved from a house where the cat could go outdoors and had more human company, to a high-rise apartment where cats were not even allowed. The apartment was sterile and the cat spent most of the day alone. My client was very distraught and worried about Misha.

Constantly projecting that her cat was upset, she smothered Misha with emotion when she returned home, which the cat pulled away from.

Misha communicated that, while she had been upset at the departure of the boyfriend, she was over that. By peeing on the bed, she really was protesting her bored frustration about her bland and isolating environment.

Since the cat had no other form of entertainment, she tried to make life more exciting by eliciting attention and activity. Her person made a big fuss about Misha peeing on the bed, getting very emotional and calling the veterinarian, the breeder and her ex-boyfriend about it. The cat loved the attention and being talked about and so continued the peeing game as the most interesting thing in her life.

Misha was intelligent and needed more opportunities to challenge herself. Her environment made her feel like a human would if locked in a closet all day. She wanted something to do and to have company. While Misha enjoyed her person's company, it wasn't fair to this active, intelligent cat to not have other activities to enjoy, especially when she was alone so much.

I advised her person on possibilities that Misha agreed would help her: to play music and other recordings for Misha while her person was gone, to make a cat jungle gym out of cardboard boxes or a more permanent construction, to play with her vigorously at least 15 minutes twice a day, to get another animal companion, to set up a window space and a bird feeder so Misha could watch the birds, and to move to a place where she could have safe outdoor time when that was possible.

The woman couldn't have another cat, since one was not even allowed, but she'd try some fish for company and for the cat to watch. There was no place to put a bird feeder, but she would set up a window space for her. My client realised she needed to calm down and stop focusing her tendency to worry on the cat, which added to making peeing in the wrong places such a game.

Have you ever noticed that when you don't understand and acknowledge someone, they may keep trying to get the message across somehow or prove it to you? Beings of all kinds generally mean well when they want their communications received and understood. Their messages can get desperate or weird when they have been ignored or rejected too often.

Misha was more relaxed after expressing her frustration, and she and her person had a better understanding. Following the suggested programme helped to resolve the situation.

Can you tell us about a few of your most memorable cat cases? Ones that have really stuck in your memory?

One that comes to mind was a cat I saw in person. A lady called me up to see her cat because she was very ill. In fact, the vet had kind of given up on the cat and the cat was dying. When I came to the apartment and sat down, I saw the cat lying down flat, with her head flat on the ground near her water bowl. She had not been eating or drinking and had been to the vet (where they tried everything), but they could not handle or help the animal. So I communicated with the cat and asked her what was going on and she understood that I could understand animals. Animals always understand when you get what they are thinking and feeling and that you are telepathic, and she started to tell me that life had gotten very grim with her guardian. The guardian had a boyfriend who was abusive: abusive to her, yelling at her and pushing her around. It turned out that when the guardian left home, the boyfriend was doing things like kicking the cat, and since the guardian wasn't telepathically listening to her cat, she didn't know that her cat was being abused by this boyfriend.

The boyfriend was obviously a very sick, hateful person and the guardian was absolutely shocked. She had no idea her boyfriend was doing this to her cat. The cat told me 'there is no point in living. I can't go on with this human abusing me'. The guardian said to me 'Oh, my goodness, I didn't know. I'm so sorry'. 'I want you to know,' she said to her cat, 'that I will cut the relationship off. He will no longer be around'. I was also, at the same time, doing some reiki on the cat, which is energy healing. After she said those words to her cat, the cat got up and went over and started drinking the water. She also started eating some food that her guardian offered her and got better from that day forward. So, this is a routine result of good telepathic communication: that the animals respond positively. You can see from this how much the cat was feeling what her guardian was feeling. What was most important for the cat was that her guardian would not be hurt anymore and if she and her guardian were going to be continually abused then life would not be worth having.

Another example that stands out was a home-visit consultation. I was called because the guardian's cat was extremely aggressive to people. The cat would lash out and bite when people came over to visit them and so she started to keep the cat away from people. She contacted me, as she wanted to know if there was anything she could do. I walked into the home very respectfully and quietly, and connected with the cat. The cat's guardian cautioned me, saying, 'she might bite you'. The cat was very withdrawn at first, but then came up to me, jumped up on my lap, started purring and rubbing against me and then sat down on my lap. The guardian was absolutely blown away, saying 'this never happens. This cat has never been friendly with other people'. It was a rescue cat, although I don't remember the specifics of the cat's background story. All I remember is that this cat had done the opposite of what the guardian had said was the problem she was having. I understood from the cat that there was a traumatic background and trauma with people. I worked with the cat with counselling and healing. The thing that happens with communication is that when you're good and you really listen – when you don't extrapolate and put in your preconceptions or your generalisations from other animals and treat the animal as an individual – then miracles happen. This is the kind of thing that allows changes. The reason why I know that telepathic communication is real – how you know that it's working – is that these kinds of things happen. Animals go from night to day and they so appreciate that you understand them.

Those are two of my most memorable stories, but you know, I've talked to hundreds, if not thousands of cats over the years. Cats are incredible. I love them so much; they are some of my favourite animals. I don't think I could live without cats.

Could you talk about one of your cases with cat aggression because it's quite a common theme in my consultations?

Sure. One time a client named Jackie called about her cat, Muffin[4], who was biting and scratching her people. Muffin had been affectionate and playful until after they got her simultaneously spayed and declawed. When I got in touch with Muffin, she had been severely traumatised. She experienced pain in her belly, severe pain in her toes and hurtful anger at the perceived cruelty of her humans toward her. She didn't understand the reason for either of the operations, felt extremely vulnerable and frustrated, and responded by attacking her people.

I counselled Muffin and had her go through the incident of being spayed and declawed to help release the trauma. It had been an excruciating ordeal for her, as her people had not explained what was going to happen. They did not realise that declawing is not a necessary operation and is accompanied by severe, often long-term physical and emotional pain. Usually, spaying is relatively un-traumatic and a cat heals from it without bad side effects and with obvious positive benefits. The pain of declawing, having the first joints in her feet removed, caused her to hold residual pain in her belly.

I explained to Muffin's people that, contrary to what some veterinarians tell you, the cats I have communicated with claim that declawing is a painful and emotionally harmful affair. It leaves the cat feeling vulnerable, since the front claws are a cat's first line of defence. Often, a cat that's declawed will begin to bite people, even in the face. When cats with claws intact scratch a tree or scratching post, they hook in their claws and stretch and align their whole spines, releasing locked-up energy and increasing circulation throughout the body, thus helping to ensure good health. It's impossible for a cat to do this well without front claws. The toes often feel sore for months, even years, from the physical and psychological trauma. Many cats that are declawed go outside the litter box, especially to defecate. It hurts their sensitised paws to scratch the litter and cats normally scratch to cover up their faeces. Out of discomfort and protest, some declawed cats will urinate elsewhere.

It's not hard to train cats to use scratching posts if they are available near where the cat naps. Cats normally like to scratch after getting up, and they prefer textures that they can really hook their claws into, like the bark of trees, sisal rope, or the backside of carpeting, rather than the fluffy carpeting that's commonly sold for cat-scratching posts. It helps to have smooth-textured furniture instead of the nubby surfaces that cats find hard to resist scratching. Even where there is irresistibly textured furniture, with gentle persistence and well-placed properly textured scratching posts, you can get most cats to leave the furniture alone. My four cats often scratched on the trees outside, but I still had four cat scratching posts of different sizes and textures strategically placed for their convenience; they had no excuse to scratch the furniture or carpets. They enjoyed their choices, and I enjoyed seeing them stretch and scratch to their heart's content.

Imagine if you got your first finger joints cut off because you did things with your fingers that someone didn't like. What suffering and inhibited movement you would have! It's just as cruel with cats. You can communicate with them, and they can learn appropriate places to scratch. There are rare cases where cats would be killed if they weren't declawed. However, mutilation of animals' bodies (declawing, docking tails and ears, and so on) for human convenience or cosmetic consideration is cruel and many animals who undergo such operations suffer behavioural, psychological, or physical disorders as a result.

The long-distance counselling and healing with Muffin was successful. She released her pain and emotional frustration and returned to peaceful, loving coexistence with her people. To aid the healing process, her people gave her gentle massages and special playtimes and most of all, they understood her position.

Do you communicate with cats that have passed to the other side and does your approach to this type of work differ from when the cat is alive?

It's telepathic communication whether they're with their body or whether they have passed on, so it's the same communication. It's the same with all beings whether they are embodied or without a body. As far as the approach and whether it differs; I always listen to the person. I always ask them what's going on and what they want. With any animal, whether doing it at a distance or whether it has passed on, I ask for the name, age, or in this case, the age at which they died. These are things to orient me to that particular individual. I also ask for a description of the cat, as they were when they were alive and then the person's question. What is it that they want you to ask their cat, or to communicate with the cat about?

I always feel the connection once the person gives me the description, and sometimes the cat comes in even before the person gives the description because that person has their attention on them, and the being comes in and wants to communicate. I can feel an animal's signature of their energy. I can tell whether I have got the right animal. Generally, from what I say, they know it's their cat that I'm talking to. People know their animals and they know what they are like even if they don't think they can communicate with them telepathically. I may be verifying information if the cat says they are missing their brother who is a dog, or he wants to show me his favourite place that he used to play in.

How do you deal with situations whereby a cat may wish you to tell their guardians that something they are doing is wrong? Do the humans respond well or become defensive?

I stay telepathically in touch with everybody involved. I'm respectful of the animal's feelings and the humans' feelings and I listen carefully to them both, to what they're saying and how they're feeling. Because it's a circle – a cooperative harmony – I'm trying to help all the beings involved come to more understanding and harmony. I find that in this space of pure presence of listening and understanding, the right words come out. The words are kind and communicate to the person, according to their understanding, what will help them. And animals are kind too: they love their people but they might say that the person ignores them when they want to have affection. The cat will show me the situation, and maybe give me images, feelings and times and places where this has happened so I will just explain it like 'it appears that you may be distracted when your cat really wants affection so that kind of upsets them'. I say it in a compassionate way, for both the cat and the human, so I don't find that people become defensive.

My priority, and this is how I teach my students, is that in telepathic communication we must show understanding and compassion to all the beings involved, so what we say comes out in the way that it's meant to. The purpose of the consultation is to further harmony and understanding; not to make anybody feel wrong. This is the attitude of some people towards humans: that humans are awful and humans are wrong. No. People call because they want to help their animals. These are people who care. Yes, they might be missing things. That's why they are calling you.

My take on it is that the person wants to understand more. They may be very vulnerable and they may be hurt about something that's happening, but when you explain it from the point of view of increasing understanding, I find that people do not get defensive and then everybody heals more and everybody understands more. The animals understand that the person understands them and that makes them very joyous. Animals are not trying to make their people wrong. They just may feel hurt that their people don't understand them. Once their people understand, they are overjoyed. They shift, the people shift and everybody gets better.

Can you highlight one of your unusual big-cat consultations?

Before I began teaching animal-communication retreats at Earthfire Institute Wildlife Sanctuary in Driggs, Idaho, I visited the wild-animal residents. I enjoyed peacefully being and communicating with individuals of many different species, but I will never forget my first encounter with Windwalker, the cougar.

I calmly approached his enclosure and watched as he crouched and began to stalk me – a response I did not expect. My body was stricken with fear upon feeling the intention of this approximately 150-pound mountain lion getting ready to pounce. My first thought was how big he was and that I would definitely not want to meet a cougar while walking on a trail in the forest. I knew I was at a safe distance from the bars of his enclosure, but that did not stop my body from quaking inside.

I talked to Windwalker and told him that I would end my visit with him if he continued to stalk and look at me as prey. He continued his stance. End of discussion. I quietly turned around and moved away to see other animals, who were not thinking about making me a meal.

Windwalker had come to Earthfire Institute through Jean Simpson, animal-handler expert and co-founder of Earthfire. Jean had a lifelong and deep relationship with animals. When he moved to the Rocky Mountains, he taught himself how to train wolves through living with and understanding them. This led to a career training wild animals for movies through his techniques based on reward and an amazing grasp of each species and each animal as an individual. In 1989 he founded The Wild Bunch Ranch so that he could train based on his unique understanding of wild animals.

Jean had Windwalker before Earthfire started in 2000, purchased from a woman who bred cougars and was going out of business. As Earthfire grew, he gave Windwalker to Earthfire.

After my first encounter with Windwalker, I had little connection with him in the following years of teaching there. We did not communicate other than a passing greeting, nor did he stalk me again. He was a healthy, contented being who was not particularly interested in communicating with me or anyone else at our retreats.

Years later, when Windwalker was an older lion nearing the end of his life, the change in his awareness from his younger days was noticeable. When I came to teach an animal-communication retreat at Earthfire, he was a featured helper by his choice for the first time in his life at Earthfire events. Before this time, he hadn't been very interested in connecting with people other than his friend and caretaker, Jean. Now he asked me if he could help people at the retreat.

He had spiritually grown, radically shifted from caring little about other beings in the world into a consciousness of what people were thinking and feeling and the importance of the human–wildlife connection. As he lay in his enclosure with all the retreat participants seated around the perimeter, he looked around intently and deeply connected with each person with a gaze full of wisdom and care.

When we talked with him, he now had things to say about the bigger world that he had not been interested in before, including the state of cougars out in the wild. He had transformed into a being of loving wisdom and made a deep impression on everyone who met him.

After that, at retreats that other teachers held at Earthfire, Windwalker gave his full attention to people, transmitted healing with his gigantic purr, and communicated his wisdom freely. Despite the veterinarians predicting he would die soon of congestive heart failure, his new connection with people gave his life meaning and instilled energy into his failing body for another year.

Has any cat ever blocked your avenue of communication?

No, because I come as a spiritual being without agendas. I come in openness to understand them, so they don't block. A good example is the aggressive cat I mention above. You might think that that cat would have blocked anybody, but that wasn't the case. They know right away that you are open to them; that you are not judging them, that you are receptive to who they are, and that your intention is to bring more understanding. There was once one cat who was just recovering from an operation, and he still was under the influence of drugs so it was not the right time to communicate with him (although the person really wanted to know). In this instance I wouldn't say the cat was blocking me. It was more that he needed a little bit more time to recover. His focus was on the healing. If I get animals that were traumatised and have had bad experiences with people they will sometimes back off at first from anybody just because they are human. I just back off too. I move back and say 'OK'. I'm not here to impose anything. I let them know my intention, what their person's intention is and why I'm there. Then they normally open up to communication because I'm very respectful and loving of them.

What do you feel cats give us in life and why do we love them so much?

They are just characters. I can speak for myself. I'm a very independent person, who likes to do things my own way and also does not want to be bugged by distractions and unnecessary things. So I'm very cat-like! And cats are incredibly beautiful souls, as all animals are, but cats… I just enjoy them so much. Their antics, their physicality, their beauty, their gracefulness. I have three beautiful photos of my three cats above my computer right here and I'm looking at them. They just blow me away. They are incredible.

They give this incredible love and understanding. Some might have more of a sense of humour and don't mind that people may be ignorant in some ways and others just won't tolerate it. They scold you, 'I don't understand, I don't have the time for you' and they walk away. They're not trying to please you so much. So, they are unique individuals and meditators.

Cats are incredibly wise beings and have wisdom when teaching us how to be present: to meditate, relax, enjoy and stretch. You really have to earn a cat's respect. It's good. I regard that as a very good thing. I could go on and on. I adore cats. They are quite amazing, as the internet shows us with the gazillions of videos and pictures of cats. It's well known that people really love their cats!

I was very inspired hearing Penelope speak. I admit that an area I struggle with is stillness of mind. That in itself is quite an art form, as is blocking out preconceptions to allow the mind and body to feel and understand the energy of another person or being. Opening up the mind to be mindful of another's journey and communication is at the forefront of a peaceful existence, and this is especially true for people who work closely with animals. Without opening the mind, we couldn't possibly have empathy for the animals we love. This chapter's Cat Chat looks at ways we can be in the moment with our pets, to give them the concentrated quality time that they need. Being mindful of what you're giving out to your pet will get you the best results back.

A CATTY SUM UP

1. Set aside your own thoughts and preconceptions and open yourself to the direct communication from animals.

2. It's better to get information from the cat than other people's opinions.

3. The changes in behaviour and healing begin when the animal feels respected and understood.

CAT CHAT

Mindfulness And Cats

The more cynical of you out there could be forgiven for thinking that my title is a calculated way of attracting maximum attention on social media. The combination of these two immense buzzwords must surely be the ultimate in gaining Twitter followers, Facebook likes and whatnot. Add a cute picture and I'm going to clean up, right?

Seriously though, practising mindfulness in our human–cat interactions is not only beneficial for our cats, it can also enhance our personal experience with these furry companions. I searched for a definition under 'mindfulness' and the KMC London website came up with a very good one. Although they're talking about meditation, it can just as easily relate to the subject we're discussing here: 'The function of mindfulness is to prevent the mind from being distracted – from wandering away from the object it's holding'. In other words, to use a more old-fashioned phrase, we should pay attention!

It's no secret that we're now a society addicted to screens – TVs, smartphones, laptops, tablets, etc. Many times I've seen someone waving a hunting toy somewhere off to the side whilst checking friends' posts on Facebook or whatever; they look around and find that the cat has walked off. Well, I'm not surprised!

My own cats look straight into my eyes when an interaction is in the offing and they decide, according to my level of attention, whether they're going to participate or not. If I'm absorbed with a movie or a programme on TV, or working on my laptop, odds are they won't. Even when a cat is very happy being petted, if someone phones me and I start talking, the cat will very often get up and walk off. They know that despite the stroking they haven't got my full attention and so they behave as if our interaction is over, whereas I might think that I'm 'multitasking' by splitting my attention between the caller and the cat.

To be fair, when my cats come to me, they are fully present. Their purrs tell me that our interaction is at the centre of this moment and rubbing their heads on my hands/face has an intensity that would be completely lost if they had smartphones to keep tabs on. Rolling over for a belly rub, they certainly aren't preoccupied with the latest crisis on TV or some cheesy throwaway entertainment. This is the entertainment and it's as good as it gets. Nothing from their point of view dilutes the moments my cats give me, except the possibility of a treat, maybe, so why shouldn't I give them the same courtesy?

It has become very clear to me that these moments are sacrosanct and I give myself entirely to them. During the whole interaction my cats will constantly look deeply and meaningfully into my eyes to check if I'm still giving them my complete undivided attention. I store the memories of these moments and have no other agenda or thoughts present. They are, to all intents and purposes, meditations.

OK, so maybe cats don't know exactly what 'mindfulness' is, but they instinctively recognise that mental state and are 'present in the moment' as Eckhart Tolle would say. He calls house pets (especially cats and dogs) 'guardians of being' – because their interactions with us aren't accompanied by thought processes (judgements, random mental noise, etc), but are based on 'pure being'. This is why he thinks that we enjoy their company so much – because they have the ability to lift us out of our thought processes. I can definitely relate to what he's saying, as I forget all my worries and other mental gymnastics when completely focused on the beautiful creatures I share these quiet moments with. I'm definitely more relaxed and peaceful too!

Now then, what if we transferred this philosophy to humans…?

CHAPTER NINE

Can Cats Be Trained?

*'In ancient times cats were worshipped as gods;
they have not forgotten this.'*

Terry Pratchett

CHAPTER NINE

In this chapter:

- Get inside knowledge on the famous Acro cats and how they were trained, in conversation with Samantha Martin.
- Find out what training works best with cats.
- Read about the history behind the most common training tool – the clicker.

Can cats be trained? This is a question I hear dog and cat lovers discuss between them and usually it ends with a 'no'. Dogs are sycophantic and, as a pack animal, wish to please their master, whereas cats care little about pleasing us and want what they want, when they want, without any considerations for our feelings! The latter is true, of course, but cats can indeed be trained, as is the case with most animals, by the use of a reward, usually food. I'm not talking about the training that occurs from extreme cruelty like training a bear to dance for tourists, breaking their spirit and will to survive, as this is what's classified as negative or punishment-based training.

The training I'm interested in is classified as positive-reward-based training and goes hand-in-hand with other forms of training such as changing an environment to 'guide' a cat back to a natural behaviour rather than an unwanted one. An example of the latter is changing a litter tray or area a litter tray is placed to train/guide the cat back to using it rather than in an inappropriate area the cat has chosen. The key to training a cat is consistency and positivity. Results are achieved if the cat is getting something out of it. It was whilst searching the internet for good examples of clicker-training cats that I came across Samantha Martin.

Samantha is a formidable woman who has inspired respect all over the US with her *Acro Cats* show, where the stars are her own pet cats. Samantha has used her show and her talents as an animal trainer to educate cat carers about positive-reward-based training. She has also helped with feline adoptions, having taken in and hand-reared a large proportion of her own cats, spreading information and adoption requests from many animal shelters and rescue facilities whilst touring *Acro Cats* from state to state. Samantha and her cats have appeared in numerous US commercials, films, music videos, documentaries and prime-time chat shows, so it was very exciting when I heard back from her with a positive response to helping us understand more about training cats.

It's so inspiring to see how much fun the Acro cats are having and the love and care Samantha shows for her feline friends. Let's find out more!

In Conversation With Samantha Martin

I know you started work as a trainer with dogs, rats and other animals. Why did you end up focusing on cats in the end?

I was a wildlife educator for 25 years and I had really wanted to make a change in my career and get back to training animals, particularly for film and television. I had started out as a dog trainer many years ago, but there were already plenty of dog trainers out there. Cats are the second most requested animal in film and television, but I knew cats were much more challenging. I'm always up for a challenge and I absolutely love cats and their independent, difficult nature.

Since I didn't really have a reputation as a cat trainer at that point, I started taking a cat called Tuna around to show off her skill set. Tuna was brilliant. I attended pet expos and other events where cats were welcome. I bought a small baby carriage for cats that could hold some props.

She was the inspiration for the show now called the *Amazing Acro Cats* and my transition from 'The Rat Lady' to 'The Cat Lady' only happened when, Tuna, a new-born, all-white baby kitten entered my life.

Awesome. Tell us more about Tuna. Where did she come from?

Back in 2002, a woman down the street had a beautiful white cat named Luna. I had borrowed her cat a couple of times for photo shoots. One day she asked if I might take care of her cat for a couple of weeks while she went back to Poland for a visit. I said of course! She never came back. Not long after, I realised that Luna was pregnant! She gave birth to three kittens. Tuna was one of those kittens. There was something special about Tuna, right from the start.

She was a bit of a loner and had a confidence and curiosity about her. When she was just a few weeks old, I got a call from a photographer who needed a white kitten for a photo shoot for Nutro Max kitten-food packaging. Strange how the universe makes things happen sometimes. I immediately thought of Tuna for the job. She settled in immediately, like she had always lived there, and within moments the photographer had all of the shots that they needed. Shortly thereafter I got another call for a kitten, this time for a Petco advert. Tuna got the job and was a natural. There was even a dog on set and Tuna was unfazed.

That's when I really knew I had a special cat. I got out my clicker and target stick, and started working with Tuna on a daily basis. As an adult cat she starred in her own little comedy film called *Zeke*, written and directed by Dana Buning and produced and edited by Mat Olmon, two students at Florida State University[1].

How did your interest in clicker training come about, and can you explain the philosophy behind it to the layperson?

I started training animals when I was 10 years old with the family dog. When I started working with rats in the 80s, I knew that you couldn't use the same methods, so I experimented with food rewards. I didn't know about clicker training at that point. I had no formal training in clicker training, until I attended Bob Bailey's chicken workshops[2].

I discovered that the techniques I was using were correct, but the clicker made things a lot easier for communicating to the animal what you wanted from them. The classes were operant conditioning and behaviour workshops that used chickens as models. Clicker training is a positive-reinforcement-based method of training. The sound is made using a 'clicker': a small hand-held device that makes a click sound when pressed.

Clicker training is a method that uses a unique sound to tell the animal that he or she has done something right at the exact moment they do it, and that they will receive a reward. The sound can be used to mark any action or behaviour that you want the animal to do. If you think of the clicker as a camera, you would want to click as the desired action was taking place. It's a very effective way to communicate with the animal what you want. There are no negative consequences. It's all positive reinforcement.

Can all animals respond well to clicker training, and do you feel clicker training can work on most behaviour issues?

All animals can be trained through positive reinforcement. However, if you were working with dolphins you would use a whistle and if you were working with fish or a deaf animal, you would use a flashlight.

Many animals have behavioural issues because they are bored. However, sometimes it may be a medical condition, so you should always get your pet examined by a veterinarian if they start exhibiting behavioural problems to rule out anything medical.

How long did the training take for the circus shows?

I can train most cats to do a basic behaviour within five minutes. Many of the tricks take a couple of weeks or more. Some tricks are an ongoing process, as I try to build duration, such as on the musical instruments: strumming the guitar or drumming for longer periods of time before rewarding the behaviour.

Have you found that all cats, despite their backgrounds, can be trained to work as an Acro cat, or does the cat need a particular personality to begin with?

All cats can be trained to do basic behaviours. The cats that have been most successful as Acro cats are the troublemakers that have excess energy. Channelling that energy into fun behaviours or 'tricks' is a great way to meet their excessive mental and physical needs.

How do you get the cats used to the stage, lights, cameras and audiences? Isn't that another level of training altogether?

All of my Acro cats start out as kittens: usually the ones that I'm fostering. I incorporate them in the show as soon as they are eating solid food. If they are really young kittens, then I keep them in a pen off to the side, so that they can hear the audience and experience the lights and music. I also take them to as many places as possible to get them used to travelling and different situations. The more situations you expose your kitten to at a young age, the more well adjusted they will be as adults. Anytime they seem a little startled by something, I immediately click and give them treats to turn the situation into a positive experience.

Have you ever had moments when an individual cat shows stress or an unwillingness to perform, and how do you respond to that?

During almost every show there are cats that decide not to do their trick. I'm constantly reading their body language and know when to bail on a particular trick. Sometimes they just need to be refocused, but they are never forced; only encouraged. Many times I just laugh and throw my arm out in a 'tada' motion, even if the cat is just sitting there and grooming. I just go with the flow and just keep smiling no matter what happens. Every show is different, depending on the cats' mood that day. I discovered people just really loved seeing the cats regardless of whether they did what they were supposed to do, so I just go with whatever the cats want to do that day. It's a win-win.

In addition to the routine feline clicker training component, there is the non-routine feline+live audience component. The cats are sometimes distracted by a light or noise or aroma and will run off stage to investigate. At the beginning of each performance, I ask each audience member to try not to pay too much attention to the cat rubbing on his/her leg or sniffing at his/her shoe and explain that eventually the cat will return to the stage and perhaps even complete the trick! Audience interaction is part of the thrill and entertainment of the *Acro Cats* performances – the stage extends out into the audience seating area.

I can see that the cats enjoy the stimulation of the shows and I feel that cats, especially indoor ones, need stimulation and enjoy agility games. Explain to people who may see the cat circus as unnatural and bad for the cats why this is different to other animals used in a circus situation?

Since it's not safe for cats to be outside unattended, hunting birds and chasing prey, they need some sort of stimulation and outlet for all of that energy. Half of training is observation. I spend a lot of time just watching my cats to see what they like to do and what their skill sets are. I base their tricks on what they enjoy doing. The props on stage are the same things that I have set up in my house. So basically my show is just an extension of what I do in my home. I'm sharing my life with my cats with the audience, hoping to inspire people to work with their own cats. None of them are ever forced or mistreated. It's all free will and many of the cats will just leave the stage and hang out with the audience members. At the end of the show, during the meet-and-greet when people come up to mingle with the cats, they have the option to just disappear or go back to their carriers. Most of them stay and seem to enjoy the attention they get from the audience.

Do you have any funny circus stories that came out of those times when things have not gone quite as planned?

Almost every show does not go as planned. One time, Tuna ran up a 20-foot ladder and I had to stop the show to climb up and fetch her. Many times the cats invent new tricks during the show. Sometimes they leave the stage but then later reappear, so we rearrange the show on the spot to accommodate their sudden appearance.

The cats do not like clowns or people dressed in costumes, so this can bring the show to a screeching halt. Also, people sometimes buy catnip toys before the show and the cats will seek them out and lay in their laps for the entire show. We discovered Albacore Tuna loves popcorn, so sometimes, if there is popcorn served, he will just leave and enjoy the concessions. We never know what's going to happen and every show is different.

A memorable moment not connected to the cat circus involved my pet raccoon on a shoot. The raccoon scrambled up a tree and refused to climb back down. I'm petrified of heights but was more scared of harm coming to my beloved raccoon. Climbing up after him, cooing words of comfort to my pet, I swayed back and forth on narrow tree limbs as I clung to branches to rescue him. After catching him, I manoeuvred down amidst cracking tree limbs to the safety of the ground. Not bad for a girl who could never climb the rope in gym class.

You do educational shows for feline lovers. What are the main feline issues you concentrate on?

Our show demonstrates that cats are not aloof, un-trainable creatures. Many people have a latchkey relationship with their cat and merely leave out a bowl of food for them. So many cats end up in shelters because they do not have a relationship with their human. This is not the cat's fault. People need to spend quality time with their cat, just as people would do with their dog.

If you spend just 10 minutes a day with your cat, it can make all the difference in the world. You'll have a cat that's well adjusted and more content. They will be less likely to display aggressive or destructive habits and training can also save their life.

All of our cats are trained to do a whistle recall to a room or their carriers. If you need to call your cats quickly in an emergency situation, you can just blow a whistle and have them come running. Those minutes that you save could possibly mean the difference between life and death.

Also if you have a routine established with your cat, you will notice if your cat is ill because behaviour change is the first sign that your cat might be suffering an illness. Cats are notorious for hiding illness. Just by establishing a feeding regimen in which you blow a whistle for your kitty to come for dinner time, you can determine if something is wrong based on how fast your cat comes to the bowl, how fast they eat and whether or not they are having problems eating.

Teaching your cats some basic behaviours can also keep you in tune with your cat's physical issues. This is especially helpful as they age.

Those 10 minutes a day you spend can tell you everything you need to know about your cat's health.

We really hope that our show can inspire people to spend more quality time with their cat and build a better bond. We also do rescue and foster, so we promote adoptions from local rescues and encourage people to foster. Since 2009 we have fostered and found homes for around 220 cats and kittens.

We are in the process of changing our company to a not-for-profit called 'Rock Cats Rescue'.

There's a joy in seeing animals stimulated with training that focuses on the animals' natural instincts and skill set. I'm not talking about wild lions, elephants or Orcas who perform in circuses or commercial establishments such as Sea World and whose natural instincts would be far removed from what they are being trained to do for entertainment, sometimes with the cruel practice of breaking their spirits. With domesticated pets that love a stimulus which centers around their natural ability to hunt, chase, stalk and climb, and which taps into their natural curiosity, training is fun.

The Acro cats are domesticated pets that have freely chosen to perform in the show or not on any given day, and are all treated as they would on the road or as stay-at-home pets. Samantha breaks the myth that has labelled cats as un-trainable and too independent to really form a close bond with us. She shows with ease how cats will do anything for food and, coupled with stimulation that's fun and exciting, most behaviour issues can be managed or erased entirely.

In 2014 I had an email exchange with the late Dr. Sophia Yin, applied veterinary animal behaviourist, and she agreed:

The biggest misconception is that cats are aloof and un-trainable. I just gave a lecture at the American Veterinary Medical Association conference, where I showed how just training three exercises – sit, target, come – can help solve a majority of behaviour issues a pet owner might come across. One of the main points I stressed was that cats are actually easier to train with these behaviours than dogs. I showed how each could be trained within five minutes! Besides training and trainability a huge issue is that people don't realise they should be socialising their kittens just like puppy owners are supposed to socialise their puppies. By doing so, they can develop a kitten that's as outgoing as the average dog and who is less likely to spray, hide from guests or be aggressive to other animals in the house.

The history behind clicker training and why it has grown to be one of the most popular humane forms of training is fascinating. Humans and their inventions to get ever closer to animals, to feel that connection, never fail to amaze me.

When was clicker training discovered, and who discovered this method of training? Find out more in this chapter's Cat Chat.

 **A CATTY SUM UP**

1. All cats can be trained to follow basic behaviours.

2. Teaching your cats some basic behaviours can keep you in tune with your cat's physical issues.

3. Channelling energy into fun behaviours or 'tricks' is a great way to meet a cat's excessive mental and physical needs.

CAT CHAT
The History Of Clicker Training

Clicker training is an animal-training method that uses a positive-reward-based stimulus to encourage a desired action. The method stems from a type of training known as operant conditioning[1]. American psychologist Edward L. Thorndike at Columbia University first studied operant conditioning using cats[2]. His studies using cats showed that behaviours followed by satisfying consequences tended to be repeated and those that produced unpleasant consequences were less likely to be repeated, proving that some consequences strengthen behaviour and some consequences weaken it. An example of classic operant behaviour can be seen in both negative and positive-based training. A negative-training response could be that an animal gets a small electric shock when touching a red button but gets rewarded with a treat by touching a blue one. Thus, they learn to avoid the red button.

Although Thorndike began the study of operant conditioning, it was B.F. Skinner, psychologist, behaviourist and professor at Harvard University, who is best known for his work on the effects of operant conditioning on animals. He invented the Skinner Box, which he used to conduct many experiments, primarily using pigeons and rats, in order to watch and record repeatable responses, as well as recording mental states. It was two students of Skinner's, Marian Kruse and Keller Breland, who took [operant] conditioning further by recognising that the reward:

> ... did not inform the animal of success with enough promptness and precision to create the required cognitive connections for speedy learning. They saw the

potential for using the [operant] conditioning method in commercial animal training.

This was the light-bulb moment for clicker training. It occurred to Kruse and Breland that they could use the sound of a click followed by an instant reward to reinforce the desired behaviour[3, 4].

Marian Kruse and Keller Breland married, and in 1947 set up a company called Animal Behaviour Enterprises, which was to be the first commercial company to incorporate operant conditioning into animal training. They tried to introduce clicker training in the 1940s and 1950s but it wasn't until the late 1980s and early 1990s that the idea really took off[5]. Behaviourists such as Karen Pryor with her training seminars and books on clicker training made the idea very popular. She wrote *Clicker Training For Cats* in 2001[6].

Clicker training has various approaches, all of which employ the principle that eventually the animal will learn to repeat the behaviour for a treat. These approaches include:

- **Capturing:** catching the animal in the act of doing something that's desired, for example sitting or lying down.
- **Shaping:** gradually building a new behaviour by rewarding each small step toward it.
- **Luring:** using the treat like a magnet to get the animal to move toward the desired position[7].

Although clicker training is a type of reward-based training, Gary Wilkes, another animal behaviourist and trainer, interestingly points out that:

> No method of training is 'all positive'. By scientific definition, the removal of a desired reward is a 'negative punishment'. So, if you ever withhold a treat or use a time-out, by definition, you are a 'negative' trainer who uses 'punishment', where 'negative' indicates that something has been removed and 'punishment' merely indicates there has been a reduction in the behaviour (unlike the common use of these terms)[8].

Most behaviourists today use one of two training methods: operant conditioning or classical conditioning. The latter was named after studies by

Russian physiologist Ivan Pavlov. Pavlov noticed, during his research on the physiology of digestion in dogs, that his 'experimental' dogs began to salivate in the presence of the technician who normally fed them, rather than simply salivating in the presence of food. Putting these informal observations to an experimental test, Pavlov presented a stimulus (such as the sound of a metronome) and then gave the dogs food. After a few repetitions, the dogs started to salivate in response to the stimulus. Pavlov concluded that if a particular stimulus in a dog's surroundings was present when the dog was given food, then that stimulus could become associated with food and cause salivation on its own. Pavlov called the dogs' anticipatory salivation 'psychic secretion'[9].

The difference between classical and operant conditioning is that, in classical conditioning, behaviours are modified through the association of stimuli, whereas in operant conditioning, behaviours are modified by the effect they produce (for example, a reward or punishment)[10]. To illustrate ways in which the two techniques are used, and the differences between them, consider these two examples.

OPERANT CONDITIONING

A cat is stuck inside a house without a bowl of food. However, it notices (in the corner of its house) a dry-biscuit food puzzle with various levers. The food puzzle is designed in such a way that only one of the levers will release some biscuits. Thus, through trial-and-error, the cat learns to touch the lever that produces the biscuits and avoids the others. This is why clicker training is operant conditioning and is a perfect training method for cats. Clicker training can also be used in many other situations, including:

- preventing incessant meowing, where a click and treat is only used when the cat falls silent.
- encouraging a cat to sit still, where a click and treat is only used when the cat sits down.
- to guide a cat on to a climber and away from a hot stove or baby, where the cat gets a click and treat if they jump on to the desired platform.

CLASSICAL CONDITIONING

A cat has had a bad experience with a cat groomer. Perhaps, on a previous visit, the cat was scared whilst it was being shaved. The sound of clippers is now associated with the fear it feels inside. Thereafter, whenever the cat hears the sound of the clippers, no matter what the circumstances, the sound will illicit a natural response of fear. Classical conditioning can be used on many phobias and fear issues, such as a cat being frightened of strangers, loud noises, traffic, hoovers and other potentially troubling stimuli. Consistently but gradually coupling the stimulus – which elicits the natural response of fear or anxiety – with something positive will eventually change the cat's response.

CHAPTER TEN

Why Do Cats Need To Be Groomed?

'I believe cats to be spirits come to earth. A cat, I'm sure, could walk on a cloud without coming through.'

Jules Verne

CHAPTER TEN

In this chapter:

- Discover why cats need our help with grooming.
- Get rare insider knowledge on the cat-grooming world from a holistic cat groomer, Sheryl Woods.
- Get step-by-step expert advice on how to train a cat to enjoy being groomed.

I spent six weeks from 9-6 p.m. Monday to Saturday, at a pet-grooming salon in London, learning my trade as a feline-only groomer. But the hardest training for me was when I left the security of the school and my teacher to face the realities of working as a mobile cat groomer. Each day was a new learning experience, as I was confronted with cats and their formidable owners in their own homes, mostly lovely but some neurotic and overbearing, watching every movement I made. If I'm honest, at first I was quite guarded about my work because I didn't want owners taking knowledge from me and then grooming their cats without the need to book me. I was warned of this by other groomers and told to groom cats in a separate room so that the need for my services would continue.

At first I started out either asking owners to go grab a coffee whilst I worked or told them they could get on with other things around the home! This didn't last, though. I quickly realised that firstly, I didn't want to keep seeing matted cats and secondly, owners needed help and guidance. Also, I wanted the owners to stay whilst I worked because their cats, on many occasions, needed reassurance and a familiar voice and face. Who knew their cat better than the owners when it came to calming a more challenging cat?

It's true that cats do groom themselves and are fastidious with their cleaning routine. You will see your cat generally clean after mealtimes or 'allo-groom' another cat as a sign of affection and closeness. So why do they need intervention from us? The non-breed generic cat, in the UK (we call them moggies), is short-haired and low maintenance in terms of grooming. They will shed fur like all cats but in general they can maintain their coat well and would probably just need a quick brush of the coat to keep it in good condition. However, long-haired breeds of cats like the Maine Coon, Siberian Forest, British Longhair and Persians need their coats combed through to prevent mats forming. This is also true of cats with short but thick coats such as British Shorthairs. As for the hairless Sphynx cat, even they need grooming in the form of regular baths, as their skin gets very oily and dirty.

Matting is when a cat's fur becomes knotted and entwined. Mats can occur when the cat's undercoat sheds (moults) and gets trapped under the top layer of fur. A build up of dirty fur or oily skin, affecting the condition of the fur, can also result in matting. The fur bunches together if left uncombed. Without proper grooming, the matting can very quickly turn into a pelt. A pelt is a hardened mat or knotting that's tight against the skin. Pelts are formed when mats start to join together, over a long period of time, over various parts of the body. More loose fur, dirt, debris and even faeces can get stuck in the already formed pelts, making them larger. Pelts cannot be combed out and always need to be shaved. Owners are always shocked when they see what a pelt looks like once it has been removed from their cat's body, because it looks like a piece of carpet.

Let me now explain, in human terms, what a pelt would feel like for a cat. Imagine our hair without being brushed or washed for months. It would start to mat very quickly and, in time, would become a clump all over. This would tighten to our scalp and become very itchy and make us irritable and hot. Imagine this clump over our bodies connecting skin from different areas as the mats become more entwined. The matting from under our armpits has joined matting on our chest drawing the two bits of skin closer together. It feels way too tight for comfort. We are hot, we itch and sores are gathering under the matting. Without being able to communicate our frustration and misery, would we then try to rip the hair off of our bodies in desperation? Some cats do just that!

But what would a cat do if they lived in the wild? Why do you never see matted wild cats? I'm asked these questions on a regular basis. The answer is: the majority of wild cats do not have long fur. Also, wild cats have larger tongues with large barbs on them to get out unwanted bits and pieces caught in the fur. Lions groom one another. But, if you go and see a lion's mane up close (not advisable!) it will be matted in places.

Frail and elderly cats are the dread of groomers when their fur is matted. It becomes an extremely stressful, long grooming session. Elderly cats are frail, have skin like tissue paper, may hurt when their body is touched, may have nails embedded in the paw pads and most of the time are arthritic. Imagine the positions a groomer has to get in to access these mats! These cats cannot be sedated, as many have kidney issues. What now? The poor elderly cat has to endure a shaving session and it's never nice at that age. The groomer is caught between a rock and a hard place and the cat has no choice but to endure what may seem to them hell on earth. Owners should try to comb their cats' fur every day, also checking areas that mat easily such as the armpits, under the chin and around the bum area. Small amounts of combing every day can make a big difference. A professional groomer can then help to maintain the coat every six to eight weeks.

It was whilst I was finding the best way to approach my work as a mobile groomer that I stumbled upon the Facebook pages of Sheryl Woods and her associate Stacey Ward, who both founded the Holistic Cat Groomers Alliance (HCGA) and who both are professional cat-grooming experts. I knew it would be a joining of like minds and a great support network to share ideas and new ways forward to deal with the difficulties of more challenging cats. A force-free way of grooming, taking into account the mind, body and spirit of the cat.

To understand the correct way to groom a cat is to understand why it's important to approach the subject with a holistic mindset, and in light of this, I asked Sheryl if she could answer some questions for us.

In Conversation With Sheryl Woods

Could you talk us through your earlier years training as a cat groomer?

Initially, I attended a grooming academy, but these schools are focused on dog grooming and cats were not a priority. Having owned many cats over the years, I felt that the needs of the cats weren't being properly addressed at the school. I had many conversations with the director and some of the changes I pushed for became reality, at least while I attended. Protocol at that time was to harness the cat at all times, muzzle most of the time, and groom in a room surrounded by dogs. Cats were also often kept in cages on the floor with dogs housed next to them. As holistic groomers, we know all this is terrifying for cats but as I was a student, I'd vacillate between thinking 'Well, what do I know, I'm just a student' to 'I know in my gut this is wrong and there are better ways'. So, having always been a rebel, I revolted against standard methods and prevailed. Interestingly, after I graduated, the director sent many cat owners to me, as those cats I had holistically groomed at the academy now would not allow themselves to be groomed by students using force methods.

While at the academy, we hosted a three-day seminar given by the owner of a cat-groomer training company. This trainer used methods that were 180 degrees from my developing holistic approach and it threw me off for quite some time, as this trainer insisted that this was the only way to be successful. That stance made me doubt my own philosophy, as once again, I was new to the field. For a time, I tried using the air muzzle (looks like a hamster ball, which is placed on the cat's head), cloth muzzles and scruffing, though in my gut I knew this was not how I wanted to groom. Fortunately, I discovered other professionals in cat-related fields who echoed my philosophical perspective, which gave me the reassurance to continue on the path of holistic grooming.

What were the main changes you pushed for at the cat-grooming academy?

It's been several years since I last taught at the academy, which is now closed, but I'll try to remember! There was a large room in which lectures were held; I pushed to have cats kept in this room, away from dogs, while waiting to be groomed. I also pushed to be able to groom cats in this room but that took more time, as there wasn't a teacher available to supervise the room 100% of the time. Eventually, the director allowed me and the experienced students to groom cats while alone in the room.

Cats were also frequently kept on the floor in their carriers, placed in a floor cage, and/or housed adjacent to or within view of dogs. This is terrifying for cats and it had to change. Most cats prefer to be up high, so more effort was made to accommodate them. Frightened cats were to be left in their carriers with a towel covering and cats in rack cages were to have a towel on the door, depending on their personality. Most students had no idea how to assess a cat when staging them for the day's grooming, but they soon learned.

I refused to use a harness on the cats when grooming or bathing as you have a false sense of control and a greater possibility of injury should the cat flip out. It's horrific to see a cat flailing at the end of a so-called 'easy release' harness because the groomer cannot safely catch the cat. When I became a cat-grooming teacher at the school, I taught students how to properly and safely hold the cat while bathing, but I had to tell them that the school preferred that they use a harness.

I also battled about the number of towels I could use; with the director thinking one was sufficient. Ha! You need at least two for drying, possibly another for covering, a folded one for comfy sitting and another to make a doughnut bed, if needed.

Some things I could do nothing about were shared bathing areas with dogs, so I'd try to wait until most of the dogs were back in the grooming room. Cats are territorial and most aren't comfortable in unfamiliar areas, so you can just imagine the stress the cats were experiencing. As my holistic approach developed, I also pushed for cat-safe shampoos and using behavioural approaches to avoid using muzzles.

I understand that schools and other institutions do things not just for liability reasons but also for economic reasons. However, I feel they just have to find other ways to make a better environment work, for the welfare of the cats.

How did the Holistic Cat Groomers Alliance come about?

Somewhere in that time frame, while I was at the academy or maybe just after graduating, I found a couple of cat-grooming discussion groups on Facebook. I figured these would be a good place to talk about the concepts of no scruffing, no muzzling and other holistic cat-grooming topics. Was I ever wrong! I found many groomers did not want to hear ideas that went against what they'd been taught or had been doing for the last 40 years. I was told I was annoying and other lovely sentiments, with some groomers being extremely nasty with their comments. Being very passionate about the topic, I was stunned by the grooming community's reaction and I felt that my beloved cats were the ones who would be suffering at the hands of those entrenched in their archaic ways. So, I did what anyone else with a cause does, and started my own Facebook group: the Holistic Cat Grooming group, which is still going strong. I was a vocal advocate for force-free grooming at a time when the idea was met with complete scepticism and ridicule by most I encountered.

Now, 10 years later, the concept is much more prevalent and integrated into a larger movement for animal rights and humane treatment. Principles I advocated were no scruffing, no muzzles, no restraints of any type, no manhandling, and to approach grooming using behavioural and psychological methods instead of force and domination. I met another holistic cat groomer online, Stacey Ward, and we found that not only did we share similar ideas (and became friends), but we also shared the dream of teaching the concepts of holistic cat grooming to as many people who wanted to learn as possible. Stacey then hosted her first Cat Grooming Symposium (TCGS), at which I was a teacher. We then hashed out our plan for the launch of the HCGA, which was done shortly after TCGS.

Can you explain to people what exactly 'holistic' means in terms of grooming?

Basically, the term refers to the philosophy of how all the small parts of the groom relate to each other and are balanced and integrated into the 'whole' or end result of the groom. Those small parts may be as broad a concept as the body, the mind and the spirit, and they break down into much smaller components, which must be balanced. 'Holistic grooming' isn't about a single technique but rather interrelated and balanced multi-platform techniques. It keeps the cat's best interests at the forefront while also taking into consideration the needs of the owner and the safety of the groomer.

For example, the cat owner's actions prior to the groom will have a positive or negative effect on the groom. Similarly, the location of grooming, the groomer and the groomer's actions will have an effect. If care is taken at all stages to ensure the physical and emotional comfort of the cat, the result will be a cat that's happy to be groomed. If an aspect is out of balance, it will cause stress, and may result in further negative aspects, which may make for a more challenging groom.

The cat is very different to the dog when it comes to handling techniques and the approach. For the layperson, how would you describe the main differences?

When I first started out as a groomer, I also groomed small dogs. A friend who owned a salon said that I groomed dogs like I was grooming cats, so I may not know exactly how to answer this question! Dogs are, or should be, accustomed to obeying commands. They should stand when told and respond to 'good dog'. Dogs generally like people and they want to be your friend. Note that I said 'in general'; there are always exceptions. Cats do not take orders and will ignore your requests. They generally don't care if they're friends with you and most likely would prefer you disappeared, unless you have tasty treats, at which point they might suffer your presence and ministrations. If you want to have a peaceful grooming session, you must either forge a truce with the cat or become friends, though they are much more discerning than dogs. To me, becoming friends with a cat I may be grooming for the rest of its life, perhaps 20 years, is a much more enjoyable prospect.

Approaching a cat is an art and can make or break a grooming session. Cats have individual preferences and it's your job to figure out if they prefer to be groomed while in your lap, laying on their side, laying on their stomach or even while walking around the table. You would never groom a dog in these positions, unless it was an elderly dog that could no longer stand.

I studied feline aggressive responses, likes and dislikes during grooming for my dissertation at university and I like to hear different groomers' opinions. What do you feel are some of the reasons why a cat may be lashing out during a groom, and what can be done to help the cat relax?

In my opinion, the primary reason is fear. I often hear groomers calling cats 'bad' or 'aggressive' and to never trust a cat. Were the groomers more versed in cat behaviour and psychology, which isn't taught at any of the schools (to my knowledge), they would recognise that the cat feels threatened and fears for their life. Cats are not 'bad', nor are domestic pet cats aggressive, unless they're protecting themselves. Too often, these groomers then muzzle, harness or tape up the paws of the frightened cat, which sends it cowering into a catatonic state of fear, which the groomers would classify as relaxed, or creates an angrier cat that will lash out as soon as the restraints are removed. Groomers were not checking heart rate, ear position, pupil size, blood pressure or gum colour. Many cats will 'freeze' or go into a catatonic state when extremely frightened. This is not 'relaxing' by any stretch of the imagination. They may have completed the groom but in my opinion, the end does not justify the means when it comes to cats.

These cats remember being treated this way, and it will affect subsequent grooms. Once you've escalated the cat's level of fear by using dominance and/or restraints, there's very little that can quickly be done during that session, as the cat now fears the groomer. Creating a bond of trust is a delicate process and cannot be rushed. Too many groomers treat cats as dogs and rush into the grooming 'relationship' before the cat is ready. The cat will give signals as to its comfort level and the groomer needs to respect those wishes to have a successful groom.

For cats that are reacting in fear from the get go, or who respond in fear to the groomer's methods, how to help the cat depends on the environment in which one grooms. I only groom in the cat's own home, which I feel is best for the majority of cats. They are territorial by nature and many become quite stressed when removed from their domain, even if just through the front door. In house-call grooming, I take my cues from the cat before I approach and pull from my experience how best to proceed, as there are many variables to consider. Groomers often ask for a list of 'rules' on what to do and are unhappy when I tell them there are too many variables involved to have set rules. With a frightened cat I may sit and chat with the owner while ignoring the cat, until it decides it's safe and OK to investigate. Other times I might work with the cat through offering treats, scratching the chin and cheeks, or massaging key areas, if allowed, until the cat relaxes. It's very important that the cat doesn't view you as a threat and sometimes this takes time. For the reacting cat, you have to figure out why it's feeling threatened and remove or alleviate that perceived threat. It could be smells, sounds, your movements, eye contact, position of carrier, the owner's mood, lighting level and type, or even illness. Slapping a muzzle on the cat is not going to remove the threat and is, in my opinion, cruel.

What grooming issues do you come across with cat owners that frustrate you, in terms of uneducated or misinformed actions that hinder your work?

If owners are going to be present while I groom (it's their choice), I generally give a few rules first. Frustrating to me are when owners reprimand cats, try to scruff, tell me what to do, talk loudly, have the TV set to a violent show or play raucous music. All these can upset the cat and/or me.

Sometimes, owners use grooming tools that are wrong or ineffective for their cats because a salesperson said that's what they should use or they couldn't find definitive information elsewhere. I don't expect people to be experts and I'm quite happy to show them what tools to buy and how to properly use them. I do expect them to follow through, though, and in a perfect world, everyone would do so. Sometimes I have to repeat myself a few times, which does leave me frustrated.

Can you name three things that you feel should be changed in the grooming industry?

The first is to encourage or mandate the study of behaviour and psychology. How can a groomer work with an animal with no or minimal understanding of it?

My second would be to stop focusing on money as the motivation and focus on the welfare of the animal. I get upset when I see cat grooming being promoted to dog groomers as a way to make the big money.

My third would concentrate on regulations. I groom in the US, and here, groomers are not licensed or regulated, with the exception of the state of New Jersey, which at this time is on the verge of passing a licensing law. I'm an advocate for thoughtfully implementing licensing and feel it's best to be proactive to make sure it's done right.

The lion cut, a cut where the cat is shaved all over apart from its head, paws and feet, is frowned upon by many people in the show-cat world and is not so big in the UK with groomers. Why do you feel it's big in the US?

I can understand it being frowned upon in the show-cat world, as why would you remove beautiful fur? In the US, people's lives are extremely busy. Studies say that Americans are the most over-worked in the world. We work long hours, multiple jobs, take short vacations if any at all, and may also have children or ageing parents for whom to care. Often, there just isn't enough time in the day and people are exhausted. It's much easier to have the cat shaved when life interferes with properly maintaining the coat. If owners just want the cut because they think it's cute, then I try to educate them on why keeping the fur is better for the cat and to perhaps compromise with a comb clip, which leaves the fur shorter but not shaved. In the US, we also have a wide range of temperatures between seasons and between regions of the country. Hot, muggy Florida can be miserable for a thick-coated Norwegian Forest cat, so shaving brings comfort for the cat.

We both know that grooming education is key for cat owners when getting a cat as a kitten. What would be your advice to cat owners?

I'd advise doing quite a bit of research and not to rely solely on what a breeder says. People should read up on breeds and identify traits they like and dislike. They also need to be realistic about how much time they'll spend on playing and grooming. I often hear people exclaim they had no idea a longhaired cat would need so much combing or that a shorthaired cat would shed so much. Whether adopting from a shelter or a breeder, the prospective cat owner should spend a significant amount of time interacting with the kitten to make sure it'll be a good fit for a lifetime commitment. People should know that a kitten would need training and a lot of interaction or playtime from its new owner.

The way we grow as individuals and as a society is to pass on and receive knowledge for the greater good, which is why I asked Sheryl Woods to contribute to this chapter, especially on subject matter so closely resembling my own moral and work ethic.

Her Facebook group, consisting of cat groomers who wish to learn a more natural and holistic approach to working with cats, as well as Sheryl herself, has been a great support for me in times of doubt, and I love hearing the opinions of my peers as well as sharing success stories along with my knowledge with groomers eager for change.

The job of grooming a cat can be very challenging. Not all cats like to be groomed. Responses can stem from many roots, such as fear from a bad grooming experience in the past, fear of strangers, dislike of being handled, dislike of feeling enclosed with no getaway, fear of pain from a badly matted coat or even fear of the groomer's table, some of which can resemble a vet's table, as mine does. Antagonistic responses can also be learned, meaning that a cat has quickly learned that if it hisses or bats away the owner's hands, the owner, most times, will give up straight away. The cat then knows this action will stop all further attempts to groom. This can happen whether the cat is actually fearful of the groom or mildly dislikes it.

Before working with a cat, the groomer must understand the foundation of the responses the cat is giving out. Only then can a plan of action be determined. With all cats it's a question of looking at the bigger picture and the desired outcome we all want to achieve. In some cases, the best way forward has been to remove myself from the situation and train the owner how to gently and slowly get their cat used to being touched and groomed. Of course, the owner cannot remove terrible matting from a cat's coat but on a freshly de-matted or combed coat, training can begin. A cat who lives with their owner is far more likely to get used to small grooming sessions over a period of two to three weeks rather than a strange groomer entering the home attempting to do the groom in an hour with the attitude 'I've been paid to do this job and I will do it by hook or by crook!'

I wrote an article entitled 'Grooming Aggressive Cats' for the Canine And Feline Behaviour Association. I used the word aggressive to describe various unfriendly responses that are recognised by owners and most veterinary professionals; responses being hissing, lashing out with claws extended or trying to bite the human handler. In the article I wanted to highlight three difficult cat-grooming cases because each approach was different, with each cat having a different reason for acting the way it was. I wanted to highlight the many variables in this job because, with some cats that have serious matting, sedation is the kindest and most humane way forward, before training and holistic methods can realistically begin. My fascination and determination to discover the best ways to work with more challenging cats led me to offer behaviour-grooming consultations in which I treated the grooming home visit like I would a behaviour case, gathering as much information as I could, including past history, medical reports from vets, and meeting the cat in their home without necessarily attempting to do a full groom on my initial visit. The first step is helping your cat to enjoy and accept the grooming process in short bursts.

The bathing of a cat is another matter entirely!

DO CATS NEED A BATH?

I recently had a discussion regarding a shorthaired moggie being introduced to the bathing process and disliking it intensely. When I said that most cats clean themselves very well without our help, the reply came 'Yes, your cat can clean himself but it's his saliva all over his body and how bad is that?'

I think that's the silliest thing I've ever heard. All animals and all humans are dirty to varying degrees and we all carry bacteria.

If one was comparing human self-cleaning methods to that of animals, I guess cats could be seen as unhygienic. However, cats are not human beings. Nature has given the cat the correct and necessary tools to keep itself clean, and these have worked very well for the cat for thousands of years. The cat has a barbed tongue with which they lick themself. The forepaws are moistened with saliva and used as a surrogate washcloth and a cat's teeth are superbly designed to dig out tougher debris.

Saliva also aids in healing wounds[1]. Dogs, cats, small rodents and primates all lick wounds. Their saliva contains tissue factor, which promotes the blood-clotting mechanism. The enzyme Lysozyme is found in many tissues and is known to attack the cell walls of many gram-positive bacteria aiding in defence against infection[2].

As well as cats being fastidiously clean animals, using their saliva like we use soap and water, they also use their saliva as an individual scent stamp. Their own personal scent gets deposited over their bodies. As scent is extremely important to cats, saliva and the process of licking is used to make the nervous or anxious cat feel safe and secure. It's the reason why a cat will lick themself in stressful situations, sometimes too much, making themselves bald in places. It is a distraction mechanism.

Another important function that cat saliva plays, during grooming, is to enable the cat to dissipate heat. They do this by depositing saliva on the surface of the coat and this helps the cat regulate their own body temperature. When a cat gets a lion cut (I admit there are several scenarios where a lion cut is needed such as aggression issues or terrible matting), it means the cat cannot naturally regulate their body temperature.

Why have a cat if you are trying to make them smell and clean themselves like a human? Why feel uncomfortable with the fact it uses saliva to clean itself? You kiss your cat, your have your cat lie on the bed and you hug your cat every day. If you didn't like the fact they deposit saliva on their body every day, you would have to shampoo your cat daily.

WHAT HAPPENS AFTER A HUMAN HAS BATHED A CAT?

The cat spends the next hour or so licking itself all over to get back to smelling like a cat and to remove the unfamiliar scent and feel of shampoo. Kind of defeats the object really. They would continue to lick themselves every day, like before, until their owner decides they need to be 'clean' again.

So… is there a situation where cats ever require bathing and do I ever bath cats? Yes, sometimes.

It sounds ironic after the last couple of paragraphs, but due to humans messing with genetics and other scenarios which I'm about to list below, some cats require a little helping hand from us.

Here are some reasons why a cat may require the odd bath from their human:

1. An elderly cat who has stopped cleaning itself and/or may suffer from incontinence.
2. Long-haired cats who have oily skin, which contributes to making the coat mat more readily.
3. A cat who has had an accident with something smelly or sticky!
4. An ill cat who cannot clean itself and has started to smell.
5. A disabled owner who may benefit from having their cat bathed and groomed (as a one-off) due to long-term lack of coat maintenance.
6. A friendly stray cat who has acquired a new home. A semi-feral cat would probably have to be sedated to be cleaned up; if a human or cat lives on the street amongst daily dirt and rubbish, they are likely to be in need of a bath.
7. Certain breeds of cat, such as the Sphynx, require regular bathing. The Sphynx needs bathing due to an accumulation of body oils, which would normally be absorbed by hair, building up on the skin.

Most cats I see are quite capable of cleaning themselves, but occasionally I have to weigh up the odds of bathing a cat versus the stress and fear a cat may have of water. I only ever do what's necessary on a groom. A long-haired cat with very oily/greasy skin is likely to suffer from a matted coat more often than a normal short-haired moggie or long-haired cat with a normal skin type. That, combined with a lack of grooming knowledge from the owner, will likely result in a coat on which mats easily form and turn into pelts.

I see many cats every week and the percentage that could benefit from or need a wet bath is minimal. The client is shown how to comb correctly and what tools to use and the anxiety of bathing the cat is side-stepped.

It's easier for pedigree cats who have been introduced to the bathing process as kittens, but for many cats the ordeal is terrifying and miserable for them. Always get advice from a holistic cat groomer who will put your cat's wellbeing first and be sensible with any bathing suggestions, and yes… cats do lick themselves!

Many clients of mine also wash their cats because they have an allergy to the cat's fur. In fact allergic reactions are not due to the fur but the protein Fel d 1 found in cat saliva and on the skin. Washing a cat makes them lick themselves more, so is hardly helping with the allergy, and as cats naturally lick every day, bathing a cat for this reason only is pretty pointless. Interestingly, Purina recently did research on cat allergies[3] and found that the immunoglobulin Y (IgY), found in egg yolks, could bind to Fel d 1, preventing its ability to trigger an allergic reaction in people who are allergic to cats. Great news for all the over-bathed cats with allergic owners: an eggy treat is on the way!

A CATTY SUM UP

1.   Long-haired or thick-coated cats need combing on a regular basis to stop the fur from matting.

2.   Matting and pelts are very uncomfortable for a cat.

3.   Make the grooming experience a positive one by gentle holistic handling.

CAT CHAT

Tips For Teaching Your Cat To Enjoy Grooming

Some cats do not like a human grooming them by combing or brushing their fur but unfortunately, in particular for long-haired cats, grooming by the owner is essential to stop bad mats from forming. One reason that cats may not like humans to groom their fur is that they do not like to be held or handled for long and may feel a sense of entrapment. Cats like to feel they have control over situations, which is the main reason why some cats struggle with a professional groomer. The groom is too long and the cat feels a sense of panic and a lack of the control that they are normally used to. It's also possible that a cat has connected a negative association to a previous grooming experience. Most cats feel sensitivity around certain areas, such as the genitals and tail area, and elderly cats are sensitive around joints, particularly if they are arthritic. Grooming not only involves combing the fur but also cleaning the ears, clipping long claws, checking the teeth and gum condition, occasional bathing and checking the general body condition of the cat.

The best time to start training your cat to enjoy being combed is when they are kittens, but it's never too late to try. Cats learn through positive association and this usually works best with food! Positive reward-based training shows a cat that grooming can actually be a nice experience and can result in tasty treats.

Step One: When you have bought your grooming tools (a moulting comb or a slicker brush), leave them lying around with some of your cat's usual toys so that your cat can have a good old sniff and familiarise themselves with the new objects. That way they can leave some of their scent on the tools and see them as non-threatening.

Step Two: Before using the tools, get your cat used to gently being touched with your hands; especially on areas of the body that can bother some cats to be touched on, such as the paws (which should be gently pressed down on, which helps when clipping the claws), hind legs and the tummy. Combine this with special treats that are used for grooming-training only.

Step Three: Start picking up the grooming tools and gently holding them against various parts of the cat, allowing the cat to sniff the tools. Reward with treats when touching the body with the tools and monitor the reactions. At this stage you can gently try and brush or comb a small part of the top layer of fur in an area such as around the cheeks or face, as cats love to be stroked there. You will probably find that your cat actually leans into the grooming tool as they enjoy the feel of it against their cheeks.

Step Four: Choose an area of the body that you wish to try five minutes of combing on. Make sure the special treats are ready. Try and comb this area gently and see how your cat responds. You can always take some steps back if your cat isn't quite ready at any stage. Make sure you always remain relaxed and that the sessions are fun and positive. Speak gently to your cat to reassure them. Kittens will not understand a comb or brush against the body for the first few times but will soon understand that grooming is fun and always results in treats. With kittens I also use fun hunting toys. I can get a lot done when a kitten is focused on the toy. Some kittens that I'm called to work on don't even notice I'm shaving out a mat on the body, because I have presented them with a mouse to focus on. Whilst they are in hunting mode, I can quickly remove the mat, no matter on what area of the body. It always works!

Step Five: Your cat, at this stage, has had fun with playtime and treats around the grooming sessions and so should be much more open to trying a proper comb now. This is where the correct technique should be introduced. Also start from the bottom upwards so that you get to comb the fur under the top layer. The top layer of fur is called the guard hair and the bottom layer is typically called down hair or underlay. Down hair is thick and much shorter and softer than the top hair. It's this hair that usually forms mats because the hair moults and remains caught under the tougher, longer guard hair. Because people focus on combing the top of the fur, the underlay or down hair usually doesn't get groomed as well as it should. If you start by lifting up the bottom of the fur and then combing in a downward motion, a little at a time, all of the fur will get thoroughly combed.

For claw clipping, gently press down on the paw pad and the claws will spring out so that you can clearly see them. The quick is the pink section of the claw, which contains the nerves and blood vessels. This is an area to be avoided, so when clipping the claw, aim for the white part and especially the tip of the claw (which slightly bends over to form a tiny hook). Many cats do not like their claws to be clipped because claws are their main weapon of defence and they do not understand why we are removing this defence. The paw is also a sensitive area. Most groomers clip claws as a protection against being scratched during the groom, so it's not really a necessity. However, some cats, such as elderly or less mobile ones, need their claws clipped because they are not being used and worn down, as they should be. The claws thicken and grow quickly, bending into the paw pads, where they can become embedded. A little help from us will stop this painful process. Most other cats can easily manage the claws themselves with the aid of a scratch post. It's always good to get any cats used to their paws being touched so that when we do have to step in for whatever reason, to trim the claws, the process is quick, easy and stress free.

For further guidance on correct cat grooming techniques, I highly recommend the grooming books of Svetlana Broussova. Her two books,

*Grooming Longhaired Cat*s and *Grooming Shorthaired Cats*, are the best I have found on the subject and come with a training DVD.

The best part of cat owners learning to groom their cats is that it can be done in short bursts over a week or two rather than one long session on a grooming table. For the future, this means if a professional groomer is sought, they will not be called in to de-mat a grumpy cat who isn't used to the process!

Claws: Confessions Of A Professional Cat Groomer, written by myself in 2017, highlights some of my grumpy cats as well as other funny-but-true cat-grooming tales.

WHAT IF MY CAT DOESN'T LIKE BEING HANDLED?

If your cat is challenging and does not tolerate any grooming, the best thing to do is call in a professional groomer who can assess your cat and their reactions to determine the best way forward. Sometimes it's best to shave the problem areas first, which are generally the tummy, armpits and nether regions. Your cat may need to wear an Elizabethan collar (a cone that's placed around the head and neck, usually used to stop cats from licking an open wound or stitches), or be held gently with a towel for the groomer to attempt this. Once these areas have been shaved, you do not have to worry about them and you can start the above training programme without panicking about mats forming on the most problematic areas. Other cats, who may be severely matted, will need to be de-matted at a veterinary practice whilst asleep under sedation. It's far better to sedate a fearful or panicked cat if they are extremely matted than spend hours battling with them, thus avoiding a long stressful day for all concerned.

I was able to discuss the sedation route for challenging cats with the late Dr. Sophia Yin, an applied veterinary animal behaviourist, before her sad parting. She agreed that:

> … these cats should definitely be sedated since grooming them without sedation can teach them to hate going to the groomer! If the hospital has a Low Stress Handling plan for getting this cat into a quiet room, and sedated quickly and skilfully, then the stress should only last a couple of seconds. Once the badly

matted cat is clipped, then the owner should work on a plan of training the cat to love getting groomed. This can be done by having short daily sessions (several minutes) where they feed the cat tasty treats (such as canned cat food) and pair the feeding with light grooming for just a few seconds at a time. Then they can groom for systematically longer periods of time and with more pressure as long as they always stay below the threshold that bothers the cat.

I always assess the cat's reactions to determine whether their aggression is fear-based or a learned response merely to get the desired effect they want from their humans, which is to make them stop the groom. The two responses should have very different outcomes. For example, a grooming professional should not be expected to walk into a cat's territory to complete a groom on a fearful cat who's lashing out at every opportunity. This type of cat should not be pushed and will not change their mind and work with the groomer no matter how gentle the groomer is being. Alternatively, a cat who pushes their human with learned behaviour can be gently worked with. So, every case is different and should be approached as such.

It's extremely important that you gently feel for mats every day. As a general part of the cuddles and stroking, assuming your cat doesn't mind being handled, feel under the armpits, tummy area, around the inner back legs, the nether regions, the hind legs and under the chin. These areas tend to get small mats forming which, if left unattended, can turn into major problems. Tangles can be gently teased out with your fingers.

An important part of helping a cat to enjoy being groomed is to know the correct combing technique so that the combing feels comfortable on the cat's body. Equally, the correct grooming tools are essential for comfort too.

Our cats are complex creatures and grooming them can be challenging, which is why I opened a part of my behaviour practice to focus on grooming behaviour issues. It's a specialised area that I'm particularly interested in. My dissertation at university was the first ever research into feline aggressive responses during grooming. It was no surprise that 100% of the small number of cats who could only be groomed under sedation had undergone some form of negative experience, such as being groomed at a dog-grooming parlour (one not used to, or ignorant about handling cats in a holistic way), or being groomed with a tool that caused discomfort and pain. A large majority of cats didn't like to be handled or stroked and hated the feeling of being kept still in one place. Many reacted badly due to grooming tools that were inappropriate and had been recommended by vets who do not understand what tools are the best, and a good percentage of cats had learned that if they hissed or showed displeasure their humans would stop straight away. Bingo! The desired result. The cats that loved the grooming process loved to be picked up, touched and mollycoddled and so it didn't matter what areas of the body were being touched. They loved the attention, so grooming was always going to be a positive experience for them.

It's very difficult to work with clients who have a young long-haired cat who is challenging when it comes to handling or combing, but what I can say is that these types of cases need to be looked at very differently and treated as behaviour cases first. It's very damaging for a groomer to be called in to complete a grooming job, irrespective of the consequences. Psychologically, after the first negative experience, it does far more damage in the long run and makes it more difficult to change the cat's response to other groomers. It can be done, though. What I have found, in many cases, is that the groomer needs to be removed from the equation and the guardians taught how to work with their cat gently and in small steps over a long period of time, to regain trust.

The Holistic Cat Groomers Alliance was born out of a real need for education and change and my wish is for cat carers to hold this knowledge as a baton of hope to pass forward to the next generation of cat carers. Hopefully with the tips above, we can go a long way towards helping (most) cats to experience grooming as a positive and pleasurable experience.

CHAPTER ELEVEN

What Should I Be Feeding My Cat?

'The greatness of a nation can be judged by the way its animals are treated.'

Mahatma Gandhi

CHAPTER ELEVEN

In this chapter:

- Hear expert veterinary advice on feline nutrition, in conversation with Dr. Pete Coleshaw.
- Understand what gives our cats optimum health.
- Get a definitive explanation on common pet-food labelling terminologies.

There are two main controversial subjects connected to the pet cat. One is the argument for or against letting a cat roam freely due to concerns over the wildlife a cat hunts, plus safety concerns from cars, foxes, getting lost and people with ill intentions towards cats. The other contentious subject matter is over the diet of the cat and whether its food should be raw meat, commercial tinned food or dry kibble. Where do I stand on the diet front? I'm an advocate of a meat diet for cats, as cats are obligate carnivores and their natural food source is animal flesh. This means they need the nutrients in animal tissue and muscles to survive. Taurine is one such nutrient.

I'm not an expert on feline nutrition but I do know the struggles I have had with my own two cats over food. Now they mainly eat a raw meat diet, sometimes a complete high-quality commercial wet food and on the odd occasion a tiny amount of kibble, which they enjoy munching. I started out trying to make the raw food myself, buying in a variety of supplements, a meat-and-bone grinder and fresh meat from a local organic free-range butcher. Being a vegan I found making their food difficult to stomach. I was horrified when one day I asked a local organic butcher to get me some free-range rabbit for my cats, only to be handed a whole dead rabbit, skinned of its fur but with the head still fully attached. Not wanting to decline the order I asked the butcher to chop it up into small pieces so it didn't resemble the animal and promptly left the shop. I was mortified all the way home and felt sick. My husband couldn't believe what he was seeing. Suffice to say my experiment in making the raw cat food myself lasted one day! Luckily, there are companies such as PurrForm that supply the food mixed and ready for catty consumption.

Reading this chapter to my husband, he reminded me of the time I bought our cats a box of dead mice to eat! Looking back, I don't know what I was thinking. Any rational person would know that a cat, given the choice of a cold, motionless mouse in their food bowl, or the chase, excitement and body warmth of a living critter, would clearly choose the latter. Still, back when I didn't know much about cats, and being non-vegan at that time in my life, I searched the internet for where to buy dead mice for pet food. I came across a website that sold the mice for pet snakes. I ordered 12 frozen mice, which I placed in the freezer, forgetting to tell my husband. It was hardly surprising that he nearly had a heart attack when he opened the freezer to get out some ice cubes for a drink. I defrosted two mice the night before breakfast time. My cats looked at the bowl in the morning as if I had just presented them with rotting garbage. That was the end of that!

I see so many obese cats in my job that when I see a slim cat of normal weight, especially when grooming a cat under sedation, I have to ask the vet to come and check whether the cat is malnourished and underweight. I'm always told no; it's a normal-sized cat. That's how many fat cats I have become accustomed to seeing.

Now's a good time to introduce a vet who is an expert on feline nutrition. Dr. Pete Coleshaw has been 40 years in practice and now runs a cat-only clinic called Jaffa's in Salisbury. He's also a founding and active member of the Raw Feeding Veterinary Association. Striving to educate his clients regarding the benefits of feeding biologically appropriate foods to their cats, I started this discussion by asking Dr. Coleshaw how he became involved with studying the feline diet?

> It all started with rabbits. I went on a weekend course in rabbit medicine and I learned by the end of the weekend that every common condition of rabbits

was caused by poor nutrition. Then I started wondering if it was the same for our dogs and cats, and of course it is.

In Conversation With Dr. Pete Coleshaw

What should cat carers be feeding their cats?

They should be feeding them a nutritious diet. How they feed their cats is a matter of choice. There's lots of different ways. I have a 'ladder of desirability' with the bottom rung being a cheap-grade kibble and the top would be a live raw-prey item. Obviously that is not a practical or humane thing, so number nine on the list would be a dead whole rabbit with fur on and guts in. We then move down the ladder with gutted portions of whole meat on the bone. Then we have minced prey-type items with the bone and all the organs that can be fed raw. We have cooked versions of that and then we have the high-grade moist wet commercial foods down to dry foods at the bottom of the ladder. It's for each of the owners to make an informed choice, but I think it's important they get unbiased informed advice to make the correct choice. The problem is in finding a good source of advice.

What are the pros and cons for a cat on a dry, kibble-only diet?

Pros for kibble: it can be cheap (but it can also be quite expensive). It's convenient, it can be left down all day, you can feed multiple cats on it, and that is as far as it goes in terms of pros. Everything else is cons. You are feeding a dehydrated diet to a species that has evolved to eat something that is 80% water, which isn't good for bladder health. Dried foods are all based on starch with all the intrinsic issues that brings, since most of the dried foods are actually 'ultra processed' – cheap ingredients of unknown origin and undetermined degree of processing. They are formulated to meet minimum requirements of fat, protein, carbohydrates and minerals, which doesn't reflect the bioavailability or biological 'quality' of the constituents. Kibble-fed cats have a very different intestinal microbiome to their raw-fed counterparts with major health implications, as in humans.

Most vets in the UK sell kibble and many recommend kibble as being perfectly OK as the only food source for a cat. Why do vets advocate this?

I can't speak for the other vets. I can only speak for myself. When I first became a partner in a practice I saw financial opportunities and I was very keen to get every cat on to the dry cat food that we recommended. Basically, I thought it was a great marketing tool but I've come to realise how wrong that is and I've done a complete about turn, hence where I am now.

What are the main ingredients a cat needs in their diet to maintain optimal health?

From the perspective of 'artificial' diets I'm not sure we really know that. What we do know is that over millions of years of evolution cats have evolved to eat a prey-based diet, so if we feed something as close to this as we can, we should meet their requirements. So, in terms of ingredients, for me, it would be fresh meat, bones and organs. Does a cat need those for optimal health? I think it does.

Some vegans say that supplements added to a non-meat diet is totally fine for cats. What are your views on this?

We have some vegans who are very concerned about their cat's diet. They are fastidious about their own diet and health and can be very committed, motivated raw feeders even though they don't like handling the food themselves. The concept of feeding a vegetarian diet to an obligate carnivore doesn't ring true to me. One might be able to keep a cat alive but that doesn't mean optimal health to me. It's only through thousands of cats being fed any particular diet over a protracted period of time that we can now get an overall picture of the potential issues. It's worth mentioning that most nutritional disease is insidious – and not always easily ascribed to any particular food. New ingredients such as pulses are creating all sorts of illnesses and we really don't have an understanding of the potential negatives until it happens. We come back to the fact that cats evolved to eat meat and prey and that is unlikely to be problematic for them.

What would you say about the fact some kibble companies sell the idea that biscuits clean a cat's teeth?

One of the big myths is that dry cat food effectively cleans cats' 'teeth'. There will be some abrasion IF they crunch the biscuits but they only crunch the biscuits with their cheek teeth. Some cats just swallow kibble whole.

In either case the teeth on the front half of the mouth are not cleaned in any way. The other big misconception is that dental disease in cats is a single entity. At least 50% of the disease I see is not caused by periodontal disease (but by FORLs – feline odon toclastic resorptive lesions) and is not, therefore, a result of plaque build up on the teeth and lack of attrition.

What's the commonest illness from a kibble-only diet?

Obesity is number one – especially when cats are given free access to unlimited amounts – and that tends to be the default setting encouraged by the manufacturers. Urinary tract disease is probably number two, contributing to stress-induced cystitis, and chronic digestive upsets would be third. Any condition that improves when swapping from everyday kibble to 'prescription' kibble can be considered to be an illness caused by the kibble.

Do you feel a raw diet is the best and, if so, what's the best way to transition our cats on to a raw diet?

Under perfect circumstances a raw diet based on whole dead prey would be ideal. This generally isn't practical for most folk – or their cats. So we need achievable solutions. But it needs to be done properly, and this is where we vets should come in and educate people in the correct way of feeding a raw diet rather than pretending it's deadly dangerous. By discouraging people, they become alienated from the profession and end up doing their own thing and risk getting it wrong. In terms of transitioning a cat on to a raw diet, that's a whole chapter in its own right! Generally it needs to be a slow process – getting them accustomed to what to them is a novel food. It takes time, it takes perseverance and it takes a plan. It's one of the biggest problems people have. Having got your cat transitioned, they may eat raw food for months and then decide they don't want it anymore. Cats are not easy. Dogs are far easier when it comes to transitioning.

Why do our cats not recognise raw meat as food?

Because they have been habituated to kibble from an early age. Those formative weeks are critical for every aspect of any animal's life. Ducks will think their mum is a dog if they are brought up by one. Food works the same way – whatever mum feeds them has to be safe as she would not have produced babies otherwise.

Any tips for making the cat food at home?

Yes, don't! Once you start trying to formulate a diet you will get it wrong. Have a much more relaxed approach and choose the correct ingredient. Don't worry too much about percentages. We want to feed meat and bone in sensible quantities with organ meat 10–20%, varied organs. There's lots of advice out there. Tom Lonsdale's Raw Meaty Bone website is a very good resource. People need to educate themselves from an authoritative source rather than just jumping on something they read on the internet and adopting it. The most dangerous thing about raw feeding is doing it wrong, thinking that it can be a meat-only diet.

What about the commercial 'complete' wet tinned diets that state the product has high meat content and no added fillers? Anything wrong with these?

They state they have a high meat content, but how processed is that meat? Is it fresh meat lightly cooked or is it waste from the meat trade, which has been high-temperature rendered? Either can be labelled as a 'meat-and-animal-derivative' yet the latter may have a very poor biological value, requiring a lot of processing by the body. So, there are good canned meats and there are poor canned meats. The problem the cat owner has is deciding which is which.

What's the biggest misconception regarding cats and diet in the 21st century?

I think it is that dried food is a good acceptable food for a cat.

Any advice you can give cat owners regarding the obesity crisis some pets face and why this seems to be a growing 21st-century issue?

The obesity crisis is a worldwide pandemic shared by people and pets alike and it has followed the introduction of processed foods as they've become more widely available throughout the world. Dried foods processed within an inch of their life and which can be stored for two to three years may have all sorts of influences on the body that we don't necessarily understand. It's a complicated topic but may involve foodstuffs that the body doesn't recognise (such as trans-fats) and therefore doesn't know what to do with, and which may have influences we don't yet fully understand. As an example, propionate is commonly used as a preservative and has been shown to have major effects on insulin-sensitivity in mice. So, it's that unknown factor. What we do know is ultra processed food, obesity, diabetes and cancer are all linked. That's well proven on the human front.

On my consultations I do come across many cats who refuse to eat meat, odd as it sounds. Any advice for cat owners on how they can encourage more moisture in their cats' diet?

Firstly, cats that refuse to eat meat – it's a case of transitioning. Taking time, and looking at different foodstuffs. Adding water to kibble will get more water into them if they will eat it, but it's not addressing one of the primary issues with kibble, which is the ultra processed starch and all the influences that has. Basically it needs persistence.

Lastly, what would you say to a client of mine who commented a cat could be eating the content in their prey's stomach that may be grains, thus no different than feeding commercial food with fillers and grains in – in other words they are not convinced that raw feeding is an optimal diet?

The natural prey of small felines is mostly rodents and birds, which have varied diets that would not naturally include grain, which is not the same as wild seeds. Any seeds eaten are not cooked and processed. Depending on the prey, the guts and contents may or may not be eaten. If your client doesn't want to see nature as optimal then you are wasting your time, I find.

Of course there are two sides to this question and many vets see no harm in feeding a dry-only diet. Certainly most veterinary surgeries in the UK sell kibble. As with everything, people have conflicting views and information to back these views up. I have decided to focus on the 'meat for obligate carnivores' viewpoint. However, it would be irresponsible of me not to mention certain pitfalls that can affect a cat eating a raw-meat diet should things go wrong at the manufacturing end, if the raw food is commercially bought. In 2018, in the UK, a large number of cats became ill, and research by Dr. Danièlle Gunn-Moore from the University of Edinburgh found that the cats were all known to have eaten a raw commercial wet food diet from the same source. The company recalled the product whilst investigations continued[1].

I asked Dr. Coleshaw to comment on these findings:

> The reason for this outbreak of TB in cats has never been determined. We don't know if all the appropriate regulations were followed (and if these regulations need amending). Nor do we know if contaminated carcasses were deliberately introduced into the supply chain at some point. No cases have been recorded before nor since, so we know that something exceptional occurred. This can happen with any foodstuff, be it wet, be it dry, raw or non-raw. That is not a reason to dismiss any particular means of feeding as being unnecessarily dangerous. There were many thousands of cats that died from melamine in the food some 10–15 years ago. There are lots of dogs dying now – maybe hundreds or more, due to pulses introduced into certain foods – so it's not the way of feeding that should be brought into question, just the cause of the 'outbreak'.

This should not deter a cat owner from supplying their cat with quality meat products and with a little research and advice from feline nutritionists and your own vet, you should be able to find the right food for your obligate carnivore pet. It need not be raw but it should be meat!

This chapter is peppered with great advice regarding our cats' feeding habits and food choices, but how many cat owners actually understand the labelling on their food choices for their cats? What does it all mean? In the following Cat Chat I will go on to explain.

A CATTY SUM UP

1. Cats are obligate carnivores, meaning they need the nutrients in animal tissue/muscle to survive.
2. A cat's teeth are designed to rip meat from bones and to crush bone.
3. A cat's diet in the wild is 80% moisture.

CAT CHAT

Cat Food Labelling: What Does It All Mean?

Take a deep breath. This chapter is a long one, folks!

Cats are obligate carnivores: animals whose survival depends on animal flesh. Their eating habits remain un-evolved like those of the wild cat[1]. Cats occasionally eat grass but this is believed to be for the inducement of vomiting. Grass also contains an essential vitamin for cats, which is folic acid. Their jaws are designed to bite down and hold prey so they have limited side-to-side movement. This means that cats do not chew food! Their sharp teeth are designed to tear meat from bone[2].

Controlled studies of the cat's unique nutritional needs, dating back at least 40 years, were a response to the cat's status as an increasingly popular companion animal and to the demand for commercial cat foods[3]. There are several large organisations that regulate the commercial pet-food industry. In the UK this is the FSA (Food Standards Agency), while in the US the regulators are the FDA (Food and Drug Administration) and the AAFCO (Association of American Feed Control Officials).

Pet owners and animal professionals should know how to read the labels on cat food so that they can make an informed choice.

The first thing to explain is the terminology behind the labelling process.

Pet-food ingredients are listed in descending order of predominance by weight, not volume[4]. One thing to bear in mind is that some companies use a practice called 'splitting', whereby ingredients, such as ground corn and corn gluten meal, can be split into two categories, therefore allowing the ingredient to appear further down the list. The consumer would then naturally assume the product contained a much lower carbohydrate quantity because the main protein ingredient appears first. Should the consumer add all of the 'split' corn ingredients together, they may find that the percentage is actually higher than the meat! Therefore, it's always worth looking at the nutritional information and where the items have been placed individually.

Let's take a look at the common terms you will see on the tins and sachets of commercial cat food.

Meal: The word 'meal' means an ingredient that has been ground or reduced to particles with water and fat removed. It's classified as a rendered product. According to the FDA's Center for Veterinary Medicine (CVM) pet-food specialist, William Burkholder:

> Meal is another ingredient that some people like to avoid. In processing meat meal or poultry by-product meal, by-products are rendered (heat processed),

which removes the fat and water from the product. Meat or poultry by-product meal contains parts of animals not normally eaten by humans... Protein quality of by-products is sometimes better than that from muscle meat.

Chicken Meal: Chicken meal is a combination of clean chicken flesh and skin (with or without attached bone) and is exclusive of feathers, heads, feet and entrails[5]. The ground-up chicken meat is dried to a moisture level of 10%, which means that the percentage of protein is higher than that of chicken meat of the same weight, due to the moisture content of the latter. The downside to this is that 'rendered meat' claims to be free of any diseases or infections due to the rendering process, so '4D' animals (dead, dying, diseased or disabled) can make up the components of chicken meal[6]. Because of the 'possible' inclusion of 4D animals, chicken meal is not considered fit for human consumption. This is against EU pet-food regulations, which state that:

> All ingredients used for the manufacture of pet food have to be 'fit for human consumption' according to EU standards. Only animals declared healthy after ante- and post-mortem examination will qualify as ingredients for pet food[7].

Meat And Bone Meal: Meat and Bone Meal (MBM) is also a product of rendering. It's typically about 48–52% protein, 33–35% ash, 8–12% fat and 4–7% moisture[8]. It's used as animal feed, but because it's considered a major cause of mad-cow disease (BSE) is no longer used to feed hoofed animals such as cattle, goats, sheep and other ruminants[9]. It's still widely used in the US as a low-cost meat for cats and dogs, as well as in some parts of Europe. In UK abattoirs, the brain, spinal cord, trigeminal ganglia, intestines, eyes and tonsils from cattle are classified as SRM (specified risk materials) and must be disposed of appropriately. Astonishingly, most countries in Europe now use MBM as a fossil-fuel replacement for renewable energy generation, as a fuel in cement kilns, in land-filling, and in incineration[10].

Fish Meal: Fish meal is a product made from fish and fish bones and takes the form of brown powder after the drying process[11]. The usual types of fish used in fish meal are marine fish that contain a high percentage of bone and oil and therefore are not seen as fit for 'direct' human consumption[12]. Other sources of fish meal can be by-catch from fisheries (other specimens caught up in the fishing net[13]) or fish waste and offal (by-products of trimmings during the fish processing). The amino-acid profile of fish meal is what makes this feed ingredient so attractive as a protein supplement.

Animal By-Products: Animal by-products (ABPs) are animal carcasses, parts of carcasses, or products of animal origin not intended for human consumption. They can present a risk to human and animal health if not used or disposed of safely. Animal by-products range from carcasses (from slaughterhouses, animal shelters, zoos and veterinarians) to animal by-product food waste (such as raw meat, fish and shellfish not fit for human consumption), to other animal by-products such as milk or eggs that are not fit for human consumption, manure and digestive-tract content, semen, ova and embryos (except when destined for breeding purposes) and catering waste. There are controls on the use of animal by-products when used as feed (including pet food)[14]. EU regulations require all pet food using by-products to add the wording 'not fit for human consumption'.

ABPs fall into three categories, which are determined by the associated risks and whether particular products can be re-used. The following categories are those noted by the Department of Agriculture, Environment and Rural Affairs (DAERA), and will assist you in understanding which ones can end up in our pet food![15]:

1. **Category 1**

   Category 1 material is the highest risk, and consists principally of material that's considered a transmissible spongiform encephalopathies (TSE) risk, such as Specified Risk Material (those parts of an animal considered most likely to harbour a disease such as BSE, e.g. bovine spinal cord). Pet animals, zoo and circus animals and experimental animals are also classified as category 1 material. The risk from these animals may also be high, for example due to the level of veterinary drugs and residues they may contain; the fact that adequate diagnoses of the exact cause of death of exotic animals can be difficult to achieve; and that some species are known to harbour TSEs and may carry other diseases. Wild animals may be classified as category 1 material when they are suspected of carrying a disease communicable to humans or animals. Catering waste from means of international transport (i.e. which has come from outside the EU) is also category 1 due to the risk from exotic diseases.

2. Category 2

Category 2 material is also high-risk material and includes fallen stock, manure and digestive content. Category 2 is also the default status of any animal by-product not defined as either category 1 or category 3 material.

3. Category 3

Category 3 materials are low-risk materials. Category 3 material includes parts of animals that have been passed fit for human consumption in a slaughterhouse but which are not intended for consumption, either because they are not parts of animals that we normally eat (hides, hair, feathers, bones, etc) or for commercial reasons. Category 3 material also includes former foodstuffs (waste from food factories and retail premises such as butchers and supermarkets). Catering waste, including domestic kitchen waste, is category 3 material.

So what ABPs can be used in pet food? According to the DAERA[15], 'Only certain Category 3 animal by-products (ABP) and products derived from Category 3 material including Processed Animal Protein (PAP) and certain imported Category 1 materials can be used in pet food'. We may be alarmed that category 1 products may be used in pet food but DAERA's position is that:

The EU Control Regulation requires operators to carry out safe sourcing (Article 37), or failing that, safe treatment (Article 38). This applies to pet food plant operators (Article 35).

Safe sourcing means using material that:

- does not present unacceptable risks to public or animal health

- has been collected and transported, or brought from the point of import, to the plant under conditions excluding risks to public and animal health.

Processed Animal Protein: Processed Animal Protein (PAP) contains protein, fat and minerals from by-products in category 3, which are animals fit for human consumption at the point of slaughter.

Meat And Animal Derivatives: Meat and Animal Derivatives is a generic term for animal proteins that avoids having to specify where the meat comes from: it can be any part of the animal. This enables some pet-food companies to use whichever meat is the cheapest, and there is no way to tell what it is. The meat is sourced from animals which have been inspected and passed as fit for human consumption and are the parts of the animal which are surplus to the requirements of the human food industry in the UK (e.g. heart, lung or muscle meat, which are traditionally less widely consumed)[16].

Crude Ash: Crude ash[17] is what's left over after the protein, fat and carbohydrate content has been completely incinerated, leaving a mineral residue. Crude ash content is normally low.

Digest: Animal digest is:

> material, which results from the chemical and/or enzymatic hydrolysis of clean and undecomposed animal tissue. The animal tissues used shall be exclusive of hair, horns, teeth, hooves and feathers, except in such trace amounts as might occur unavoidably in good factory practice and shall be suitable for animal feed[18].

Any kind of animal can be used including the now infamous '4D animals', goats, pigs, horses, restaurant and supermarket refuse. Digest is used to 'flavour' kibble so it becomes palatable to the animal. A miniscule amount of digest can be used for the manufacturers to then label the food 'chicken flavour'. Digest is usually sprayed on to kibble.

Corn: Corn is the main ingredient for many cat and dog dry foods. The list of corn products that can be used is extensive but I will list a few below, from the AAFCO website and the book *Food Pets Die For* by Ann N. Martin.

- **Corn Gluten Meal:** This is the dried residue from corn after the removal of the larger part of the starch and germ, and the separation of the bran in the wet-milling manufacture of cornstarch or syrup, or by enzymatic treatment of the endosperm.
- **Corn Flour:** This is the fine-sized, hard flinty portion of ground corn, containing little or none of the bran or germ.

Wheat: Many cat foods include wheat which, like corn, has several definitions. Here is an explanation from the AAFCO website:

- **Wheat Flour:** Wheat flour mixed with wheat germ, bran, flour, and the 'tail of the mill'. The term 'tail of the mill' means the floor sweepings of leftovers in the mill after everything else has been processed from the wheat.

Maize Gluten: Also known as corn gluten meal (CGM), maize gluten is a by-product of maize processing. Gluten is prepared by centrifugation, filtering and drying of the slurry received from the primary and secondary stages of corn refining. It's high in protein and is cheap, so historically has been used for animal feed.

Sodium Chloride: Sodium chloride is salt, and is used for fluid balance in pet food. The National Research Council lays down guidelines on sodium levels for cats and dogs.

Potassium Chloride: Potassium chloride is a salt containing the compounds potassium and chlorine. It's used as an added source of potassium in pet foods when other ingredients do not supply enough. It's also used as a gelling agent in canned pet food.

Calcium Carbonate: Calcium carbonate is a chemical compound with the formula $CaCO_3$. It's medicinally used as a calcium supplement for humans and is widely used in pet food as an inexpensive source of calcium.

Yukka Extract: Yukka is a perennial shrub from the family Asparagaceae. Yucca extract is used to control the smell of animal waste. This is possible because saponins bind to ammonia to prevent the smell from passing into the air. It's commonly found in food for cats and dogs and may also be found in cat litter.

Chicory Extract: The chicory plant is a member of the dandelion family and acts as a digestive aid.

Tomato Pomace: Tomato pomace is a cheap by-product of tomato manufacturing. It's what's left over from the making of foods such as tomato juice, tomato sauce and tomato soup. It's used in pet food as a dietary fibre as well as a source of A and B vitamins. It's known to be rich in powerful antioxidants such as lycopene, and has a high level of soluble fibre, which, according to Wellness Pet Food, 'helps create excellent stools, gut health and a strong immune system'.

Taurine: Taurine is an extremely important component in cat food. It's an organic acid found in animal tissue and plays a role in the development and function of the skeletal muscle, the retina and the central nervous system, and is essential for cardiovascular functioning. Taurine is also found to be important for fetal development, growth, reproduction, neuro-modulation, sight, hearing, blood platelets, immune response, antioxidation and bile acid. Most mammals manufacture taurine from other amino acids. However, cats cannot manufacture an amount sufficient for their needs and, therefore, must source enough taurine through their food. It can only be naturally found in muscle meat; however, it can be synthesised in a lab.

Vegetables: Many pet foods have a small percentage of vegetables added. Vegetables can provide a good source of vitamins, minerals and fibre.

Natural: As defined by the AAFCO, natural feed is:

> a feed or ingredient derived solely from plant, animal or mined sources, either in its unprocessed state or having been subjected to physical processing, heat processing, rendering, purification extraction, hydrolysis, enzymolysis or fermentation, but not having been produced by or subject to a chemically synthetic process and not containing any additives or processing aids that are chemically synthetic except in amounts as might occur unavoidably in good manufacturing practices.

The use of the term 'natural' on the label is false and misleading if any chemically synthesised ingredients are present in the product. Two common examples of this are propylene glycol and BHA, or butylated hydroxyanisole, which are chemically synthesised ingredients found in some pet foods.

Premium/Ultra-Premium/Holistic: These terms have no official definitions within the AAFCO and should be taken as a clever marketing tool with little value.

Veterinarian Formulated: It only takes one veterinarian to support the claim 'veterinarian formulated' or 'veterinarian developed', assuming that fact can be sufficiently documented.

Complementary Vs. Complete Cat Food: Complementary and complete cat food are worlds apart in definition. In the UK, the term 'complete' means a balanced diet with a range of nutrients, whereas complementary cat food ultimately means a 'treat' to be served in moderation with a complete food substance. Gourmet foods are like treats, with a smaller range of nutrients, and should also be given in moderation.

So these are the main ingredients found in cat food, although there are many more to be found if one investigates all of the many brands on the market in what has now become a very competitive billion-dollar industry.

What I have noticed is that many of the well-known brands defend themselves on their websites regarding labelling and why they use certain products, because the internet is awash with people alarmed by what they have found after doing their own research into pet-food manufacturing and the ingredients that are allowed. Rules and regulations vary from country to country.

There are also many myths and poorly researched or out-of-date facts, so it's important for the reader to try and do as much journalistic digging as possible and follow up on references and citations. Even with this method of research, the reader needs to be aware of the background of the writer and who that person might be 'backed' by, influenced by or whether they put forward these views for financial gain, paid by the manufacturers of the pet food brand itself!

Let's look at a few hot-debate topics from both sides.

DEBATE ONE: THE USE OF BY-PRODUCTS

By-products are bits of the animal that humans don't normally eat and because of this, and the fact that the guidelines on what exactly can end up as a by-product have many grey areas, people are alarmed. They see it as morally wrong and compare it to being offered an inferior product. In some cases the consumer has no idea what meat has made up the finished product in their purchase and this can be bad in the case of a pet with allergies or an illness. Consumers also object to 'inferior' unknown meats in a product sold to them with deceitful marketing and with a higher price tag.

People view the parts of animals that humans would not consume as repulsive and equal to 'garbage': not 'real' meat but offal/tissue. This shows a lack of cultural awareness. We only think of cuts that we don't typically eat as 'garbage' because we don't typically eat them. In other cultures, where humans eat almost the entirety of an animal, this concept of 'real' meat would make little or no sense.

Pet carers began to investigate more about pet-food manufacturing after the 2007 pet-food scare in the US, when thousands of pet foods had to be recalled due to many animals falling ill and dying. The upshot of the investigations was that samples of wheat gluten mixed with melamine, presumably to produce artificially inflated results from common tests for protein content, were discovered in many US pet-food brands, as well as in human food supply. The adulterated gluten was found to have come from China, and US authorities concluded that its origin was the Xuzhou Anying Biologic Technology Development Company, a Xuzhou, China-based company[19].

In the US, many years back and highly unlikely in 2020, certain rendering plants were found to be using euthanised pets from animal shelters and vets' practices. Although manufacturers claim not to do this, in 2012 the practice was still not illegal in some states in the US. In 1990 there were several articles written for the *San Francisco Chronicle* on the subject of deceased pets in pet food[20]. Within the article, the FDA, the American Veterinary Association and the California Veterinary Medical Association confirmed this to be correct. The article went on to state 'veterinarians at the University of Minnesota warned in a paper that the sodium pentobarbital used to put pets to sleep survived rendering without undergoing degradation'. They concluded, however, that the residue would be too small to cause a problem so long as renderers mixed euthanised pets with other raw materials throughout a day's production runs. It would certainly be illegal in the UK, and no reports of euthanised pets being used in pet food has ever been linked to any UK rendering plants.

People are also alarmed by the vague terminology on the AAFCO website when defining 'by-products' as being 'exclusive of feathers, hair, horns, teeth, hooves except in such amounts as might occur unavoidable in good processing practice'. In large factories that deal with thousands of dead carcasses, the word 'unavoidable' becomes very realistic. Also, nowhere on the AAFCO site does it define 'good processing practice'.

The side of the debate that casts by-products in a more positive light is the one that argues that most feral or wild cats are not fussy about which parts of the animal they eat and we, by being appalled, are only projecting our own human hang-ups/bias. The quality of 'protein' in by-products can sometimes be better than that of muscle meat, and the heart, liver, lung and brain of animals are known to be nutritionally beneficial. Why should so much of an animal, already slaughtered for human consumption, go to waste when most of the animal that's left can be recycled into perfectly edible animal feed? Also, something to bear in mind is that people in the West may find chicken feet repulsive (chicken feet can be classed as a by-product) and yet people in the East eat them as delicacies. Food for thought. A totally muscle-based meat diet with no other ingredients would not be a healthy diet for a cat.

DEBATE TWO: WET FOOD VS. DRY FOOD

I am for a wet meat diet, which is why I enjoyed speaking with Dr. Coleshaw. Meat is the natural food source for the feline species, but I admit I give my cats a tiny amount of kibble on occasions, as they seem to like it.

The debate for wet food is that cats are obligate carnivores and need the vitamins from animal flesh to survive. Their anatomy is designed for meat eating, their teeth designed for ripping flesh from bones and their jaws designed for downward movement for the crushing and holding of prey. Cats in the wild do not eat biscuits, and seeing as a cat's evolution has not changed significantly over millions of years, why should they eat them now? Dry food is higher in carbohydrates and contains far less moisture so can be seen as an unnatural food source. It's a clever marketing ploy that dry biscuits help to maintain healthy teeth and gums. What would keep teeth clean and free from plaque is ripping big clumps of meat from bones and disembowelling small rodents, for example, although the inner-city pet cat would not necessarily have the means to hunt and kill in this way, and if they did, would more likely bring their catch home as a gift to their carer than eat it.

Some cheap dry brands contain a high percentage of grains and other carbohydrate fillers that some cats show allergic reactions to or find hard to digest. A high-carbohydrate diet is not a natural diet for a cat, whose daily intake of protein from animal kills is far higher.

However, more reputable companies ensure that their dry food is a complete balanced meal for different stages of the cat's life cycle. The price of the food should help determine its quality, although reading the labels and especially the small print should also help.

Most cat owners that choose a dry-food diet for their cat do so as a convenience so that they can leave food out all day for the cat to graze on. Dry kibble does not smell, does not attract flies in the summer, and can be easily stored. Cats on a dry-food-only diet can become obese due to the high carbohydrate content and the simple fact that their carers leave huge piles of food out for them to constantly graze on. Cats will eat when not hungry and will continue to graze if food is available. A high-grade dry kibble from a reputable company may be better than a low-grade cheap wet brand, so it's not always the case that wet food is better.

Complete dry food from companies such as Hills or Science Plan have perfected their dry kibble to meet all of a cat's needs but I still think it's unnatural for a cat to eat kibble as its main source of food as this goes against what cats have historically eaten throughout the course of their evolution, and what they currently eat in the wild.

It has been noted by Lisa A. Pierson, doctor of veterinary medicine[21] that:

> The protein in dry food, which is often heavily plant-based, is not equal in quality to the protein in canned food, which is meat-based. The protein in dry food, therefore, earns a lower biological value score. Because plant proteins are cheaper than meat proteins, pet-food companies will have a higher profit margin when using corn, wheat, soy, rice, etc.

Another important factor to consider is water content. Prey would naturally have a high water content and this is so important for a species that obtains most of its water requirements from the ingestion of solid food rather than liquids and therefore needs to get water from its food source to remain healthy. Wet food addresses this 'problem' with its high moisture content.

One last factor to consider regarding a dry-food-only diet is that of weight. Research on feline obesity found that one of the contributing factors for the percentage of overweight cats was a dry-food-only diet, especially when weight gain started at a young age[22].

Many cat carers have taken to feeding their cat raw-meat meals and many new companies have materialised, offering commercial pre-packaged raw meat. Most of the meat is organic and lists where the animals originated, such as from local farms, which pet owners find reassuring. There is nothing wrong with feeding a cat raw meat and ground bones but not all cats will take to it. My two Norwegian Forest cats took a long time to accept it, and ironically pure meat (protein), without including ground animal bones, lacks essential calcium and vitamins.

Of course our cats dictate to us what they enjoy eating but we must always guide them to food with the best quality ingredients. The main diet of a cat should be meat, either raw or commercial tinned 'complete' foods with a high percentage of meat rather than fillers. If a cat enjoys kibble then ensure the kibble is high quality but given minimally in very small amounts with plenty of fresh water to hand. Discussing food options with a vet is always a good idea should a cat have any medical symptoms or obesity issues that dictate a special diet.

CHAPTER TWELVE

How Can I Enrich My Cat's Living Space?

'I wish I could write as mysterious as a cat.'

Edgar Allan Poe

CHAPTER TWELVE

In this chapter:

- Get guidance on how to stimulate your cat by changing their environment, in conversation with Kate Benjamin.
- Understand why cat furniture is so important.
- Learn how to keep an indoor cat happy.

There are so many factors to making the life of a cat the best it can be within the perimeters of our homes, and I would say that territorial transformations hold the biggest key to opening the door to behavioural changes. The smallest of changes to a cat's environment can make a world of difference, and sometimes cat carers need reminding that their cat's territorial needs should hold the same importance as their desire to have lovely aesthetics in the home. There is no excuse now, what with the choices online for the most stylish designer cat furniture, with leaders in the field like Hauspanther bringing these catty delights to our attention. There's even a website called Ikea Hackers[1], which shows you how to change Ikea furniture into something practical for our cats. When I visit a client's home on behaviour consultations, it does leave me a tad frustrated when there is nothing in the home to tell me a cat resides there, apart from a food bowl.

Years back, when I first started running my cat-sitting business, I remember one client who lived in a flat on the top floor of a house. The windows were high and with no climbers in the home, this beautiful British Shorthair had no view of the outside world. Although it wasn't my place to be giving advice I decided to go around the home on all fours, mimicking the posture of the cat, to take photos of their cat's view. Walls, walls, furniture and walls. I had no idea if my client had a security webcam, but I'm sure if they had they would have been thinking 'What the hell is she up to!' When the owners arrived home from their holiday I emailed over the photos and advised they get a couple of tall climbers to give 'Melody' visual stimulation. They thanked me but ignored the advice.

Hauspanther is the brain-child of Kate Benjamin, environmental designer for Jackson Galaxy's TV show *My Cat From Hell*. She also co-wrote the two brilliant books *Catification* and *Catify to Satisfy*, which focus on how to transform your home for a cat using a DIY hands-on approach.

Kate has transformed the lives of thousands of indoor cats with her innovative cat furniture, which she either makes or sources from outside vendors, and has given new hope and encouragement to thousands of cat owners. For cat behaviourists like me, Kate Benjamin was a godsend. Cat owners can tap into the evolutionary behaviour of their cats by understanding the thought processes and detail of Kate's work. From wall steps to cat caves, Kate seemed to be the furniture equivalent of Jackson's advice, visually showing cat carers what it means to make one's cat mentally and physically content. Many cat lovers who watch *My Cat From Hell* will be in the know regarding the buzz word 'catification' and I caught up with Kate to ask her more.

In Conversation With Kate Benjamin

Can you tell me where the word 'catification' came from and what it represents?

Catification is Jackson's term for environmental enhancement for living with cats. It encompasses everything that cat guardians do to accommodate the needs of our indoor cats: building climbing structures, providing scratching surfaces, adding beds, drinking fountains, feeding areas, litter boxes and other resources that cats need to live comfortably. An essential part of catification is understanding your own cat, because every cat is different. All cats have basic instincts and needs, but because each cat has a different story and life experience, cat guardians need to cater to their own individual cats.

Jackson and I started to call ourselves the Catification Team. We bring together his cat-behaviour expertise with my design background to create environments that work for both cats and humans. We're here to tell you that your house doesn't have to look like a crazy cat lady lives there just because you have cats! Catification can be done with style and anyone can do it. That's exactly what our books are about.

So, how did you initially get into designing furniture specifically for cats?

In 2007 I was working as the Director of Marketing for a modern children's product company, Boon Inc. We were making beautiful, innovative items for babies and parents. I don't have children, I have cats, so I started searching for similarly designed products for my cats. I came across a few companies and designers who were making designer cat furniture, but I couldn't find a single media source focused on design for cats. So, I started blogging about my finds and I quickly gained a large following. From there I started making my own line of handmade cat toys, scratchers and beds while I continued to cover feline design finds from around the world on my blog.

In 2013 I created the Hauspanther brand around the same time that I started working with Jackson Galaxy on his show *My Cat From Hell*. We developed the concept of catification, which led to *Catification* and *Catify to Satisfy*, both showing people how they can easily catify their homes to accommodate their cats' needs as well as their own personal style. I currently work with Texas-based Primetime Petz to design and manufacture a line of cat furniture and toys under the Hauspanther brand, which is sold internationally. I continue to write about design for cats at **hauspanther. com** and I have been involved with several cat-shelter makeover projects, bringing the concept of catification to shelters in order to benefit rescue cats awaiting adoption.

What are the main things you feel a cat needs to enrich its environment to the maximum?

A truly catified space definitely needs areas for climbing, lots of scratchers, beds and hideaways, easy-to-access resources including food, water and litter, and toys. If you can add a catio or a nice window perch for your cats to look outside, even better. All of these things will keep a cat active and engaged while giving them a sense of territorial ownership, resulting in a happy, well-behaved cat.

In terms of cat trees, most, I feel, focus too much on the cat sleeping. Have you found any good cat trees that encourage climbing and playing on too?

Modular cat trees provide the most flexibility for creating a structure to accommodate climbing and playing. One of my favourites is the Katt3 system from Canadian company BeOneBreed. The Katt3 is a system of cubes with different-sized openings that can be configured in endless ways. They have add-on accessories including scratchers, ramps, toys, hammocks and more that allow you to create the ultimate climbing, playing and sleeping zone for your cats.

Can you talk us through the different materials you use when catifying a home, and what are the benefits to the cat in using those materials?

Two of my favourite materials for catification projects are carpet tiles and yoga mats. Both can be easily cut to any shape and used as non-slip surfaces on climbing surfaces. They also have the added benefit of absorbing a cat's scent to create a sense of ownership, plus they can be easily cleaned or replaced as needed.

Cat furniture finishes need to be easy to clean, durable and attractive. I'm always looking for that perfect material, and each one has its advantages and disadvantages. I do like plastic because it's easy to clean, but for a higher-end feel wood or wood laminate with a durable clear coat on top is a good choice. I also look for colours and finishes that are in keeping with current decorating trends (that's for the humans, not so much for the cats!).

Clients often tell me that they don't need cat furniture because they have high sofa backs or tops of wardrobes their cat can climb on. Can you explain why cats need their own specific furniture?

I advocate for including existing furniture in what we call the 'cat superhighway', a path that allows a cat to navigate around the entire room without touching the ground. However, it is important to add some pieces that are specifically for cat use only. Cat trees and shelves can include toys or scratchers for added enrichment, plus cat furniture should have soft surfaces where cats will leave their scent, creating a sense of ownership.

In a multi-cat household, what is your criteria for changing the territory and how would you go about it?

I live with double digits of cats in an 1,100 sq ft condo, so I've learned how to maximise space! You definitely need to take advantage of vertical space, adding the superhighway with cat perches, shelves and lounging spots overhead. We have lots of places for cats to rest, some out in the open and others that are semi-hidden, but I've blocked off any spaces where we can't reach the cats, like under the bed or the sofa.

I also use what Jackson and I call 'diffusion posts' to keep the cat traffic circulating nicely. I have a large scratcher, the MaxScratch, in my furniture line that makes the perfect diffusion post because it has a sturdy perch on top. When multiple cats are in the room, one will often jump up on the top of the scratcher to get out of the way of another. This is just one of many scratchers throughout the house, which you need with multiple cats so they have a variety of places to scratch, leaving visual and scent marks of ownership.

In the UK many homes are flats that have difficult hot-spot tension areas like narrow hallways. Any tips for these areas?

We have some of these in our home, too, like in our front entryway by the door to the kitchen. The cats congregate in this space when it's feeding time, and there can be conflict. I added small cat shelves on both sides of the space and a scratcher on the wall. Some of the cats know to jump up to the shelves so they can have a little more space when the area gets too crowded. The scratcher is also a nice distraction for some of the cats while they are waiting for their meal.

You're a huge advocate for designer furniture to please the humans

too. How difficult is that balance and how do you cater for both so that the human gets the aesthetics but equally, the cat gets what they need too?

This is the core concept behind catification, considering both the cats and the humans in the design, because if the people don't like how something looks, then they won't have it in their home, which could result in a less-than-ideal environment for a cat. Also, we're trying to bust the 'crazy cat lady' stereotype here. You can have cats and a sense of style!

It's really not hard these days to find functional, durable and beautiful cat furniture that coordinates with your décor. Major manufacturers to small design studios are producing all kinds of products for cats that are nicer than most human furniture. The other option is to create something yourself, but modifying a piece of human furniture for a cat to use. This allows you to start with something you love and make it totally customised. Jackson and I call this a catification hack and it's one of my favourite things to do.

Can you tell us a story about one of your most challenging cases on the design front?

Small spaces are always a challenge, especially in a multi-cat household. On the very first episode of *My Cat From Hell* that I was on, Jackson and I worked on a small apartment in New York City. The two cats were not getting along. One was attacking the other cat, who in turn acted like prey. Lots of the conflict took place in the tiny kitchen that had a dead-end corner. It took us a while to figure out a solution, but we eventually came up with the 'revolving door' concept. We added a spiral cat tree in the corner of the kitchen that allowed the timid cat to get up and away, escaping over to the top of the refrigerator and the upper cabinets if she was cornered.

What do you feel is the biggest misconception that people have about keeping cats?

I think that a lot of people feel that cats don't need anything: that they are completely independent and reclusive. That's not the case at all! For cats to live fulfilling, rich lives, they need the proper environment to thrive. That really is at the heart of catification: giving your cats what they need to be happy. Also, love and affection, play and stimulation, proper nutrition and quality vet care are so important to keeping your cats happy and healthy. It makes me so sad when people adopt a cat and then never do anything for the cat because they think it will be fine on their own.

I'd love to hear about any other recommended products, and your opinion on the reason for their success?

Cat trees are such an important part of catification, but many people picture beige-carpet-covered monstrosities the minute they hear the words. There are several companies that make beautifully designed, sturdy cat trees that anyone would be proud to have in their home. The one I have in my living room is one of my favourites – the Acacia Cat Tree in bamboo plywood from Square Cat Habitat. I love everything about this cat tree, from the look and style, to the size and the way it works for the cats. It's quite easy to clean and has proven to be incredibly durable. It's a bit of an investment, but it really is more like a piece of high-quality furniture, not a disposable item.

Another important thing to provide for your cat is a bed or hideaway. Some of my favourites are the Pod Bed from Hepper and The Cat Ball. Both come in modern colours and the cats absolutely love them.

Scratching surfaces are also a must-have for all cats. As mentioned previously, you'll need to determine what kind of surface your cat likes to scratch on. Does she prefer cardboard, sisal, carpet, wood? One of my most recommended space-saving cat products is a wall-mounted cat scratcher. You can place them at any height to give your cat a good stretch, and they don't take up floor-space. My favourite design, the Wallflower Scratcher from Marmalade Pet, is no longer available, so I designed something similar: a modern wall-mounted cardboard scratcher in brushed steel which is available in my online shop.

What is most challenging when catifying a home?

The biggest challenges are usually the people. A lot of people are scared to catify because they are afraid that their house will start to look like the cats have taken over. My job is to find that balance between giving the cats what they need and making the people happy. There are plenty of ways to integrate cat features into an environment in a seamless way, so visitors wouldn't even know it's for a cat until they see one walking overhead or scratching on something that looks like a piece of modern sculpture.

The key to successful territory sharing with a cat is getting the environment right for the species so that they can act, within reason, as naturally as they would outdoors. I say 'within reason' because it's impossible to create everything that a cat would get from being free-roaming, such as fresh air, fulfilling their natural curiosity and hunting, as well as the natural guarding of territory, but we can come pretty damn close. With dedicated cat-loving creatives like Kate, there's now no excuse for living in the dark about our cats' unique needs.

We may assume that having cats means that they should easily slot in with our way of living and our time schedules, but having this mindset shows a lack of respect for another species' needs. I once had a client ask me 'Why do I need vertical space for my cat? They have the back of my sofa. They wouldn't know the difference between cat and human furniture!' It's true that cats like to lounge on our furniture – especially the highest sections like the backs of sofas and shelving, the latter of which can be unfortunate if cluttered with ornaments – but many also like to be higher than our furniture so that they can safely look down on their domain. They choose their own specifically designed furniture because it can offer options such as getting away from us when they choose and being out of reach of our children's hands or unwanted attentions. Specific cat furniture also gives a suitable outlet for a cat to leave their scent on, as well as providing the correct material for optimal scratching.

When it comes to cat furniture, it's also important to consider the multi-cat household because providing adequate resources for every cat is an important aspect of peaceful feline coexistence.

Many practical functions can be served by delving into the psychology of our little tinkers. An important part of choosing cat furniture that I consistently mention to my clients is the need not to look at cat trees and climbers for the sole purpose of your cat sleeping. Depending on the type of tree, some offer high vertical beds and platforms and other designs should encourage climbing and provide fun for your cat, promoting stimulation. A cat does sleep many hours in the day and that's completely natural. However, a bored cat will sleep far more than necessary due to lack of stimulation or a view.

Living in London I come across a high percentage of indoor cats who live in high rise blocks or on busy urban streets. One staple of my behaviour consultations is advising cat guardians on how to keep their indoor cats happy. Read on to the next Cat Chat to find out more.

 **A CATTY SUM UP**

1. For cats to live fulfilling, rich lives, they need the proper environment in which to thrive.

2. All cats have basic instincts and needs, but because each cat has a different story and life experience, cat guardians need to cater to their own individual cats.

3. A bored cat will sleep far more than necessary due to lack of stimulation or a view.

CAT CHAT

How To Keep Your Indoor Cat Happy

Catification may be a buzzword but I feel it's the most important word of the 21st century for cat owners hoping to learn all about the pet they love and making sure they get it right first time around.

For cats who are kept exclusively indoors, or ones who used to roam freely but have since been moved into a place with no outside access, it's essential to provide lots of stimulation within their own homes. This is where understanding catification can make for a more contented cat, and thus happier owners too.

It's extremely important for the wellbeing and happiness of your cat that you understand their basic needs. You and I are able to go outside every day and be stimulated by hundreds of different sensations – sounds, sights and smells – but it's a different story for the indoor cat who only has their owner and home as the daily focus of life. When confining a cat indoors, owners commonly make the mistake of providing no stimulation and this can lead to your cat sleeping for most of their life through boredom, which can lead to obesity, anxiety and depression. It's important to remember that cats are animals first and pets second, and the natural state of a cat is to hunt, kill, eat and sleep.

Here are a few important pointers to encourage cat owners to think about their cats in a new way, and to help them improve the environment that their cat lives in. Catification isn't just about climbers and walkways. To me, the word represents living with a cat and making sure that every aspect of that life is shared with a cat's perspective. With this in mind, here is my catification advice, covering everything from toys and climbers to food and litter trays.

PERCHES

To create the illusion of the outdoors, you should provide a 'tree' or two. When I say 'tree', I mean an elevated place for a cat to climb and perch. Many cats feel more secure off the ground and like to sit up high and

look down on their domain. The elevated space can be a cat tower or climber, or even a space on a high shelf, with the ornaments removed, of course! Vertical space can help cats who are nervous of strangers or help them to get away from the tiny hands of excitable kids. This enables them to build up confidence, but at a safe distance. Vertical space can also help with the introduction of a dog because they enable your cat to be up high whilst your pooch is trained not to react to it. Of course, it's a given that a multi-cat household should have lots of climbers and walkways to aid peaceful cohabitation.

SCRATCHING POSTS

Cats usually keep their claws in good shape by scratching tree trunks or fence posts. As well as keeping their claws trim, cats naturally scratch to exercise the muscles in their paws and to leave their scent, so it's a basic and natural need. The indoor cat will scratch your furniture and carpets if a scratching post is not provided. Most cat trees have numerous scratching posts incorporated into their designs but they are usually small posts in between platforms. It's a good idea, combined with these climbers, to buy a large tall scratch post so that your adult cat can get to fully stretch. For cats that like to scratch horizontally, try furniture that doubles up as a scratcher, like cardboard cat loungers. Corner scratching posts that attach to the side of a sofa are another ideal solution if you're not able to deter your cat from their chosen area.

A ROOM WITH A VIEW

Next, we come to windows. An indoor cat loves to look out of the window to watch the birds outside and to keep an eye on their territory. This is a great way to stimulate your cat and to relieve long hours of boredom. Window perches can be found online in many varieties. If you have a property where it's difficult to make any alterations to the walls using screws and nails, there are specially designed window perches to combat this problem. This type of window perch uses suckers to connect to the glass itself, and are still strong enough to hold most cats' body weight. If space allows, then place your cat climber by a window. If you own your own home, consider building a window box for your cat so they can safely sit outside. A window box is a DIY structure connected to an outside windowsill. People use window boxes typically for flowers and plants but a larger window box can be made for a cat to sit outside in. It can be rectangular or square in shape and be made safe by enclosing the box with netting at the sides and top.

TOYS AND BOREDOM

If your cat sleeps all the time, it may be that you are not providing enough stimulation. You may think that your cat doesn't need to play or doesn't like playing, but you will be surprised once you have found the 'right' toy to suit your cat's personality. Playtime is imperative, not only to relieve boredom and frustration but also to tap into a cat's natural hunting instinct. Playing furthermore helps strengthen the bond between you and your cat. Once you have found the correct toys for your cat they should be rotated to keep the cat interested. Leave out some fun little toys for your cat to enjoy on its own, such as ping-pong balls, open paper bags, cardboard boxes and catnip. Most people get the wrong kind of toys and then wonder why their cat is not interested. Another mistake that some owners make is thinking that once their cat gets old, it no longer has any interest in playing. Not true.

Many times I have shown cat owners how much their elderly cat does want to play, simply by showing them toys that get them excited.

HUNTING TOYS

The toys I like to encourage owners to get are what I call hunting toys. Cats are successful predators and their natural hardwired instinct is to hunt and kill things, so any toys that stimulate this type of behaviour are highly beneficial for the indoor cat. Toy mice, bugs, spiders, birds or feathers on a wire or string make excellent toys. To excite your cat, place and move the toy under a newspaper, the edge of a rug or a cardboard box and watch as your cat enjoys the hunting process. Reward your cat with a treat afterwards or a little piece of meat to finish off the hunt. Moving a toy too near to a cat's face will become a boring game for them. Cats need to enjoy the tease and the chase, so make the game as realistic as possible to emulate the hunting of prey in the wild.

BEST TOYS FOR BLIND CATS

I often work with cats who are blind and it's important to get it right when it comes to toys, which can greatly improve their quality of life. Just like a human who is visually impaired or blind, other senses become stronger, and it's no different for the feline species. A cat will rely on smell, hearing, touch and vibrations to survive, and blind cats do very well indeed. It never fails to amaze me, actually.

Whilst blind cats can cope extremely well indoors, memorising where objects are placed and remembering distances for jumps on the bed or width and depth of stairs, toys and playtime can become a tad boring because the wrong toys are considered. What we have to remember with a cat who no longer uses their eyes is that the other senses kick in, so toys with a strong sense of smell, such as catnip and valerian, or toys that make a sound, such as rod toys with a bell on or a ball with a bell, can perfectly entertain. Even textures such as fur or cardboard puzzle toys such as a toilet roll sealed either end with holes in the middle and treats inside, can be a great fun toy to bat around, with the smell of the treats as a guide. Some cats who are not totally blind can see some light, so any ball toys that give off light are great.

Words to use when searching online for the best toys for blind cats are: *cat toys with bells on, cat balls with bells, cat balls that light up, Crinkle cat toys, real fur hunting cat toys (with a bell on), catnip* or *valerian toys.*

When it comes to climbers, cats can judge distances extremely well and blind cats are no different. To give a helping hand I would concentrate on cat trees that have a ramp or ones that have platforms close together. You can guide your cat on to a cat tree by scent such as catnip leaves, the smell of favourite treats or the jingle-jangle of a favourite toy. They will soon love exploring their new cat tree and will become familiar with the distances of the platforms.

Some cats can even be walked on a lead when blind. There are plenty of examples of YouTube of sightless cats loving the great outdoors. It very much depends on whether the cat is confident and showing signs of wanting to go outside. If the street outside is quiet and your cat has taken well to lead training and shows an interest in wanting to explore a little outside, then why not! Let them guide you.

Life doesn't stop with a blind kitty. Get the right toys and climbers and your cat will love you for it.

CATNIP AND VALERIAN

I'm constantly surprised at how many owners never supply catnip or valerian for their cats. Both are fun treats, which harmlessly 'intoxicate' your cat for somewhere between 5 and 15 minutes. Both are completely safe. The main constituent of catnip is nepetalactone, which is an oil contained in the leaves of the catnip plant. It's believed that cats react to the nepetalactone because it resembles a chemical in tomcat urine. Valerian (Valeriana officinalis) has tiny, sweet-smelling flowers that grow in clusters and have jagged leaves. However, in the case of valerian, it's the root of the flower that excites our cats rather than the flower itself. Both plants provide a much-needed experience for an indoor cat and are wonderful ways to get overweight cats to kick up their heels a little!

GRASS

Grass is essential and your cats will love having the opportunity to eat it as a normal outdoor cat would. They love to rub against grass too. It's easy to grow and you can buy special grass tubs for cats from any pet store. Pre-made grass garden squares or rolls can also be bought to line a tray, which your cat will enjoy lying on. Cats regurgitate grass due to the fact that they cannot digest it. This is because they lack the enzymes to break down vegetable matter[1]. There are many theories as to why cats eat grass. It's supposed that it encourages the act of vomiting, which clears their system, that they benefit from the folic acid contained in the grass because it's an essential vitamin for a cat's body, and even that it works as a natural laxative. For whatever reason cats eat grass, it's good to give them the opportunity to do so.

LASERS

This toy is a wonderful addition to the hunting-toy collection. Perfect if you're feeling physically too tired to play with your cat in a typical 'thing on a string' scenario that demands a certain amount of physical effort, cheap laser pens mean that no one has an excuse not to do their duty!

Play with your cat for short bursts of 5–10 minutes, and they will go nuts trying to catch the light. Because it's frustrating for the cat that the light can never be caught, take care not to use this kind of play for long periods of time. Sessions should be finished off with a hunting-type game where your cat can actually catch something. And of course never shine the light directly into the cat's eyes.

CAT-DREAMS DVD

Check out the various cat TV DVDs or the many YouTube videos featuring singing birds, squirrels foraging for nuts, fish swimming back and forth, and other critters that your cat would love to get hold of and eat! YouTube also has many fun cat games that will keep your little tinker focused with hours of fun. These games and critter videos can be played on an iPod, which could be fitted on a cat tower with a specially made bracket. That way your cat gets its very own TV. It may seem over the top, but hey, we are cat people!

FEEDING

Make sure that the food dish is wide enough for your cat's face and is shallow. This can be a plate or saucer, but what's important is that your cat's whiskers do not hit the sides. A lot of owners buy dishes that are too deep and more appropriate for dogs or too small in diameter: more suitable for the face of a ferret. Just look at the length of a cat's whiskers to get an idea of the best width for your cat's food dish. My cats, two big Norwegian Forests, use a bowl called The Wetnoz Studio Scoop 5 cup. It's a dog's bowl but perfectly suitable for their needs. The large size suits most cats' faces, especially large breeds such as Persians, Norwegian Forests and Maine Coons. This bowl is particularly suitable for the extreme flat-faced Persians as the bowl is tilted upwards at a slight angle. Food should be placed away from water and definitely as far away as possible from the litter tray. You can make drinking water fun for your cat by buying a water fountain. If you have a multi-cat household, then set up separate feeding stations, as cats like space away from other cats to eat. This will also help stop unwanted behaviour such as food bullying.

Small regular food portions throughout the day is better for cats than free feeding, which cat owners often do when their cat's diet is kibble. I have seen bowls with so much food in that I wondered whether owners were feeding a horse rather than a small cat. Food in the wild isn't available all day, and your cat's digestive system needs time to rest! Without a proper feeding schedule many cats will eat all day, even when full, which can lead to obesity. A feeding schedule also breaks up the day for an indoor cat and you will begin to notice your cat getting much more excited at meal times when scheduled feeding times are introduced. Ceasing free feeding also helps with any behaviour issues because food is usually the main incentive for animals during training. If you wish your cat to eat regular but small amounts of wet food throughout the day then consider a food timer with ice trays.

Treats like freeze-dried chicken, shrimps or prawns are great, and 100% meat or fish snacks can be fun in a treat puzzle ball or given as a small bedtime snack to see your cat through the night. 'Bedtime' snacks are also great for cats who wake up too early in the morning and cry excessively to be fed or for attention. Engage in a chase/hunt play session at night and finish with a meaty treat and this should satisfy your kitty enough to sleep through until you wake up the next day. Hopefully!

LITTER TRAYS

Many owners buy litter trays that are too small or too gimmicky. Ensure that you have a large enough tray for your cat to move around in and dig properly. They should also be able to collect litter from another area of the tray to cover their waste. Large plastic 'under-the-bed' storage trays are great for this as are kiddies' plastic paddling pools or baby baths, depending on the space. Don't line the tray with plastic bin bags or paper. This makes digging harder for the cat and is a totally unnatural material for them to have in their toilet area. Plastic bags and paper collect urine, which will turn rancid quickly and be very unpleasant for a cat, whose sense of smell is far more developed and therefore more sensitive than ours. For this reason, most cats who have litter trays lined with bags or paper do not cover their waste. One litter tray per cat is the general rule, plus an extra one in separate areas of multi-cat households, in case one cat blocks another. Cats do not need hoods over their trays. These are mainly for humans. Although a very shy, timid cat may feel more secure with a hooded tray, most cats do very well without them. They like to see what and who is around them without getting a surprise from another cat or human. If you do need to get a tray with a cover, make sure the litter tray is especially large so that the hood does not restrict movement.

ONE-ON-ONE ATTENTION

It's simple. Don't come home and get straight on your computer or crash in front of the TV without giving kitty some attention. The days can be very long and boring for an indoor cat, so they will be very excited to see you when you get home from work.

Time put aside for play is absolutely essential for your cat's wellbeing. To be honest, it's also good for owners to wind down after a hard day with some good wholesome kitty love! Spend some time showing your cat just how special they are to you. After all, your cat isn't just there for your entertainment or to look pretty sitting in your home.

THE MULTI-CAT HOUSEHOLD

Territorial stress is common amongst multi-cat households. The core home territory is the most important aspect of a cat's life. It's connected to survival and within it a cat experiences warmth, food, human attention and the feeling of safety. All of these things are precious resources and cats can get protective over them. Even a human caretaker is a resource. Some cats can become much more territorial over the home turf and need to be able to live with their humans without other cats encroaching on their space. However, there are many circumstances whereby cats can share space.

Harmony is possible as long as there is enough space in the home for the cats to coexist, and the personalities of the cats are suited to the situation. A multi-cat household needs to create space for the cats to get away from one another. Just like a large human family need space away from each other, so do our cats. To help create a harmonious multi-cat environment, think about a cat's natural behaviours and then each cat's individual personality. They need plenty of escape routes and hidey-holes placed high and low. These can be cat trees, shelving, boxes or floor pods, as a few examples. Look at hot-spot areas that can create tensions such as exit and entry points to any outside access and try to think of ways to help the cats. An example is a cat flap. Have several cat flaps in different locations if possible so that no one cat can block it. Other hot-spot areas may be toilet locations, narrow hallways or the human bed, the best location in the home as it carries the strongest smell of the humans. Feeding stations should be in separate locations to give the cats space to relax and feed in peace. Play should be given to all cats individually with different toys, as there is always one cat who takes over the play, leaving other cats sitting by the sideline frustrated. Toys can create tensions between cats too. Another reason to buy plenty of them so that each cat gets to play in separate areas and with that special one-on-one attention.

Understanding your cat, its origins and its basic natural behaviour will help you to see what needs to be done inside its home environment, and will enable your cat to find all the happiness and fulfillment that it deserves.

CHAPTER THIRTEEN

How Much Touching And Attention Do Our Cats Really Like?

'I have felt cats rubbing their faces against mine and touching my cheek with claws carefully sheathed. These things, to me, are expressions of love.'

James Herriot

CHAPTER THIRTEEN

In this chapter:

- Learn why some cats do not like much attention.
- Get expert advice on how to live with cats who prefer limited touch, in conversation with Sarah Fisher.
- Read a true case study on a cat called Juice who had special needs.

Two common issues I come across both in my cat-behaviour and grooming practice, is low petting aggression and cats who do not like being picked up or having too much attention lavished on them. Both issues rely on a change of expectations from owners when it comes to how a cat 'should' be. It's a difficult area, especially when it comes to living with and grooming these types of cats, because, of course, a) cat owners want and expect something back from the animals they care for, and b) grooming is a necessity for cats with long fur.

First of all, let's look at a behaviour condition called low petting aggression. It's actually becoming a common feature of my visits, leaving owners feeling rejected and scared of their cats. Low petting aggression happens when a cat is conflicted by the need for closeness with their humans and the dislike of being stroked for too long. This causes inner conflict, which erupts with an aggressive response in an attempt to stop the physical touching. This type of aggression can also be due to over-stimulation and arousal but still leaves the cat with conflicted emotions. Some cats have a very low threshold, which can be seconds, whilst others can go for much longer before lashing out. The usual signs of irritation from a cat are: swishing of the tail, rippling of the back (over-stimulation), ears back or flatter, and hissing. Sometimes the cat will show no signs of irritation but will simply lash out, seemingly without reason and leaving the owner feeling shaken and with a bad scratch or bite wound.

Other cats prefer to be near us, like sitting next to us, or in the same room as us but don't necessarily want to be fussed. The cat may want to engage with the room and the people in it, but on their own terms. This is fine but some cat carers may mistake this honour as the cat being aloof and not affectionate.

Sarah Fisher is one of the UK's highest qualified Tellington TTouch instructors, a gentle touch-specific therapy that helps animals gain calmness and confidence, enabling them to move beyond a typical fear response. The Tellington TTouch therapy also aids circulation when working on specific joints, which in turn leads to a more active healthy animal. It was originally developed by Linda Tellington Jones over 32 years ago when it was discovered that massage and bodywork, using gentle, non-habitual movements with the intent of activating unused neural pathways to the brain in humans, proved successful on horses too. Having studied with Linda to become a leading light in the UK on this subject, I couldn't think of anyone better equipped to contribute to this chapter than Sarah.

In Conversation With Sarah Fisher

How does Tellington TTouch work, and how can we use this with cats in particular?

Tellington TTouch is a unique method that includes a variety of non-invasive body TTouches that can provide an illuminating and respectful way of introducing contact at a pace to suit each cat. A skilled TTouch Practitioner will pay attention to the nervous system responses, and 'drip-feed' body contact with the back of the hand, the back of a finger, or other items such as artists' soft watercolour brushes to find areas where the cat does enjoy contact, and areas of sensitivity that may warrant further veterinary attention. By chunking down the learning process it's possible to identify if contact in general is the issue or if it is the type of contact that is concerning to the cat. Some cat carers do tend to handle too vigorously and too quickly and miss subtle signs that the cat is becoming concerned. If we take it slow, the trust will grow.

Do you think cats like the amount of touching and attention we think they do?

In my experience, many animals, including cats, are over-handled, as we have an innate desire to show affection through tactile interactions. I don't think it is a coincidence that many cats gravitate towards visitors that are anxious about cats, as that person, due to their own fear response, is not actively trying to engage with the cat. Whilst this is obviously concerning for the fearful human, this lack of interaction probably makes the cat feel safe in the company of a person who is avoiding eye and hand contact.

Why do you feel some cats don't like tactile attention?

Some cats will have had poor experiences of being handled, some will not have had any experience at all (good or bad) and those early learning experiences can be contributory factors to avoidance of tactile attention. I have also worked with several cats that had underlying physical problems including hip dysplasia, luxating patella [knee-cap dislocation or un-normal movement of same], arthritis and old fractures in the spine that had not been diagnosed until the guardian asked for help with their cat's behaviour. Pain, or pain memory, can increase touch sensitivity for obvious reasons. Cats that are stressed, have digestive disturbance, and/or are highly frustrated are also less likely to enjoy being touched. A cat that is content and relaxed is more likely to find appropriate body contact truly rewarding.

What can we do to connect to our cats without touching them too often?

I have had a great deal of experience working with animals that do not enjoy contact from the human hand. I use a combination of approaches including Animal Centred Education (ACE) Free Work aimed at influencing the sensory system by introducing novel textures such as carpet mats and rubber mats for the cat to walk over, and treat-seeking mats and rummage boxes that the cats can explore and touch with their paws, their noses and tongues. This approach gives cats the opportunity to engage with new tactile experiences at their own pace. Observing how a cat moves and interacts with the different textures can be illuminating in itself as the guardian may start to recognise the cat actively avoids specific textures. An action that involves stepping up or over low-level poles on the ground might show that the cat has physical problems that need veterinary attention. The cat may avoid soft textures underfoot as this can create more movement through sore joints or sore, soft tissue, and stepping up on to a raised surface or over poles may not be possible or may seem awkward if the cat has pain or underdeveloped muscle due to compensation patterns as a result of an old injury, or undiagnosed physical problems. I also use Chirag Patel's The Bucket Game, and Counting Game to build the relationship and to learn more about the animal before introducing contact.

Many cats struggle with laminate flooring and providing non-slip mats in the home where the cat can rest, play without slipping, and engage with other sensory items such as interactive food toys, can be an integral part of reducing body sensitivity and tension. Modifying the games we play with cats can also help. Cats are hardwired to follow movement and if we play fast, arousing games with toys, not only are we increasing arousal and body tension in the cat, we are pairing our own hand movements with those experiences of arousal. We may be actively teaching the cat that hand movement signals the start of arousal and increased body tension, and this can be a contributory factor to how the cat responds when we then extend a hand to touch them.

What should cat carers look out for in their cats in terms of understanding how much they are giving us compared to our expectations of them?

A desire for companionship should not be confused with a desire for contact. We need to understand and meet the individual needs of every animal that shares our lives, and give them as many choices as possible, whilst bearing in mind those choices are usually limited to the options we've chosen to give them. I encourage all my clients to start looking at the world through the eyes of their cat and to really consider whether the cat finds our interactions and lifestyle rewarding, or if those interactions and lifestyle choices are aimed more at fulfilling our own needs. As with any partnership, a rewarding relationship is based on mutual appreciation and trust. If we want cats to change their habits and interactions, we usually need to change ours first.

All behaviour has a function and there are patterns with all behaviour, including movement and the posture of cats at rest. If we watch more, and 'do' less, these patterns become more apparent. Always ask whether the interactions we choose are truly rewarding for the cat. Is the cat more touch-sensitive during or after a specific event such as visitors in the home, or after eating, or after eating a particular type of food or treat perhaps? Does the cat enjoy or avoid contact in a specific room or at a specific time of day? When sleeping, does the cat only ever lie curled up or stretched out on the same side that might indicate some body discomfort? What smaller nervous-system responses are we able to observe, such as the more subtle movement of the whiskers or ears, or the blink rate, etc, and when might we see them change? Avoid jumping to conclusions based on one observation, avoid taking the reactions of the cat personally, and question everything – but never, ever question the cat as the cat is always right.

There are many ways to build connections without using our hands through treat-seeking games, and by establishing calm foundations on which further learning can be built. If we find something that the cat truly enjoys, we have something to go back to if we do have to do something that concerns the cat such as veterinary checks or worming, for example. The more positive experiences a cat can have, the quicker the cat will recover from something that unsettled them.

What types of cat situations and cat personalities can the Tellington TTouch method help with?

The Tellington TTouch can be beneficial for every cat at any stage of life provided the guardian really 'listens' to the cat. TTouch offers ways to deepen understanding and increase awareness of a cat's individual needs and to introduce body contact a little at a time. We ideally need to handle cats for health reasons and if we are diligent in our approach and listen to the 'whispers' of the cat we can build confidence and let our cats know we 'hear' them so they never need to 'shout'.

Do you have one cat story that stands out in your mind where TT helped with a difficult/challenging cat?

There is one particular cat who stands out in my mind. I was teaching a feline workshop for a rescue organisation and one of the cat pods in the area was covered by a towel. The resident of this pod was a long-stay rescue and had handling concerns that had escalated. She would fly at the door of the pod if anyone walked past, or if she saw any cats exploring the free-roaming area opposite the pods. Feeding and cleaning the litter tray were overwhelming experiences for her as she could not tolerate hands in the pod and if anyone tried to touch her she would grab and bite the extended hand.

In that particular organisation, the environment was limited but the care-givers had set up her pod as best they could to give as much privacy as possible, and somewhere to hide. I was asked if I would try to help her and we started the steps to connecting with her during the lunch break when the cattery was a little quieter.

By 'listening' to her, and gradually moving the towel across the door, I was able to build her trust and open the door to her pod a little, ensuring at all times she could hide whenever she felt the need. I used a long feather to initiate contact, letting her first see the feather, sniff the feather and touch it with her paw. These steps took several mini-sessions as it's vital each animal is given breaks and time to process what they are experiencing. As I was teaching a two-day event, I was able to spend moments with her during the course of the afternoon as well as the following day.

In a relatively short space of time, this beautiful girl was rubbing her face into the feather and I was able to continue to build our relationship with the pod door completely open. She could advance and retreat at her own pace, and when I finally put my hand into the doorway of the pod, she walked forward and pushed her face into my open hand. I was watching her blink rate, her whiskers, her ear set, her tail and her body posture all the time. One thing that really stood out was the quality of her coat in the middle of her back; it was raised, and coarse. Whilst many factors influence the appearance of an animal's coat, and it is something that certainly warrants further research, I have seen correlations between coat patterns and mobility issues many, many times.

Towards the end of my time at the shelter, this little cat was sitting watching the activities in the cattery with her door fully open. I could do TTouches around her head, neck and shoulders but if I moved my fingers past her shoulders, her posture would change and I would take my hand away and return to an area where she was more relaxed being touched. She didn't scratch or bite once – just stopped blinking for a moment and her ears would flatten slightly. It was evident that contact wasn't an issue, but contact on her back most certainly was.

The cattery team were incredible and one by one began to connect with her using the same approaches I had shown them. They listened to my observations and took her for an X-ray after my visit. The X-ray revealed there had been damage to her spine at some point in her life, right under the area where her coat was raised. She was given pain relief, and the brilliant team continued to build her trust.

I can only imagine how painful it must have been to be touched, picked up, and to experience the human habit of stroking along the back and then along the length of the tail when her spine was damaged. Even the slightest 'pull' on the tail must have been unbearable for her. I injured my own spine in a riding accident, and I know all too well that acute pain can make every single centimetre of your skin hurt; contact from even the softest of fabric can be too much to bear, never mind being stroked or ruffled by a human hand.

I still think of her often as it was such a peaceful and rewarding experience connecting in this quiet way. Her whole world opened up as her confidence in humans grew and she enjoyed exploring the cattery and free-roaming area. Best of all, this little long-stay cat was successfully rehomed.

It's very rewarding helping cats live by our sides, and Sarah's work in an area connected to touch and handling is vital in a world whereby we put so much on animals to expand our own daily experiences. Below are more tips to help with common behaviour issues I deal with.

LIVING WITH A CAT WITH A LOW-PETTING THRESHOLD

The biggest challenge when living with cats who don't like too much stroking is to recognise that not all cats like to be touched the way we think they do. And this is where respect and lower expectations come into play. First of all, a cat may like to come and inspect their human and to place their scent on them as a way of greeting them or certain guests that visit the home. This is not a green light to reach out to stroke the cat with a low-petting threshold. This is a greeting that the cat likes and can 'handle'. It's best to get on the level of the cat and to relax the arm downwards so that the hand is there for the cat to rub against. A cat may like to do this several times, purring away to show contentment.

Some cats may hiss and attack straight away should that relaxed hand then reach above them to stroke their head! So, first things first. Watch and listen to your cat:

- What makes them relaxed?
- What are their likes and dislikes?
- How long do they enjoy a stroke before you see signs of discontent?
- Do they actually look like they enjoy being picked up?

Understanding a cat's body language and respecting what your cat wants and feels is the way to achieving a balanced relationship without the human caretaker getting harmed.

One such cat I was in regular contact with was called Mish Mish. She had low petting aggression and would purr happily on your lap until you went one second over a few seconds stroking her, appearing one minute to relish the attention and the next hissing and swiping like a feral cat.

BUT MY CAT LOVES ME AND WANTS ME TO TOUCH THEM

I hear this many times but again it's down to reading signals from your cat and not assuming that just because they headbutt your leg that they wish to be rubbed frantically on the head and scooped up like carrying a baby. Some cats will flop over and show their belly to you. This is a sign that a cat is feeling very comfortable within their territory and within your presence, but is not a green light for a human hand to suddenly start doing the jazz-hands rub over their most vulnerable area!

The best thing we can do for our cats is be mindful of their body language and understand touching and handling from their perspective. With all of the above in mind, my top tips are:

1. Be aware of body language and stop touching if your cat is getting twitchy or too aroused. A nip or scratch will be forthcoming if you continue to ignore the signs.

2. Don't be disappointed if your cat isn't a lap cat. Many of the long-haired breeds of cat overheat when sitting on our laps and prefer to sit beside us. As Sarah Fisher (Tellington T Touch Instructor) rightly points out: 'When your cat sits on your lap, it's likely he just wants your body warmth and to be close to you. He doesn't necessarily want a lot of fuss while he's there'.

3. Accept that sharing the sofa with your cat is a compliment from that individual.

4. Accept the compliment if a cat remains in the same room as us.

5. Get on a cat's level and loosely hang the hand down for a cat to rub against it with no attempt to stroke the cat. Cats with low-level handling tolerance love this approach and feel comfortable with it.

Remember that some cats from rescue centres view the hand approaching them or reaching above their heads with trepidation. Perhaps the movement is connected to a negative association from experiences in the past?

An example of this is very timid or shy cats who are still very nervous of the cat–human relationship. These types of cats need plenty of patience and a low-expectation approach. Don't attempt to stroke them at the beginning of your relationship. That honour will come when your cat shows you they are OK for you to be tactile with them. Sitting quietly in a room at a distance from your cat, reading a book or quietly watching some TV will help gain the trust of your timid or shy cat. You can use treats scattered from their place of safety, such as a box on its side, to halfway towards where you are, to try to encourage exploration. For cats who have a phobia towards strangers (and some actually do), quick consistent daily exposure to humans quietly paying no attention to them, combined with something positive such as food or a catnip mouse, can help build trust and lessen fear. Exposures should be varied in length of time as part of a long-term therapy plan.

A cat's life can be saved with a long-term therapy plan. Meet one cat called Juice in the following Cat Chat.

A CATTY SUM UP

1. Many animals, including cats, are over-handled.
2. If we take it slow, the trust will grow.
3. A desire for companionship should not be confused with a desire for contact.

CAT CHAT

Juice: The Special-Needs Cat

Juice didn't know an angel was watching over him the day he was taken to the vet's to be put to sleep. That angel guided him into the arms of Silvia, the vet-on-call, who refused to euthanise him. All Silvia knew was that Juice shouldn't die. She couldn't look into his huge emerald eyes and push a needle into his veins to end his short life

when he hadn't experienced the joy of life with humans who cared.

For a seven-year-old, Juice had experienced his fair share of trauma, including an abusive home where it's suspected a child threw him out the window. In turn, Juice became distrustful and fearful, being rehomed twice due to aggression. After his latest outburst, the owner decided he should be euthanised.

However, Silvia disagreed and Juice spent six months in a cage at the veterinary practice in St Albans while the team explored options other than ending his life. This long stint at the practice was due to Juice's escalating aggression. No one could get near him, especially at the beginning, which made it difficult to find prospective fosterers or owners. After all, who would want a cat displaying this type of aggression? The sad fact was, the longer Juice remained at the vet's, the more his behaviour declined. Still, his stunning marbled tabby coat and bright green eyes tugged at the heartstrings of the practice staff. They all agreed his aggression was due to emotional baggage as well as unsuitable homes, where owners weren't equipped to deal with his behavioural issues.

Silvia ended up taking him home, but even for an expert like her, Juice's behaviour proved a challenge. His outbursts came with no prior warning and he would often lie in wait under the sofa, launching attacks on whoever happened to walk past. Silvia believed the only way to stop him was by scruffing his neck. Unsurprisingly, Juice's behaviour didn't go down well with Silvia's friends, and it also impacted her vet flatmate, Andrea, who eventually recommended getting a cat behaviourist to assist. Silvia duly dropped me a query via email.

Silvia is a true animal lover who especially loves cats. I could see that she adored Juice but felt overwhelmed by what to do next. Sometimes she regretted bringing him home, but she also longed to understand his unpredictable outbursts better. It was all causing Silvia immense anxiety.

When Juice wasn't being aggressive he was a perfect gentleman and extremely affectionate. When I arrived for my first home visit he rolled over to show me his belly. 'Ha, I'm not falling for that one, Juice,' I thought. 'One touch and you'll have my arm for lunch!' I knew this much because Silvia had scars on each arm from succumbing to the temptation of giving Juice a jazz-hands belly rub.

Although Juice played with all of my hunting toys, I noticed he was extremely nervous of sounds. Silvia's home was a small flat that backed on to a car park and the noise of cars coming and going made him anxious. On some occasions the noise was enough to prompt an attack on Silvia, Andrea or a guest. Silvia revealed Juice's latest aggressive response occurred when he was woken by a mobile phone and that Juice also become agitated with neighbouring cats, who would encroach on the territory outside his cat flap. In addition, Silvia admitted the long periods Juice spent alone made him overexcited when a human appeared. If he was fussed over and petted for too long, he would attack.

After discussing Juice's history, I diagnosed him with redirected aggression and low petting aggression. Both are explosive and the former can appear to come out of nowhere. Juice's attacks were usually short. It was reassuring to know he could be stopped if the outbursts were disrupted, when Silvia scruffed him, after which he would run away rather than persist and his behaviour would quickly return to normal.

While we were chatting, Silvia revealed that once while Juice was being scruffed he had screamed. It's worth noting that contrary to popular belief, scruffing adult cats can be painful. Mother cats scruff their kittens using only light pressure on the neck to move them from danger. They don't scruff to reprimand. Owners who scruff their cats can antagonise them, causing an already agitated cat to become worse because they feel the need to act defensively. I always advise against scruffing, but I do understand why so many owners resort to it. After all, it's only natural to do whatever you can to halt an attack from an animal.

I now knew that Juice's problems were rooted in his environment. Silvia bought new stimulating toys, large climbers for indoors and modified the area around the cat flap so he could sit outside and still feel safe. Silvia also chose to put him on mild anti-anxiety medication, using her expertise as a vet to decide on the dosage.

While Juice's behaviour greatly improved, deep down we knew he needed a larger garden as well as humans who could be there for him more than his present carers. With Silvia's long working hours, Juice was lonely on his own. No amount of playtime could compensate for the hours he spent scared of noises and being intimidated by other cats roaming freely outside.

When the decision to rehome Juice was made, we were all thinking the same thing. I assisted with a flyer and YouTube video, and came up with the title 'Special-Needs Cat'. There was no other way to describe him; he had special needs and the list of requirements for his future home was rather long. We required an experienced cat lover with the time and patience to work with Juice, as well as a large open space for him to roam in. It was also important that they had no other cats. It was a tall order.

To help Silvia understand life from Juice's point of view, I asked her to write a brief paragraph speaking as him. I had seen Jackson Galaxy, the highly regarded US cat behaviourist, use this method on his TV show *My Cat From Hell*. It was a great, original idea and I made a mental note to use it when the right time came. Silvia's statement went on his poster, and I helped by writing the first line: 'Hello, my name is Juice and I'm looking for someone special to love me'.

Days later, Silvia sent her moving contribution.

It took me two days to write Juice's behaviour report, which is an essential part of the rehoming process. I didn't hold back on the level of aggression he sometimes displayed. Unfortunately, some early interest from one apparently perfect lady came to nothing. Whilst she was retired, wealthy, lived in a large home with huge grounds and had cared for cats all her life, she quickly distanced herself from taking on a 'project' (her words) like Juice after receiving the report. With our hopes dashed, Silvia spent the next 10 months continuing Juice's behaviour-modification plan, while we continued to search for his ideal home. It was a difficult time, with emotions running high. Silvia was wracked with guilt for leaving him alone while she went to work. Many times we wondered if the right person for Juice actually existed, while also knowing we just had to find them, for all our sakes. With the posters being shared all over social media, many people declared an interest, but then chose not to take things further.

Time was running out. Silvia was making plans to leave the UK to go travelling, which meant Juice would either have to go to another rescue centre, and perhaps remain there forever, or worse still, be put to sleep. The immense pressure was felt by both of us.

Just when I was on the verge of giving up hope, Silvia texted me to say she'd had interest from someone at her veterinary practice. They'd seen Juice's poster and, what's more, they seemed the perfect match. We had been there before but we waited for further news and prayed it would all work out. That weekend, Silvia visited the home and rang me afterwards, hardly able to contain her excitement.

'They are perfect!' she screamed down the phone.

'Have they read the report?' I asked cautiously.

'Yes, they said it doesn't matter. They will work with him'.

I still couldn't quite believe the good news. The prospective owners were a retired couple, who were passing the vets and saw Juice on the poster staring out at them. They read his story and fell in love, knowing they could offer just what he needed: empathy, time, patience and two huge hearts. They also had no other pets. It was a dream come true.

As a precaution, we arranged for Juice to spend the weekend with the couple to see how he would respond. He arrived with his toys, bedding, bowls and special blankets. By the end of the first day, Silvia had forwarded me several photos sent from the couple. One of them showed Juice basking in a sunspot in an armchair in the conservatory, which looked out on to a lovely large garden. He looked like a different cat. I was astounded.

'Has there been any aggression?' I asked tentatively over the phone.

'None at all,' said Silvia. 'They said he was very affectionate with them and straight away appeared relaxed in his quiet new home, relishing constant human companionship'.

Silvia was almost in tears. She no longer had to carry such guilt around and I told her she should be immensely proud of saving Juice's life when everyone else had given up on him.

Soon Juice was introduced to his garden and became a perfect hunter. His behaviour mellowed, and he even made friends with the gentle female moggy next door. His new owners haven't experienced any serious aggression.

I will never forget the compassion Silvia showed when she decided to save a young animal's life. That took courage and selflessness and Silvia will always be a star in my eyes. Meanwhile, Juice the Special-Needs Cat has two special owners and is living a very special life indeed.

CHAPTER FOURTEEN

Can Cats Be Therapy Pets?

*'I love cats because I enjoy my home; and little by little,
they become its visible soul.'*

Jean Cocteau

CHAPTER FOURTEEN

In this chapter:

- Discover the world of the therapy cat.
- Get inside knowledge from Isabel Serafim, the owner of famous mog London, who travels to hospitals to help clients.
- How to help pets who struggle with various issues themselves – what can we do to give back?

It's there for all to see. How animals make most of us feel. In moments when I'm enjoying people-watching over a coffee at a cafe, I zoom in on the delight that washes over the faces of animal-loving humans when they encounter a dog, and I hardly ever see someone walk past a cat on a wall without saying hello to them and reaching to pat their head. Animals make us feel something, and generally, if one isn't afraid of them, the emotion is joy. They help us to forget any worries in that moment for we understand that the animal we are greeting is living in that exact moment with us. They hold no malice or grudges and do not have the weight of life's tribulations, which we all seem to carry on our shoulders. Personally, I speak to all animals I encounter. The fact they cannot understand my light banter matters little. My words are an extension of my meaning and my meaning is love and connecting. When I'm feeling anxiety I walk to my local park and quietly watch the dogs running after their toys like it was a matter of life or death. Their excitement and pleasure is infectious. It's the same with watching cats play with the toys we bring them, or watching them rolling around in the sun.

It's now undisputed that animals help us emotionally and physically, with cat and dog owners volunteering their pets to companies such as Pets

As Therapy. The charity was founded in 1983 by Lesley Scott-Ordish. Originally called Pat Dogs, Lesley formed the charity because she recognised the misery and fear elderly dog owners felt when having to give up their pet to go into residential care[1]. Pat Dogs has expanded from nursing homes to hospitals, schools, hospices and other establishments, with support from the nursing field, who have seen massive differences in moods when their residents spend time with the animals.

Something magical happens to us when we stroke cats, especially when we hear them purring. It's said the purr has healing qualities, not only for the cat, but for the humans receiving it. Scientific studies have proven that the presence of a cat has been associated with reduction of stress and blood pressure, and therefore may reduce the risk of cardiovascular diseases[2].

Not that the cat, London, can reduce my stress levels when trying to groom him, but I'm pleased to announce my feline client recently received his certificate to fly the flag for the cats at Pets As Therapy. London's mummy, Isabel Serafim, was close at hand to answer some questions on London's work at the London Royal Hospital, an internationally renowned teaching hospital based in east London. I asked Isabel what made her decide to volunteer London as a therapy cat?

'I was looking for fun things that I could do with London and I just came across Pets As Therapy on the internet. I always thought that if I could spend more quality time with my cat, we would have a beautiful bond and he would be happier…'

In Conversation With Isabel Serafim

What's the criteria for deciding if a cat will be a good candidate for this type of work?

Firstly, as a cat guardian, you need to ensure that this would be something your cat would enjoy doing. London likes people. He likes the attention. He doesn't mind being fussed over by strangers and doesn't get stressed in new surroundings. When he does his volunteering as a Pets As Therapy

(PAT) cat we are sometimes in contact with vulnerable people. The PAT cat needs to be calm and relaxed and not to strike back if uncomfortable. It's of utmost importance for the cat and their guardian to have a strong bond, so the guardian can understand any signs of distress from the cat. It's also important the cat knows that their guardian will keep them safe.

Can any cat be a therapy cat?

Yes, providing they pass the assessment, have all their medical affairs in order, are at least nine months old and have been six months with their guardian. If they pass the assessment they will get a PAT certificate.

How does the process for certification work?

Once you are sure this is something that would make your cat happy then contact Pets As Therapy. You will have to submit your and your cat's application, but before you do this the cat needs to pass 'the exam'. This assessment can be conducted by a certified vet such as The London Cat Clinic. The cat will be tested in a variety of categories such as reaction to touch of strangers, reactions when facing an unfamiliar room, cleanliness and grooming, and overall behaviour and demeanour. When the cat passes the exam the application is submitted along with the medical records. There's also a vetting process whereby two people who know you well are asked to provide references.

What do you feel is the role of a therapy cat?

Cats have the ability to calm people. Dogs are wonderful PAT pets, but cats have a different energy about them, more relaxing.

We have been volunteering visiting more mature humans and people who have gone through trauma. In both these scenarios a cat visit equates to a gentle 'loving cuddle'. The biggest achievement is always the number of big smiles.

What would London's day look like on visit days?

On the day before the visit we turn on 'cat-calming perfume' at home. There are several products that help your cat to cope better with unfamiliar things such as Felliway and Pet Remedy. A thorough grooming session takes place as we need to ensure that London's claws are clipped so they are not sharp, and that he is clean. On the day of the visit he has an early breakfast to ensure no accidents happen whilst visiting. Then we put the harness on and pick up an outfit. My London is a very stylish cat, but the outfit is not only a fashion statement but also another coping tool for the cat. The outfit is sprayed previously with calming cat perfume, and once again we are just giving all the tools for the cat to be able to better face unfamiliar situations.

Then we go to the hospital. As soon as we leave home he is working, as he usually gets the attention from people on the street and on public transport. He doesn't travel in a traditional cat carrier, he goes in my shoulder cat bag. It's like he is carried on my lap.

He likes to see what the surroundings are, but at the same time feels safe as he is on my lap. Every time we leave the apartment he wears the harness and he is on a lead. The shoulder cat bag also has a clip inside to attach to the harness, therefore he has learned earlier on that there's no benefit to trying to escape. Also, the view from the bag is better than from the floor.

When in the hospital London is put on the floor and he is free to inspect what he wants and greet everyone in the lobby.

When we go to the wards we always have the company of someone from the hospital. My first obligation is to look after the cat and our institution partner's job is to look after their patients, in case of an unexpected occurrence.

The volunteering team from the hospital always checks with the wards beforehand if a PAT cat is welcome. It's very important to bear in mind there are protocols in place that we all need to follow to ensure we protect the patients' and health professionals' wellbeing as well as the cat.

The volunteering team have been wonderful showing us the ropes and taking us through all the protocols. For example: being mindful of allergies; every time someone strokes the cat we need to ensure we clean up the patient's hand with wet wipes to avoid cross contamination. Another example is whether London's visit to a person suffering from a mental illness will be beneficial to them, or could it trigger an unsettling state of mind whereby they may think the cat is there to attack them or that the cat is theirs, and I'm stealing their cat.

London is now familiar with the hospital and he walks around with his tail up like the hospital is his, and visits his friends on the ward one at a time.

What type of places has he visited so far, and can you talk us through some human responses?

Currently we visit the hospital, and given this is our first assignment we are working on building a routine. Once this activity is well established in his life, then we could consider other institutions.

The response has been amazing. The expression 'London made my day' is something we hear regularly. London provides an escape for patients and family members who are going through a difficult time. London's presence triggers happy conversations about our pets, how much we love them and how happy they make us.

It's interesting, London has an instinct about reading certain situations. He will walk on to the wards with his tail up, but we have also seen him refusing to enter a room. When we picked him up to take him to the patient in that particular room, the patient told us he was not a cat person so wasn't interested in seeing London. I have also seen the reverse whereby London didn't want to leave the side of a lady. The nurse told us that this lady in particular had just received bad news and could use some cheering up… how did he know?

Another lady 'runs' on her walker to fuss London and funnily enough, he runs towards her too.

The hospital can be a very lonely experience, especially if you don't speak English. London understands universal language and kindness. A lady who didn't speak English had a long conversation with London whilst fussing him and I'm sure he understood it all as he was there for her and she had the biggest smile.

All the stories have the same ending… big smiles.

All animal lovers get it. We all talk about how pets make us feel and there's no denying that being with our cats makes us happy. Mars Pet Care and the Human Animal Bond Research Institute conducted a study in 2019 on pets and human attachment connected to wellbeing, and found that a high percentage of people said their pets have helped with feelings of loneliness and helped them to cope or recover from mental-health or anxiety issues[3]. Other friends speak of this bond as 'companionship and loving acceptance of who I am', whilst others describe it as 'feelings of love, laughter and comfort'.

The perfect end to this chapter is something said to me by a very close friend, Mandy Bell, when talking of her relationship with her cat Pickle:

> Sharing life with Pickle has taught me one of the most important lessons a human can get: the realisation that actually, it's not all about me...how can it be? Because in the nicest possible way, it's all about him.

 **A CATTY SUM UP**

1. Cats have the ability to calm people.
2. A cat visit is a gentle 'loving cuddle'.
3. The biggest achievement is always the number of big smiles.

CAT CHAT

When Cats Need Therapy From Us

In this chapter we learned about the role of the PAT cat, who is confident and friendly and loves human attention. However, many cats struggle to shine. This could be because of past experiences with humans, or fear in an unknown place such as a rescue centre, or because a cat has spent much of their life as a feral street cat. There are so many situations and the context of each individual situation is important to determine whether a cat actually wants or needs a little helping hand from us. A perfect example of this is a semi-feral versus a feral cat. Semi-ferals or strays are much like feral cats in that they live on the streets. However, semi-ferals are usually more comfortable being close

to a human, with some having been owned in the past and, for whatever reason, now find themselves living on the street. Ferals are born free-living and are classified as wild and impossible to get close to or handle. The latter has never socialised with humans. A semi-feral cat may appear in your garden or close by your back door waiting to see if food is left. If you step close to this cat, it will run or hide, but if food is left and once the human has disappeared, the cat will step closer to enjoy the offering. It's possible that over time and with a tremendous amount of patience a street-living cat can become a pet. It takes effort from the human to shake off any expectations and work only with what the cat is giving out. Little by little you may see the smallest of steps towards trusting you. What may seem like very slow progress is huge from the cat's perspective.

When I use the word 'pet' it shouldn't be read as a cat we can suddenly start to furiously stroke or pick up on a whim. Getting a street cat to step inside a home is a big feat for them. They are moving one step closer to being a pet that enjoys a home as well as enjoying the great outdoors. Shutting a street cat in can cause huge distress and then trust is broken down again.

Other cats that need a great deal of understanding are the hissing, fearful, nervous cats that everybody walks past when visiting a rescue centre. These cats are overlooked because who would want to take on a challenging cat with behaviour issues? Most of these issues arise from past experiences and to help a cat get past them we must understand that the present has been written from the past, and because of this we are seeing a cat cloaked in fear and distrust. In time cloaks can be lifted. Take Nelly, for instance.

Nelly was rescued from a neglectful situation and lived partly on the streets and partly in a home where she was fearful of the dogs and other cats. When a friend of mine, Cathy Ocelot, decided to approach the owners to ask if she could give Nelly a loving home, the cat was frozen with fear in a gap behind the washing machine. The owners agreed that Nelly could go. Poor Nelly continued to be so scared in her new home that Cathy hardly ever saw her. We would all ask 'Where's Nelly?' on a daily basis, as Cathy struggled to keep up on her hiding places. Whenever Cathy discovered Nelly's hidey-hole, a new hiding place was established the following day. After months of this behaviour Cathy phoned me for advice.

On the day of the call, Nelly was discovered on top of a high cabinet in the living room. With a small bundle of fur showing, Nelly was curled into a tight ball and so far back she may as well have been glued to the wall. I knew this could go on forever if Nelly couldn't understand or feel the loving intentions of her new humans. She would only ever eat at night when no one was around and was never seen during the day, so how could Nelly ever be helped to get past this stage? She couldn't if the paths of cat and human never met. We had to go to Nelly, on her terms, and progress with tiny benchmarks.

I advised a ladder be bought. If Nelly could never get past the fear of coming down from her high spots when a human was around then we had to go up high to her level. It was a jackpot moment. Cathy purchased a ladder the moment our call ended. Upon climbing to the top of the cupboard and with Nelly not able to run, she slowly laid down some food and then held her hand out for Nelly to sniff. Suddenly, a little purr rang out and Nelly bravely head butted the hand. Nelly wasn't an aggressive cat. She was extremely timid but with a small challenge to help her trust the situation she slowly blossomed into the most loving cat.

She is still very shy with strangers and runs when there's a noise she doesn't like outside, but Nelly now sleeps on Cathy's lap and 'owns the room' with confidence when she feels particularly brave. It took months of perseverance to get to this stage but the breaking moment was helping her to see that there was nothing to fear and helping her to feel there was nothing but love and kindness being channelled her way. Naturally, every cat is different. Some distrusting cats will hiss and lash out if cornered, so context and cat personalities always dictate how one should approach a situation that needs healing. Funnily enough, Cathy messaged me saying: 'Nelly has started acting like a cat and sitting at the balcony window watching the birds! It's only taken her a year'.

When I was younger and ran a cat-sitting company, I was asked to care for a sweet Persian cat called Anouse. Anouse was an indoor-only cat and terrified of visitors. Her mummy had to work away from home on a regular basis and so began the journey of sitting Anouse and trying to earn her trust. It took at least six months for her to allow me to stroke her and then, bingo! – she was all over me. I will never forget her slithering close to the ground like a snake, trying to get to her food bowl in the kitchen, as I sat in the living room quietly and at a distance. By making herself small she was telling me she was frightened and not a threat. Any movement on my part would see her turn to stone like a statue, looking into the distance as if hoping to become invisible. Walking towards her would be met with a hiss and growl and then a frantic rush for the nearest bed or sofa to belly-crawl under.

Before I cared for Anouse I met her on several occasions with the one person she trusted, her human mummy. When it was time to care for her I would sit quietly reading a book to allow her to feel relaxed walking past me to where her food bowl was placed. After time I began to introduce her to smelly toys that excite cats, such as catnip and valerian, and would toss them to the other side of the room. These toys would be placed closer to where I was sitting as time went on. Gradually, Anouse became less afraid and bolder. She would still hiss but I think it was more habit and not knowing what to do than a real threat to me. After months of her becoming more accustomed to my presence I started to hold out my hand for her to sniff. One day, whilst she was sniffing my hand I slowly wiggled my finger to stroke under her chin. She liked it, I could tell. Any more and she would have backed off and so I continued with slow steps, moving from her chin to her cheeks.

The biggest moment for me was when she flopped down relaxed and invited me to stroke her tummy. Now, this could have gone either way. We all know the tummy game whereby we are given a green light to stroke this area, only to be sent off with a red card and a scratch. However, I decided to see what would transpire and rubbed her belly. Anouse loved it. She couldn't get enough! It was a moment I will never forget. She still needed a box on its side as a precaution to play with me. The box gave her a retreat and was her safety 'castle'. She would sit in the box and play with a rod toy for the whole visit.

With both of the above examples, it's trust that helped these cats take a step further into our world. Everything depends on building positive new experiences to get past negative ones. Sometimes, a happy compromise for both cat and human is a cat who is comfortable sitting close-by without wanting us to encroach further into their space. An unspoken language is being understood and respected and that's pretty cool in my eyes.

When starting the journey of healing with a timid or frightened cat, it's best to encourage play and bonding, using gentle toys such as pipe cleaners or a piece of string so that the toys are not threatening to them. Food offerings should be irresistible like chunks of warm roast chicken or smelly fish like pilchards, mackerel, prawns or tuna (the latter unsalted and in spring water). Anything that is not the typical daily food could be very enticing and could help break down barriers more easily. But first of all, start by sitting quietly with the cat and make no attempt to touch. Allow them to feel a calm presence. Keep the sessions short and leave behind a treat for them to eat when you leave. Over time and with the cat gaining confidence, gentle play sessions can be encouraged.

For feral cats, leaving food and a warm shelter, near to your home, can be enough to aid survival in the winter months. Ensure the food and shelter are placed sufficiently away from the home so that your cat doesn't react to other cats within its core territory.

Caring for and loving another being outside of yourself is something everyone should try to experience. The world would be a much better place if we truly understood that life is all about love and we, as the human race, have a duty to make this planet better for all of earth's creatures, not just the ones we recognise as pets.

A mouse fully relaxed in my company seeing a toy mouse for the first time

CHAPTER FIFTEEN

How To Care For Elderly Cats

'Prowling his own quiet backyard or asleep by the fire, he is still only a whisker away from the wilds'.

Jean Burden

CHAPTER FIFTEEN

In this chapter:

- Get definitive expert veterinary advice on caring for elderly cats, in conversation with Dr. Amy Bergs.
- Get expert tips on how to give medication to cats and food to fussy eaters.
- Learn how to cope with the emotional trauma of losing a pet.

I love the elders. They are my favourite grooming clients for sure. Some are deaf, some have painful joints and some have stopped grooming. I am most thankful for the ones that don't have teeth. The elders can still be feisty little tinkers! Older cats need a helping hand, just like humans do, and this includes: checking claws on a regular basis to ensure they don't grow too long and embed into the paw pad; grooming on a regular basis to clean the ears, eyes and coat; checking the gums and teeth to ensure there are no nasty surprises (bad breath can mean there's something not right either in the mouth or the tummy); and buying movement aids like pet steps so that they can join their humans on the sofa or bed without the need to jump. It's easy to forget how old our cats are but this should help: At the age of 6 months your cat is 10 human years; at 2 years, 24; 6 years, 40; 10 years, 56; 14 years, 72; and at 20 years they are 96 human years[1]. Comparing their age in human years can give us empathy with their daily challenges.

I recently worked with an elderly cat called Harley. When I first met Harley, a beautiful 18-year-old Persian, he was matted all over with the most shocking clumps I have ever seen. He was so skinny that it took two separate visits to de-mat him. Unfortunately, his delicate age meant it wouldn't have been wise to sedate him. From that moment forward Harley became the cat who I would take under my wing. I never wanted to see Harley suffer again and, seeing that the owner was an elderly gentleman who could little afford my services regularly, I offered to visit Harley every month free of charge. This went on for a year until, sadly, Harley passed away. On my visits I would clip his hardened claws, wash his face and check over his body to ensure no matting had formed. He couldn't walk by the end of my visits so Harley was seen on his favourite bed in the living room. The owner, a Muslim gentleman, didn't know how to thank me. On one occasion he clasped my head in his hands and gently kissed my forehead. He then said sorry for having broken a protocol.

I saw my visits to Harley as special, and Harley's owner saw me as an angel, although I was always embarrassed when he called me this. Now I know Dr. Amy Bergs' visits would be looked upon in the same way by her clients. An angel with a calling.

Dr. Amy Bergs is a veterinary surgeon with a special interest in feline internal medicine and preventative healthcare. She is also the founder of The Cat Doctor, an at-home veterinary care service. She was kind enough to chat to me about caring for our elderly furry companions, something she does so well.

In Conversation With Dr. Amy Bergs

Can you tell me a little about common illnesses in our elders?

The two most common diseases we see in our practice are arthritis and dental disease, which many people don't think of as illnesses. Nearly every elderly cat we see has some degree of pain in their joints, with the lower spine, hips, knees, shoulders and elbows often affected. Because it comes on slowly and cats simply adapt their lifestyle to their increasing pain levels, many owners are shocked to learn that their cat has been coping with a considerable amount of pain on a daily basis. A study in 2002[2] found radiographic evidence of arthritis in 90% of cats over the age of 12.

Dental disease is also incredibly common. I cannot remember the last cat over 10 that I saw without some form of it. Cats can get periodontal disease just like humans and dogs, but they also get a special type of dental disease called 'tooth resorption' where the body decides to eat away at the teeth from the inside, resulting in painful holes and broken teeth. Much like arthritis pain, cats with dental pain rarely show it and they will continue to eat normally. It isn't until you go looking for it that you uncover the true extent of the disease and realise how painful it must be.

After arthritis and dental disease, the next most common illness is chronic kidney disease. Cats can have the early stages of kidney disease for several years before it becomes clinically apparent, so unless a cat has been tested to rule it out, we almost have to assume that they have some degree of kidney failure. Kidney disease causes weight loss, decreased appetite, dehydration and lethargy, all things that people often incorrectly associate with 'normal' ageing in cats, and can have a considerable effect on both longevity and quality of life in affected cats.

Other illnesses common in older cats include hyperthyroidism (excessive growth of the thyroid gland resulting in a dangerously high metabolic rate), pancreatitis (inflammation of the pancreas with associated gastrointestinal signs), diabetes, hypertension (high blood pressure), cognitive dysfunction (feline dementia) and cancer. It's worth noting that aside from arthritis and dental disease, which have almost no clinical signs, most of the common illnesses that older cats present with similar symptoms, making screening tests such as blood samples, urine testing and blood-pressure measurement critically important.

What should cat carers be looking out for in elderly cats?

The most important thing to remember about elderly cats is that they won't show any signs of illness until it becomes absolutely necessary for them to do so. Cats are both predators and prey animals who assume that every other creature is out to get them, so the last thing they want to do is to appear ill in any way. This means that most signs of illness in cats are very subtle.

Keeping an eye on body weight and muscle condition is very important. Although a bit of fat and muscle loss can occur, visible changes almost always indicate that something is wrong. We sometimes recommend carers obtain a set of baby-weighing scales to keep a closer eye on their cat's weight, as changes that seem small to us can actually equate to a large percentage of a cat's body weight, indicating a problem. Appetite is another thing to monitor, although – I cannot stress this enough – most cats experiencing pain eat normally.

One of the phrases that upsets me most is 'But, he was still eating so I thought he was OK!' This has resulted in countless cats suffering unnecessarily. Cats eat to survive, often regardless of how much pain they are in. Some illnesses increase the appetite (such as hyperthyroidism, diabetes and inflammatory bowel disease) while others decrease it, usually due to nausea (as in the case of kidney disease or pancreatitis) even if they are not actually vomiting. Appetite may or may not correlate with weight loss, as several diseases cause cats to eat more yet still lose weight.

Going off particular foods after several days can also be a sign of nausea or abdominal pain and changes in the way cats eat (not chewing on one side, suddenly preferring wet food to dry, dropping food out the mouth, etc) can indicate dental pain. So, although it is important to monitor how much your cat is eating and how they do so, it is not the only measure of how ill your cat is.

Most cats (unless they are on an exclusively dry diet) don't drink from water bowls often. As a desert species, they naturally evolved to get most of their fluids from their prey. Their thirst drive is actually quite low, so in today's world of processed dry cat biscuits, it is easy for them to become dehydrated, especially as they get older. However, many of the illnesses above result in increased thirst. If you see your cat at the water bowl more regularly or notice the water level going down faster than before, or perhaps they are hanging around the sink more often in search of a dripping tap, you should consult your vet as it could be a sign of illness. The phrase 'Oh, yes, she has been drinking very well lately' sets off alarm bells because carers often don't realise that cats don't normally drink much. However, different diets can result in different levels of water intake, so pay particular attention to sudden changes and long-term trends, not just the actual amount your cat is drinking.

It's also helpful to monitor your cat's activity levels and other daily routines. Have they been upstairs as much lately? Are they hesitating before jumping up where they used to do so with ease? Have they changed the way they get down from the sofa? Are they spending less time with the family and more time under the dining table? Or have they recently become more 'clingy', following you around the house? Subtle changes in their daily routine are often the only sign you get that your cat may be in pain or unwell.

Similarly, changes in behaviour can also indicate illness. Have they started to howl at night? Do they no longer seem to hear their dinner being prepared or startle easily when you approach? Do they seem to forget you have just fed them or spend long periods of time simply staring at the wall? Behavioural changes such as these are not necessarily a normal part of the ageing process and can indicate sight or hearing loss, high blood pressure, cognitive dysfunction or other illnesses.

It's also worth noting any gastrointestinal signs your cat may be showing. Vomiting – even if it is 'just' grass or 'just' hairballs – is probably not normal if it occurs more than about once a month, and can indicate intestinal disease. Similarly, changes in stool consistency can be a sign that not all is well. Diarrhoea is often seen with illnesses such as inflammatory bowel disease or cancer, and many metabolic diseases cause dehydration, which results in hard, dry stools. Constipation is particularly common in older cats and, although rarely life threatening, can have a significant effect on the quality of their life.

Name a common misconception about our elders?

'Well, he is getting older so I thought it was normal...'

Age is not a disease. Although some changes do occur with age, the vast majority of weight loss, changes in appetite, decreases in activity level and behavioural changes are NOT normal and actually indicate treatable illness. Dental disease is not normal, even in very old cats, nor is joint pain. It's very important for carers of older cats to realise that just because a particular condition is common, that doesn't make it normal. Some of the most common diseases of older cats can be managed very effectively to make them much more comfortable.

What can a cat carer do when their elderly pet refuses medication and is a fussy eater, so won't eat any special food to aid their condition?

Although it's a natural instinct for cats to change their dietary preferences occasionally, being a very fussy eater may not be normal and can indicate illness. This, of course, does not help when it comes to treating an illness as the easiest way to give a cat medication is to put it in their food, or when the food itself has been prescribed to treat them.

Prescription diets can be tricky as they're usually meant to be fed exclusively (i.e. no treats or other types of food allowed) for maximum efficacy. Although they can work well if the cat eats them, there are many times when the cat refuses. If your cat eats the food but without great enthusiasm, there's a chance that perseverance will allow you to successfully transition them on to the diet. If, however, they refuse and go on 'hunger strike' for more than 24 hours, it's not safe to continue trying and you will need to feed them an alternative or consider introducing the diet more slowly. It's also not acceptable for your cat to lose weight, energy or muscle condition on a prescription diet because they will only eat enough of it to barely survive. Many vets put too much emphasis on prescription diets in my opinion. If your cat will happily eat them, great. If not, try to look at the bigger picture, as starving them or forcing them to eat something they dislike is probably not in their best interest. If your cat hates or fails to thrive on the food that your vet has prescribed, ask for a different treatment option.

Although there may not be an easy alternative for medications, there may be a different brand that your cat accepts more. Most carers find liquids easier to administer than tablets, although if the tablet is well hidden that can sometimes be easier. Many tablets and liquids come in flavoured versions, which can enhance their palatability. Some medications even come in transdermal gels that can be rubbed into the skin of the ear.

As a feline-only practice, we hear about cats not wanting to take their medications on a daily basis. In the vast majority of cases, a solution can be found. If there are no alternatives and you have to give a particular tablet, here are some of our favourite tips and tricks:

1. Hide the tablet in a treat – there are various pill putties, pill pockets and soft jerky treats on the market which very effectively mask the flavour of medications, provided you fully conceal the medication (use tweezers to avoid handling the medication and transferring the taste if you have to). If those fail, soft human foods, in very small quantities, may often be used such as soft cheese, butter, Marmite, pâté or a single prawn (cut a slit in the middle and insert the tablet). Your cat may take the treat directly, or you may be able to hide the treat itself in a small amount of food.

2. Hide the tablet in food – most tablets can be crushed (check with your vet first) and mixed into a small amount of wet food or cat milk or those little cat yogurt sachets. It's OK to use special treats that you wouldn't normally want to feed a healthy cat, just use the smallest amount possible. For best results, give the small amount of medicated food first thing in the morning or just before dinner, as they are more likely to eat it if they are hungry.

3. Cover it with catnip – if your cat won't take the pill wrapped in a treat on its own, try rolling the medicated treat ball in catnip (or crushed dry cat treats if they prefer) to make it even nicer. You can also sprinkle dried catnip or crushed treats over food to encourage them to eat it.

4. Chill the medication before giving it – cold medications don't taste as strong as warm ones, so try keeping the medicine in the fridge before administration.

5. Hide the tablet in a gel cap – you can order empty gelatine capsules from your vet or online and place the tablet into them. This hides the flavour of the medication as the gel cap itself is relatively tasteless.

By far the best way to give a cat medication is for them to take it willingly, which is why we prefer the first five methods. If, however, you simply have to get a short course of medication into your cat and they absolutely refuse to eat it on their own, there are a few other things you can try:

1. Take advantage of your cat's desire to be clean – crush the tablet and mix it into hairball paste or another paste-like treat and rub the mixture around their lips or on to their paws where, most of the time, they will lick it off. Beware though, they may instead choose to shake it all over your walls and, to be fair, I can't say I would blame them…

2. Syringe it in – most tablets and capsules can be crushed and mixed with 1–2 ml of nice tasting yogurt or cat milk or tuna juice to create a liquid that can be syringed directly into the mouth. Keep an eye on them for a few minutes after giving it, however, as if your cat finds the medication particularly distasteful, this may result in excessive salivation and foaming at the mouth. Although not pleasant, this is generally not harmful and just means you need to move on to plan B (or C, or D…).

3. Administer the pill directly into their mouth – some cats don't seem to mind it too much, but this is probably my least favourite option. If none of the other tricks work and your cat's health depends on it, it is certainly worth trying. Holding the cat between your knees or gently wrapped in a towel (some cats feel more comfortable that way, others hate it), pop the tablet covered in a small amount of treat directly into their mouth either by opening their lower jaw and putting it in the front, or sneaking it in the side (provided you can do so safely). There are many resources on how to do this safely and effectively online, so do your research first and remember, this really is a last resort as it probably has the greatest impact on the bond you share with your cat.

If you make it all the way down to the bottom of the list without luck, or you are able to administer the medication but you feel that your relationship with your cat is suffering as a result, then it's worth having a discussion with your vet about whether or not the medication they have prescribed is really necessary. Ask your vet what would happen if your cat didn't get this medication, to make an educated decision together about what is in the best interest of your cat. In some cases, your cat may actually be happier overall without the medication. Whatever you do, don't be ashamed and hide the fact that you can't give the medication from your vet – it's much safer if your vet understands the real situation so they can work with you to find another solution. It may be that surgery or an alternative treatment method may actually be less stressful for everybody involved.

Can you talk us through palliative home care? What does it involve and what are the main benefits?

Many carers, and sadly still many vets too, think that once a cat gets very old or has been diagnosed with a terminal condition, there is 'simply nothing else we can do' for them. This is rarely true. Vets are very good at diagnosing and treating illness but have a tendency to back away when treatment options start to dry up. At this point, when symptoms persist despite medical treatment, it is particularly important to look at the cat as a whole rather than just a disease, and ask if there is anything else we can do to make them more comfortable. Some vets are better at this than others, so it is often up to the carer to look after their cat's comfort level and advocate for palliative care.

All cats deserve palliative care so if you request this and are refused, it is absolutely acceptable for you to seek a second opinion. There are now veterinary practices, usually mobile, that specialise in palliative care so if you are fortunate enough to have one in your area, give them a ring.

Although some clinic visits may be necessary, the best place to provide palliative care is usually at home, where the cat is already most comfortable and where they spend all of their time. If your vet or vet nurse is able to provide home visits, this is a brilliant way of getting your cat the care they need without the stress of travelling to the surgery. At this stage it's all about quality of life.

The focus of palliative care is on comfort rather than cure. The first thing people usually think of is pain relief, and this is indeed a large part of palliative care at home. Pain care can come in many forms, from tablets and liquids to injections, acupuncture, massage and other complementary therapies. Your vet can prescribe pain care, although you may need to offer suggestions if they are not particularly forthcoming. Again, if you request pain care and are refused, or are told that there is no 'safe' option for your cat, consider a second opinion, as some vets are more knowledgeable in this area than others.

When considering palliative care, it is important to remember that there is more to quality of life than just pain relief. Nausea is extremely uncomfortable and unfortunately, many of the illnesses cats get later in life can cause them to feel sick. There is effective treatment for nausea that can be given at home, so if your cat starts to turn away from their food (especially if they seem hungry) or lick their lips when presented with food, consider treatment for nausea. Dehydration is another condition that can result in considerable discomfort. Extra fluids can be provided orally or even given by injection under the skin at home to relieve this with excellent success, especially in the earlier stages of illness.

Despite everyone's best efforts, there is a limit to what palliative care can provide, because the underlying condition will continue to progress despite it. There is also a limit to what some cats will tolerate, so you have to pay attention to and respect your cat's wishes. If, after trying all the options which are acceptable to you and your cat, you are still told that there is nothing else that can be done, it's worth taking a moment to step back and reconsider the quality of your cat's life. It's so easy to focus on trying every available option while at the same time losing sight of the sentient being you are trying to help. Remember, it's all about comfort and happiness and if that is no longer possible, no matter how much we may want our cat to keep fighting for our sake, carrying on isn't always in their best interest.

What can cat carers do to help their elderly cats live comfortably?

Take time to observe their routines and make notes – has anything changed recently? If mobility is a problem (and you can pretty much assume it is the older they get), make sure they have a litter tray on every level of the house, so they don't have to climb stairs or use the cat flap every time they need the toilet (would you send your 90-year-old grandmother down the stairs and out of the back door to use the toilet at 2 a.m.?). Similarly, keep food and water bowls on all floors for easy access. Raising the food and water dishes up to head height can ease pressure on a sore neck and back. Pet-safe heat pads and cosy beds near the radiator can work wonders on sore joints. For cats with severely decreased mobility or those that cannot see, shrink their world (i.e. their core resources such as litter tray, food, water and comfortable place to lie) down to a level that they can cope with, with close monitoring to make sure they are still able to get up and change position and get to where they need to be. Sore joints also make grooming difficult, so help them out with a brush or comb and be prepared to spot-clean any areas that require particular attention (especially the backside!).

For cats with underlying metabolic disease, offering wet food instead of dry will not only make it much easier to administer medications but also help treat dehydration. Changing the food to something that is easier to eat, watering it down or blending it can make life easier for cats with dental disease. Heating the food and switching foods regularly can help cats with poor appetites, as their sense of taste and smell declines in old age. More frequent vet and nurse checks (preferably at home to minimise stress) can help pick up new ailments before they have a chance to negatively affect their quality of life.

Finally, remember that older cats hate change and take great comfort in routines. Avoid moving the furniture around or introducing new things (especially new animals) into the house, as new things are a source of stress. Regular routines for feeding, napping, etc are incredibly comforting for older cats, so try to avoid changing their schedule whenever possible. If it is a particularly busy household, be sure to provide safe places around the house where your cat can retreat when needed. Calming pheromones and catnip can ease anxiety naturally.

Don't forget to play with them from time to time too. It's important to not only address their changing physical needs, but their psychological needs as well.

What are your personal thoughts regarding home euthanasia and surgery euthanasia?

Euthanasia (which literally means 'good death'), if done well, is usually more stressful on the carer than it is on the cat. Although cats feel pain and anxiety and have great concern for what happens to them and those around them, they do not have a sense of their own destiny and do not fear death itself in the same way we do. They do not think of how empty the house will feel without them, or how much their human companions will miss them when they are gone, nor do they spend time contemplating all of the things they should have been able to accomplish during their lives that they probably won't get a chance to do. These are human thoughts, and it is very important that we do not project this fear on to our cats.

Euthanasia is used to end suffering, and is an incredibly valuable final gift that we are able to give to our feline companions. As long as it is performed as respectfully as possible, with as little pain, anxiety and inconvenience for the cat as the situation allows, then it has been done well. This can take place in a clinic, or it can take place at home – different situations may necessitate one choice over another, which is fine.

Because many cats find the journey to the clinic itself stressful, it seems natural to assume that home euthanasia is best. This is not because the procedure is any different. It just removes all of the other anxiety that comes with a trip to the surgery. As a mobile vet, I feel that our home euthanasia visits are some of the most important visits we make, as it is usually a calmer, quieter environment, away from strange people and animals, and both the cats and their carers feel more comfortable as a result. I advocate home euthanasia whenever possible, but must stress that there are times when this is not practical or sensible and that is OK too. If the cat is already in the surgery at the time the decision to euthanise them is made, for example, it would be more stressful for that cat to return home. Home visits are often more expensive so if it simply isn't something that you are able to provide, you should not feel as though you have let your cat down as a result. There may also be times when the vet is simply unable to attend a home visit at the time euthanasia is required (and as a result, a planned euthanasia is usually far less stressful for everyone involved than waiting until the very last minute) and the prolonged suffering required to wait until they are available may not be in the cat's best interest. Overall, a 'good' euthanasia is the least stressful one for your cat given the circumstances you are presented with at the time, whatever that may be.

What is your criteria, moral stance, etc when guiding cat owners to the hardest decision they will have to make – which is that it's time to say goodbye? Do you make that decision for them or just guide them towards it? What do you look out for in terms of knowing it's time to let go?

I've always thought that knowing when to say goodbye to your beloved companion is one of the hardest decisions you will ever have to make. Sometimes you just 'know'. They look at you one day and the sparkle has left their eye and they just tell you they have had enough. Other times however, particularly if their decline has been slow and steady, it can be difficult to know when enough is enough. I am, therefore, often asked 'What would you do?'

One of the most important things a carer can do is completely remove their own emotions from the decision-making process. Easier said than done I know, but if you can do it, the answer is often more obvious. I have heard countless times from owners who seriously regret not electing euthanasia for their cat sooner, because they ended up 'keeping them going' for their own sake, not their cat's sake. Acknowledge how much you will miss them, tell them how much you love them, then return your focus back to their needs, not yours.

But what are their needs? They can't tell us how they feel and what they want. They can, however, display certain behaviours that, once we interpret them, do give us a good idea of how they're feeling. When attempting to determine your cat's quality of life (which I recommend you do regularly as they get older), there are certain questions that can really help:

- What does your cat most enjoy in life, and are they still able to do those things?

- Think about their normal daily routines – are they sticking to them or have they changed significantly?

- Do they appear to be in more pain than we can reasonably expect them to cope with, and how often are they experiencing that pain?

- Are they able to eat with their usual level of enjoyment or has it become a chore for them?

- Are they keeping themselves clean or have they lost interest in or the ability to groom? Are they urinating/defecating in inappropriate places because they are not able to get into the tray?

- Are they spending their entire day in their bed, only getting up to eat and toilet?

- Do they seem happy, quick to purr when stroked and acknowledge your presence? Or do they seem depressed, disinterested in what is going on around them?

- Are they still happy to interact with the family or do they prefer to hide away? A cat who is very near the end of their life will often take themselves off away from people and other animals.

The answers are unique to each individual cat, and what is acceptable for one cat may be unacceptable for another. As a result, it is the change in behaviour that is perhaps most important, especially when multiple changes come together to form a steep downward trend.

It's worth noting that, although decreased appetite can certainly be a sign of declining quality of life, the association does not work the other way around. Cats with a poor quality of life may eat normally; this just means that they are hungry, not that they are happy or comfortable. Measure appetite, but realise that in some cats their quality of life becomes unacceptable long before they lose their desire to eat. Equally, the fact that your cat is purring does not always mean that they are happy. A happy cat will start to purr as normal when we stroke or talk to them, but cats can also purr when they are in pain or scared. A softer more constant purr often unrelated to your actions can actually be a sign that your cat's quality of life is dangerously low.

Interestingly, some cats seem to show some improvement a few days before death. We're not exactly sure why this happens (the same thing happens in people) but if your terminally ill cat seems to rally for a day or two then take a sudden turn for the worse, this is a good indication that it is time to say goodbye.

If a carer is unsure whether or not the time is right for euthanasia, I always discuss their cat's situation using the guidance above and help them come to their own conclusion. It is very important that they feel they are making the right decision, even if they are incredibly upset by it. That said, I understand how difficult it can be to take responsibility for the death of a loved one and sometimes carers are unable to do so. If they simply cannot make the decision themselves and ask for my assistance, I will take that responsibility, advocate on behalf of my patient and tell them when I feel the time is right for their cat.

With this amount of valuable information, our elders can rely on us to recognise when things are not going according to the cat plan and guide us through all the ups and downs of cat care at the senior end of the scale. The palliative cat care that Dr. Amy Bergs gives really is worth its weight in gold. Not only does she understand cats but she also understands the humans who have invested a good number of years in that companionship. Thus, a delicate path has to be trodden.

My most senior grooming cat was called Flower, who reached the grand old age of 102 human years. She was so tiny and light you could fit her in a giant's eggcup but she was also feisty and stubborn, telling me off on every visit. At the age of 20 (100 in human years), I convinced the owners to write to the Queen to see if we could get her a card. If anyone outside of the UK is baffled by this then let me explain. When any UK resident reaches the age of 100 they automatically get a signed card from the Queen congratulating them on their 100th birthday. Why should it be any different for cats? Unfortunately, we didn't get a signed card for Flower but we did get a letter from Buckingham Palace.

Flower's letter from the Queen's Lady in Waiting

A CATTY SUM UP

1. Age is not a disease.

2. The most important thing about elderly cats is that they won't show any signs of illness until it becomes absolutely necessary for them to do so.

3. Cats eat to survive, regardless of how much pain they are in.

CAT CHAT

Saying Goodbye

Saying the final goodbye to our pets is the hardest decision some of us have to make, and it was no different for a friend of mine who owned a sweet cat called Boris.

Boris was a young, grey, skinny stray cat when found by Shana. Having been a street cat for most of his life, his health was in a shocking state. Due to malnutrition, most of his teeth had fallen out, with the exception of his canine teeth, which led to a lifetime of mashed wet food. Kibble hurt his mouth too much, so he avoided it.

He was the love of Shana's life and rather than leave him in the US, Boris was flown over to join her when she decided to move to the UK. When I met Boris he was 13. He was so skinny that

I initially thought something was amiss. Boris was a fussy eater and refused to eat most brands of commercial wet food, but I was assured that he had always been underweight. For most of his life, Shana and other professionals thought of ways to fatten him up.

Boris was 15 when he started to show signs of deteriorating. He became so dangerously underweight that it was making him ill and lethargic. When Boris reached 16, Shana knew she was in trouble. Boris was now showing signs of dementia, forgetting where his food, water and litter tray were. To get Boris to eat he had to be physically placed time and time again in front of his food bowl, as he would wander off mid-meal. Shana sought help from a mobile vet and chose one that offered feline end-of-life care and guidance.

It's not an easy decision to make, to know when it's the right time to euthanise your pet. I know because I had to make that decision with my cat Figgy, who had kidney disease. Whenever my husband and I decided on the day to say goodbye, Figgy would awake with a spring in her step, purring away. Then a day later she would be hiding again with no purrs to be heard. Shana was guided every step of the way with Boris, as the vet would visit the home and give her encouragement and advice. Shana told me that she really wanted someone else to say when the time was right to say goodbye, but the vet presented the facts to allow her to make that final and difficult decision that we all dread. I guess vets do not want to be held responsible should the client have any regrets, but to hear expert advice and continued support in these circumstances is priceless. As Professor Noel Fitzpatrick rightly states: 'When faced with questions of ethics, it is at both the hearts of the vets and the families to determine the best quality of life for their loved ones'.

The time to finally say goodbye to Boris was when a low level of morphine was being injected every day to help alleviate the pain he was feeling from arthritis and when he became incontinent. Reminiscing, Shana knows she probably went on for too long with Boris, battling for months with the final decision.

Euthanising your pet is painful and many people cannot face the procedure at home, preferring to take their pet to their veterinary practice, but it is important to try and help them in their last moments on earth by making decisions on what is best for them overall. It is far better for your cat to remain within the comfort of their home, if this option is available and circumstances allow, where they have experienced love, joy and closeness, and for you to remain by their side as they slip peacefully to sleep. All vets offer a home visit for this type of service so don't be afraid of asking.

When your pet has been put to rest, there are various options to consider for your final goodbye and for the mourning process. My choice was to take Figgy to a pet crematorium where we arranged for a solo cremation. We were given a private chapel where Figgy was laid out on her favourite blanket and my husband and I were given time to say our final farewell before she was taken away for the cremation. Her ashes were put in a sculptured pet urn and I put a tiny amount of ashes in a jewellery locket, which I wear on a chain around my neck. Others use their gardens to bury their pets or scatter ashes on a place favoured by their pet or themselves.

Whatever is decided, it is important to realise that new emotions will brew a horrid concoction that will need time to surface, breathe and then evaporate.

Psychiatrist Elizabeth Kübler Ross examined the five stages of grief in her 1969 book *Death and Dying*[1]. The emotional stages – denial, anger, bargaining, depression and acceptance – described how people may cope with death and illness, but was extended to any form of serious loss upon later reflection. Whether all five are experienced when we lose a pet is irrelevant. Emotions change drastically and we could even add guilt to the above because some may feel guilty about making the final decision or, indeed, leaving that decision too long as in Boris's story above.

Eliza Henry-Jones, a psychology, grief, loss and trauma counsellor, states:

> For many of us, deciding when to euthanise a pet is the only time we are confronted with a life-or-death decision. This decision is compounded by the fact that we cannot ask them what they want. We make the choice entirely on our own and the responsibility and guilt of it can be crushing[2].

Our pets are our constant companions and they leave behind a huge void, so it's inevitable that the change will unsteady us and temporarily turn our world upside down. Indeed the *New England Journal of Medicine* reported in October 2017 that a woman experienced 'broken heart syndrome' after her pet died – a condition in which the response to grief is so severe the person exhibits symptoms that mimic a heart attack, including elevated hormone levels that can be 30 times greater than normal[3]. Our pets play a role in our lives just like the humans we become close to, yet why do we become embarrassed when expressing grief at the loss of that important role in our lives? In many ways, grief then becomes much harder when it does involve an animal who we have become close with, because we feel silly expressing such deep emotions of grief that aren't connected to the loss of a human life.

This is where friends and family can help. Recognising and, more importantly, understanding, the devastation a person can feel when losing a cherished pet and offering a listening ear is crucial. Who would think a pet could cause someone to feel so bereaved? Luckily, in the 21st century, we now recognise the loss of a pet to be a heartbreaking time for the humans involved.

Support is on offer from many organisations who now realise how devastating pet grief can be, and many independent psychotherapy counsellors also offer one-on-one support for the loss of a pet. Never be afraid to speak out about what you are feeling because trying to hide the dread and fear that follows loss is a sad journey that needn't be taken alone. The websites of the Association For Pet Loss And Bereavement, Pet Loss, the Ralph Site and Support Line all offer invaluable information. Also speaking with other grieving pet owners will help you know you are not alone. Facebook has many pet-loss support groups for people to connect, share photos and talk through their feelings.

In the home many things will remind us of our pet, including their bedding and bowls, so you may wish after a while to remove these items from the home.

Getting a new pet helps us with the grieving process but your new companion should never be looked upon as a replacement. A new pet brings us new life and joy, when we are ready. These pets sometimes get a hard time as expectations of personality are compared to that of the deceased pet. Allow your new pet to show you their individuality and start afresh with new things for them, should this be financially feasible.

Caught up in grief, we must also not forget any companion animals left behind. They may not grieve the same as us, but they will be coping with a change in their territory and will have little understanding of where their daily fur companion is. I discuss cat grief further in Chapter Seven.

The companionship and care given to a pet should help us find the courage to move forward. To know our pets had the best life possible and any decision, if euthanasia was decided, came from the greatest love and respect one can give another. Until that time, their memory and ever-lasting connection will help our hearts beat stronger every day.

CHAPTER SIXTEEN

From Syria With Love:
The Cat Man Of Aleppo, Mohammed Alaa al-Jaleel

'Inside us lies every possibility that is available to a sentient being. Every darkness, every light. It is the choices we make that decide who or what we will be.'

Charles de Lint

FROM SYRIA WITH LOVE

One man's quest to help our feline friends during the most challenging of circumstances left me brimming with admiration and a renewed hope for humanity towards the sentient beings we share this planet with. His name is Mohammed Alaa al-Jaleel, or as he is now known, the Cat Man Of Aleppo.

Mohammed Alaa stayed behind to help the local feral and pet cat population in the middle of a fierce civil war, setting up a sanctuary in Aleppo with the help of Il Gattaro Di Aleppo Organisation[1], a Facebook page set up by Alessandra Abidin in November 2015. Mohammed Alaa's work became famous all over the world.

His journey with cats is one few would be brave enough to make.

In Conversation with Mohammed Alaa al-Jaleel

What's your first memory of cats? Did you have them in your home as a child and do you remember how they made you feel?

We used to visit my grandparents, who had a cat called Bailasan. Every time she had kittens, the rest of our family – 22 uncles and nine aunties – used to reserve one kitten in advance. When it was our turn to take a kitten, my sister, Nailaa, and I were extremely excited. We named our kitten Loulou. It was white with blue eyes just like Bailasan. I was five years old and she was my biggest joy. We did not have a television as it was rare for a Syrian family to have one, but we were happy as we had a kitten.

My sister and I would fight over who would feed, bath and spend time with Loulou, but I felt like Loulou loved my sister more and I started to feel jealous. To solve the problem, my father decided to bring home another cat; a feral one from his workplace. Of course, the two cats did not get along, and to sort out the problem, my father assigned us a task. My sister would clean the new feral cat and I would feed her. This lasted for three years and my sister managed to win the cat's love over me as she normally did.

We had Loulou for seven years, until one day she became ill and disappeared. We felt so sad. I waited for her at the door to come back every day for 15 days. My father tried to comfort us, saying that when a cat falls ill it goes away to die so that the humans who love her don't feel sad.

Three months later I was walking to the ice cream shop when I found a small kitten at the gate of one of the buildings next door. I asked the ice cream man if the kitten belonged to anyone. When he said no, I spoke to my father and we went back together to take the five-month-old kitten home. After we gave her some meat, she felt secure and jumped into my father's lap. We named her Jongar, after a cartoon we used to watch, and she became a big part of our lives.

Before we had our own cats we always looked after the street cats. My father always taught his children to feed them, as they didn't have owners to feed and care for them. He also said the cats couldn't express their feelings or tell us they were hungry and that we should be the ones who take the initiative. That was the family's approach with us children, I guess to make us feel responsible.

What was your life like before the cat sanctuary?

At 21, when I had completed military service, I started to work with an electrical engineer during the summer, and four years later opened my own shop. Wherever I went on a job I carried luncheon meat to feed any street cats I saw. Carrying the meat felt as essential as my house key. I wanted to be a role model and wanted people to see this. I like helping, regardless of whether it's helping an animal or a human. At the time I was caring for three cats called Zeer, Antar and Aflatoun in my shop, as well as the nearby stray cats.

I got married at the age of 25. It was vital that my wife liked cats and would tolerate them in our house. Luckily she did and our first cat was called Alia. I was still working as an electrician, computer programmer and satellite repair engineer when, in 2011, the Syrian civil war broke out. In 2012, my wife and two children, Maram, 12, and Abdouljaleek, 11, fled the country to Istanbul, Turkey, but I stayed in Aleppo. There were not enough ambulances, since most of them were owned by the Syrian regime, so I started working as an ambulance driver, using my own car to take patients for medical treatment.

When did the idea of the sanctuary come into your head and how did you make it happen?

A British journalist was writing a report about the White Helmets[2] and heard about how I was looking after the cats. He decided to do a report on me too. That was the first time in my life that someone wanted to write about me. The article was for the *Telegraph* and it was about how an ambulance man was rescuing people alongside looking after cats.

People around the world read the article and wanted to know more. They were asking the journalists and media people in Aleppo, so I created a Facebook page, and in no time at all it was published on numerous news websites like Smart News and Aleppo News. People were asking me to post about my rescues on a daily basis so they could follow what I was doing.

In the first three days I received 2,500 friend requests, the vast majority of whom were cat lovers and sympathetic about the Syrian crisis. There were diplomats, supermodels, astronauts, artists, and even a member of the Italian Parliament.

Eventually, the Facebook supporters asked me to establish a cat sanctuary, including my good friend Alessandra Abidin. The idea of the sanctuary grew from this seed. After much support from many people, I started to collect the stray cats and managed to secure a house that was previously lived in by a family who fled the war. I adapted the house to make it suitable for cats and started to search for strays that looked in need of help. My Facebook friends helped me with funding for the cats' food and medical supplies. I did encounter some hardship with some of the cats that were once domestic pets, as they kept trying to return to their empty houses, looking for owners who fled the war. Cats often tend to return to where they used to live, but the stray cats stayed. The Il Gattaro Di Aleppo bought a power generator for €3,000, which wasn't only used to process the cats' meat, but also helped out the neighbourhood.

Can you describe your neighbourhood to us? How badly was it affected by the war?

Following the crisis and in 2012 and 2013, I lived in an area called Hanano. It was a residential area which contained more than 300,000 people. The area was lively, busy, peaceful and full of life. It became the destination for lots of people during the war until its population grew to 600,000 people. People came to this area fleeing the severe bombing from the suburbs and from the heart of the city. Following the bombing, life became difficult. During this time, I was looking after the cats, and my supporters asked me to establish the shelter as it was relatively the safest area and was full of parks. The sanctuary was an abandoned park full of rubbish, which I managed to fix and refurbish so that it would be a nice place to look after the cats and to attract the local children. It took us about three months to establish the sanctuary and the play area. In 2016, however, Hanano was subject to severe bombing. The cat sanctuary was completely destroyed: the fence, the trees, the walls and even the ambulance car. Most people fled.

Were the cats already a feral colony in the space made into the cat sanctuary or did they gravitate there? I understand people fleeing the war were giving you their pets also?

Once I started to feed the stray cats, many others started to gravitate to the feeding area. I also started to rescue stray cats from different remote areas since they would not have been aware of my sanctuary. When people found out about the cat sanctuary, many of them brought their pets for me to look after. Others reported abandoned cats that needed help. I would go to the area and call them, or sound my car horn. They became familiar with that and would come out towards me and around my car.

How did the sanctuary run on a daily basis in terms of food and medical resources?

The first original cat sanctuary in Aleppo was bombed by chemical weapons and about 30 cats died, so we had to set up another one. We chose a suburban area and it was much more organised, with funding from Il Gattaro Di Aleppo and various artists in Spain and the USA. They painted me and sold the pictures, with proceeds going to the sanctuary. To get food for the cats I would go to the Turkish-Syrian border to buy meat from the traders. Money from the fund secured the cats' food for about a month in advance. I was in charge of feeding the cats with help from two other people while the local vet took care of the cats' medical needs.

How did your family feel about the cat sanctuary and your decision to remain in such a dangerous situation?

My wife did not appreciate my choice. She asked me to leave with her and told me that if I decided to stay we must separate, which we did three years ago. My children knew how much I loved cats and how keen I was to care for and help them. My family left the border with great difficulty under incessant bombing. I did not want them to leave and they were concerned about me in such a dangerous place.

Are you in touch with them now?

I struggled for the first three months after my family left, and I felt very lonely. My heart remained with them. However, my work here is making up for this loneliness. The fact that I am helping these helpless and powerless creatures, and the many homeless human families, orphans and children; all that makes me less lonely. If they knew the extent of my work, I am sure that my family would be proud of what I am doing and they would understand. I am still in touch with them, but sadly not much.

Have you ever been criticised for staying with the cats rather than leaving with your family?

Of course there were people, mainly relatives, who have been judgmental and critical of me for leaving my family, saying that I could have gone with them. But equally, there are many people who are supporting and encouraging what I am doing. I am sure those criticising me know deep inside that I am doing the right thing. I am certain the right thing for me is to stay here to help people and the cats that I adore. It means a lot to

288 | Chapter Sixteen

me when I see the look in the cats' eyes, waiting for me in anticipation of their food.

Your sanctuary was a ray of hope at such a dark time in Syria and I have read that many children came to visit the cats. Why are cats so important to people, and does this have anything to do with the respect for cats that Islamic culture teaches?

The cat sanctuary became a shelter for the children seeking what they have lost. They gather, play and laugh in this place. In this sanctuary my aim was to teach the children how to love the animals and look after them. I believe that if you want to teach a value to someone, you should start at a young age. I wanted to teach them how to look after these animals and not to harm them and how to have responsibility. Also, I felt that this sanctuary could be a place for the children, to help them forget all their pain and anguish. The children's parents were very happy about this idea and they have noticed the difference in their children's attitude.

Islam, similar to many other religions, strongly advises that we should take care of animals, look after them and feed them. Islam strictly prohibits humans from harming animals and asks that we do not let any ill animals suffer and that we need to put them to sleep if there is no hope of recovery. Also, my family has always believed that cats bring good luck to their people.

Do you care for any other animals besides cats?

I am ready to help all animals in need and have rescued several monkeys who were kept in a birdcage. I offered their owner money to buy them and he agreed to give them to me. The monkeys were in critical condition and about to die. In my attempt to rescue them, one of the monkeys got scared and bit two of my fingers. I have been struggling with the injury for eight months and meanwhile received some funds from my friends to help build a proper cage for the monkeys.

I once heard about some animals in an entertainment park called Magic World that were about to die. There were four lions, three tigers, three jaguars, two dogs and an Asian bear. Initially I said I couldn't help, as it would take a big budget to feed them and to keep them in the right environment. I was also a bit scared to go into the area, as the extremist group Al-Nusra Front made it extremely dangerous to approach. However, I eventually went to visit the animals, and two months later met the person in charge of the park. I did what I could; I told my supporters and they launched a rescue campaign. The Four Paws organisation rescued the animals[3], although other animals at the zoo like the deer, monkeys and the female pregnant bear sadly died due to the bombing and hunger.

How do you juggle fears for your own safety alongside your need to care for and nurture the cats?

One of the difficulties that I encountered as an ambulance man was trying to help people when the areas were being bombed and it was too dangerous to attend. As for the cats, the difficulty was in the shortage of food, medication and vets to provide them with medical care. Many times I had to delay helping them due to the shortage of medical supplies, and I wasn't always able to save them.

One of the other difficulties was the shortage of food. I used to collect leftover meat from the butchers' shop to feed 17 cats. Because of the siege on the area, it was hard to secure food for me, my family and the rest of the people around me. I told my 25,000 online supporters and they suggested a food campaign. Within a week we managed to collect £18,000 towards helping animals and people. I made a list of basic supplies like rice, oil, luncheon meat and sardines for the cats. Part of it was paid for in cash and the rest I borrowed until the funds were transferred. My supporters were really fearful after the siege. What happened in Ghouta[4] regarding food supplies was looking like it was going to happen over here so we arranged to buy the food from several traders who were monopolising food. The price of food was going up due to the monopolisation so my supporters asked me to buy and secure food from the traders until the fund arrived.

Can you describe the original cat sanctuary that was bombed? Did you actually sleep on site, nearby or travel to visit every day?

The sanctuary was located on a piece of land full of stuff that people dumped. I managed to clean it up and planted some trees. I also built a play area for the children and as I was living next door, I visited every day. Often the cats would come and visit me at home, so I was with them on a daily basis; day and night.

Could you stroke the cats or were they feral and unapproachable?

This depended on whether they were strays or had previously lived as indoor pets. There were cats that were approachable, and I was capable of getting close to them whilst others were wild. They would only come over at meal times when I would stand away to let them approach. It was the pet cats that I managed to gain the most trust with. I found no difficulty dealing with them.

Were there any special cats who you became really attached to?

There was a young cat called Teresa. She came to the sanctuary all by herself and was very beautiful with long fur. During mating time I used to bring her all of the kittens so that she could feed them; there were 15 in all. I called her Teresa after the Catholic nun, Mother Teresa, who looked after poor and unfortunate people. The feline Teresa used to sleep in the sanctuary office next to me. People would visit to watch her feeding other cats' kittens.

What was given to the cats for food as time went on and things became more and more difficult?

When I was feeding the cats from my own pocket, I used to buy leftover meat, as that is all I could afford at the time. After receiving funds from my supporters, I started to get them poultry meat and instead of one feed every day, they would get two or three. We had 170 cats at this time, but due to the war we were short of human doctors, never mind vets.

The original cat sanctuary was bombed in 2016 and things became impossible to manage. What was it like?

On 16 October 2016 a fierce raid hit Aleppo. The area where the sanctuary was located suffered the worst of the bombing. We could not move around freely to save people and encountered difficulty securing food. After five days of continuous bombing, the sanctuary was completely gone. The sanctuary dog, Amal, which means hope, was killed, along with a large number of cats. My friends advised that I should move the rest of the surviving cats somewhere safe. I started to collect them and gradually moved them to a storage space beneath a building where it was safe away from the bombing, which had terrified most of the cats and made them run away.

You've started a new sanctuary in a different area. How did you pick yourself up to start again?

I started to evacuate people from the area when the fire from the bombing ceased. I also started to collect the cats and asked departing families moving out of Aleppo to the suburbs to take one or two with them.

On 16 November 2016, I too left Aleppo for the suburbs and in December met my supporters in Kilis, a city in south-central Turkey near to the Syrian border. It was very overwhelming and emotional. One of them said they did not expect to see me after what I'd been through. I was encouraged to travel to a European country, but I refused. They didn't expect that. I refused to travel and told them I would like to start all over again.

In the end we agreed to establish five projects: a sanctuary to save animals, a children's play park, a centre for the disabled and an orphanage, plus a clinic for animals and people. So far we have managed to get four out of the five projects off the ground. We have done the animal sanctuary, a hospital for both humans and animals, a centre for the disabled called Amal, and the children's play park. As for the orphanage, we've started on the building but this has been stopped due to the funds coming into Syria being suspended.

When I decided to return, people supported me very generously to achieve my goal. The financial support reached €20,000 within one year. With this amount we were aiming to expand our support circle to help as many people and animals as we could. The funds were to support many poor families, schools and more. However, I would like to add that, as of 2018, this amount has not been released from the bank accounts. Some charity organisations used to assist me in transferring the charity funds that I received through them and they used to charge me 15% of the amount for doing this. They also wanted me to use their logos by wearing their t-shirts (so that they gain all of the credit). When I refused to wear their logos they stopped helping me with the fund transfer. The reason why we were transferring the donated money through certain charity organisations was because the funds needed to be transferred via registered and authorised organisations to prove that they were not for terrorism purposes.

Did any of your cats suffer trauma from the war?

The cats' behaviour changed when the bombing started to get bad. They were terrified and ran away and those that returned were not approachable anymore. They had lost confidence in humans. The cats started to sense when there was going to be a raid or a bombing and started to act differently. I saw how they would anticipate the hazard before it happened, such as running away before it all started, and missing their meal times.

The cats that I used to bring from the destroyed areas struggled a lot. They were too terrorised and it was difficult to gain their trust again, which could take weeks. I think somehow they knew that what was happening was a result of man.

What would you like the world to know about you, the cats and the war in Syria?

War does not distinguish between strong and weak, elderly or child, animal or human. I know that war is brutal. It financially and spiritually drains everyone, but especially the poor. The poorest and less fortunate are the biggest losers in war because they cannot afford to flee it. The people who are richer manage to escape as they can afford the travel expenses.

I believe that when man is merciful toward the poor and less fortunate, God will stand beside him. Although I faced certain death on many occasions, God saved me each time. Despite all the difficulties I have continued with what I started. With each setback I am more determined to go until the end. War is the worst thing that could happen to humanity. Before this, I never imagined that the impact of war could be so dramatic.

I believe that if we have to be merciful towards each other, we have to be the same towards everything around us. People used to judge me and blame me for trying to save the cats rather than people. I always told them that cats are also living creatures, just like us, and we have to help them.

Cats can bring good luck, as the tales say. I want people who have a good heart, like I feel I have, to know that as a result of my work with cats, I got to know remarkable people all around the world, the people who supported me. As a result of my passion for cats I achieved many things that the government could not do during this critical time. People started to follow my lead. For the first time, the government has issued a directive to establish similar sanctuaries.

What does the future hold for you?

I am aiming to build a hospital for animals and humans. I would like to save all sorts of animals, not only cats, and I would like people to help and support me with this. I would like to spread love and compassion rather than hate and resentment. I want people to help me build things up rather than destroy them. I want people to help humanity by adopting a noble cause and trying to achieve it – despite all odds. My hope was to build a Child Academy, which was going to be launched in August 2018. The philosophy behind this project is to provide everything for the child, which will help to promote their skills and talent and establish a healthy generation of children that can reach their full potential.

Mohammed is a simple man who possesses the type of wealth that money can't buy and wars can't win. A spiritual wealth that holds true riches. A soul that has love. This alone is priceless, for these souls save the world and all who live in it. The interview was conducted with the help of the skilled Arabic translator, Rana Hapal, whose help and patience has been invaluable to me. My heartfelt appreciation and thanks.

EPILOGUE

Whilst waiting for a train on an overground platform at Blackfriars station, I looked out of large glass windows across at the Thames, admiring its skyline and unusual, tall glass-shaped buildings. It was a grey, dreary day of pale light and, being quite early in the morning, nothing stirred.

Then something caught my eye. On the right side of the river where the Thames reveals some of its sand banks at low tide, two small children and a little black dog piqued my interest. The children were running up and down the 'beach' playing with the dog, who seemed mesmerised by their movements; each one of them caught in the moment and seemingly having fun enjoying each other's company.

It dawned on me then that the humans and the dog were engaged in a deep communication, a mutual language that we have taken the time to learn. In this country, we are besotted with the animals that we have labelled 'pets', such as dogs, cats and rabbits. Other animals have sadly been labelled 'food', and so their language has been largely ignored. This book focuses on cats because that's my area of expertise, but I'm painfully aware that the language of others needs to be learned too.

What would they tell us – and would we listen?

ACKNOWLEDGMENTS

Let's Talk About Cats has been two and a half years in the making with plenty of ups and downs. The 'ups' were when the Madeleine Milburn literary agency signed the book, the 'downs' were when most publishers turned the book down, not seeing a market for it, and thus the book was sadly put out to drift again. Rather than allow another year to pass I put my big girl pants on, having shed a few tears, and decided the time was now or never to let my hard work see the light of day. I decided to self-publish and was very moved by the encouragement I received from friends, family and many cat lovers via my social media platforms. As with all books, there are a plethora of helpers and contributors behind the scenes and this section of the book is dedicated to shout-outs to those people, because without their input there would be no book.

I would like to send heartfelt thanks to all of the expert contributors who helped make *Let's Talk About Cats* special: Jackson Galaxy, Briony Smith, Kate Benjamin, Penelope Smith, Sheryl Woods, Samantha Martin, Dr. Pete Coleshaw, Dr. Jessica Walker, Sarah Fisher, Kim Freeman, Dr. Susanne Schötz, Dr. Jennifer Conrad, Dr. Amy Bergs, Isabel Serafim, David Teie and Mohammed Alaa al-Jaleel. Thank you also to people who I cited for their knowledge and expertise. Every effort has been made to correctly acknowledge those individuals.

Let's Talk About Cats originally started as a book of interviews about the lives of cat professionals and people whose lives had been transformed by cats. After feedback from Madeleine Milburn I teamed up with editor Anna Hogarty and the book was rewritten to finetune its message and give it more of my voice than it previously had, answering cat questions along the way. During the rewrite I had to say goodbye to some fantastic interviews but here I would like to thank the contributors for their time and efforts in speaking with me: Temple Grandin, Jo Brand, Jean Philipe, Eliza Katz, Georgina O'Neil, Marc-André Runcie-Unger and Caroline

Paul. I initially was advised to remove the interview with Mohammed Alaa al-Jaleel, the Cat Man Of Aleppo, for reasons of continuity, but his interview was incredibly moving and took so long to get that I decided, seeing as I am now the boss of my own book, to add it at the end as a bonus chapter. The 'lost' interviews were and will be uploaded to my website for all to read.

For encouragement and support along the way I would like to thank, in no particular order, Sharon Williams, Mandy Bell, Jane Lester, Svetlana Broussova, Mohammed Nazam, Marketa Zvelebil, John Palmer and Shana Westfall. I would also like to thank my clients who allowed me to write about their cases and gave me permission to use photos. Thanks also to my very good friend Alexis Countouris. Our walks mean the world to me, especially when I need to step away from the computer to feel some calm and positivity. You exude both.

Special thanks to David Lowe, the editor of my debut book *Claws*, who has been championing me every step of the way in my writing career and who never fails to see the positive in any situation. Thanks to Angelica Tunstall Campion who told me how easy it was to self-publish and gave me the lift I needed to finally take the step into an unknown world. Pushes like these are always needed in life.

Thank you to Dr. Andrew Carmichael, Wendy and Sarah Parish at Addisons Vets who allow me to work at their practice with my most challenging cats and who also take excellent care of my own two cats. Thanks to Jane Wenham Jones for encouragement and for introducing me to publicist guru Katrina Power, who then introduced me to social media guru Anita Chapman. Your work has been hugely appreciated. I thank literary agent Madeleine Milburn for her efforts in trying her hardest for this book and for stating she will always champion me from the sidelines. This kind of support is always needed for the self-publishing author. Also, a special thank you to Sarah Hartwell who gave me her blessing to cite numerous quotes from her extraordinary website Messy Beasts, and to Dr. Lauren Finka for giving me her blessing to cite a paragraph of her work. A big thank you to Giles Clark of the Big Cat Sanctuary for allowing one of his keepers to chat about their work in this book and for use of photos. A huge thank you to Rana Hapal, interpreter, who helped me with the Cat Man Of Aleppo interview. Without her assistance the interview would not have been possible. She went above and beyond to help me when I need further clarifications. Also thanks to Michael Hallam, editor of *Your Cat*, who continues to be really supportive of my writing and who seems a lovely guy to boot! Tony Royden. You are a star. Thanks for guiding me through the minefield of self-publishing and Amazon. Having navigated the maze yourself with your fantastic book *The Dealer* you stopped me from totally freaking out and guided me whenever I ran to you for help. Thanks also to my A team: Deborah Ripley for design skills, not only on the book's cover but also inside, and for assistance with uploading files to Amazon, and Amanda Crook not only for her meticulous final stage line proofing but also for the last minute editing, which has improved the book tremendously. Thanks also to Greg Heath for my author's photo and to the numerous other photographers of the cats that feature in the Cat Chat sections, all of whom have been credited.

Lastly I thank my husband Gordon Hulbert who, with hands tied behind his back, read this book numerous times, checking for mistakes before the manuscript was passed on to a professional. His support and faith in me never wavers. He lifts me up when I'm down about events and he pushes me forward when I lose courage. He is my rock upon which my whole life has been given a solid foundation. I couldn't have had a career with cats without him.

Liked the book? Use hashtag #LetsTalkAboutCats to give a shout out. Would love to hear from you too. Do drop by to say hello:

Twitter @catbehaviourist

Instagram: cat_behaviourist

Facebook: www.facebook.com/catbehaviourist

Mailing list: www.catbehaviourist.com/subscribe

OTHER BOOKS BY ANITA KELSEY

Claws: Confessions Of A Professional Cat Groomer

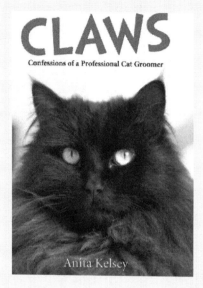

'Laugh out loud funny stories. Definitely a book for cat lovers'
Your Cat magazine

'A real insight into feline behaviour. Hilarious'
Love Sunday magazine (*Daily Mirror*)

*'Great little snapshots into the ordinary lives of the average cat owning
Great British Public!'* – Amazon 5 ***** reviewer

*'The book is beautifully put together, so it would make a lovely gift for the mad
cat person in your life'* – Amazon 5 ***** reviewer

*'I found myself laughing out loud on many occasions and more than once shed
a tear for the sad plight of a cat she was helping'* – Amazon 5 ***** reviewer

Throughout her years visiting people's homes as a cat groomer, Anita Kelsey has
amassed a vast array of funny, cute and ridiculous stories about cats and, of course, their
owners. In *Claws*, she picks out just a few of her favourite tales to share with the reader
from, 'Sammy the Swooner' to 'Tubbs: The Fat Cat Caught in His Flap'.

Claws is a must-have book for all cat lovers, written by an author drawing on a lifetime
of living with and professionally caring for cats in their various guises and with their
eccentricities. In the pages of Anita Kelsey's entertaining and heart-warming book, you'll
meet 20 of the most characterful cats, all eventually calmed and preened to their natural
beauty and animal magnificence by the author. Meet their owners, too, and enjoy Anita's
take on the individual relationships between pet and owner.

AVAILABLE IN HARDBACK AND KINDLE EDITION FROM AMAZON

REFERENCES

Chapter One: How Can I Bond With My Cat?
1. Bugler, C. (2013), *The Cat: 3500 Years Of The Cat In Art*. London: Merrell Books, p.8.
2. Wright, M. and Walters, S. (1980), *The Book Of The Cat*. Pan Books, p.238.
3. Ibid, p.239.
4. Norfolk Mills: www.norfolkmills.co.uk/Watermills/briggate.html [accessed 15 August 2013].
5. Mill Restorations: www.angelfire.com/journal/millrestoration/cat.html [accessed 15 August 2013].
6. Wikipedia, 'Ship's Cat': https://en.wikipedia.org/wiki/Ship%27s_cat
7. Loxton, H. (1990), *The Noble Cat*. Portland House, p.238.
8. Tabor, R. (1991), *Cats: The Rise Of The Cat*. London: BBC Books, p.31.
9. Pohutu (2012), 'Women And Cats: Enemies Of The Church', Three Wise Women: http://threewisewomen.wordpress.com/2012/01/12/women-and-cats-enemies-of-the-church [accessed 15 August 2013].
10. Tabor, R. (1991), *Cats: The Rise Of The Cat*. London: BBC Books, p.52.

Cat Chat: The Cat–Human Relationship: Starring Dicey Doos
1. The Cat Fanciers Association: http://cfa.org/Breeds/BreedsKthruR/Ragdoll.aspx [accessed 13 May 2018].

Chapter Two: How Similar Is My Cat's Behaviour To A Wild Cat's?
1. The Big Cat Sanctuary is based in Smarden, Kent, and is dedicated to the captive breeding of endangered big cats within the European Endangered Species Programmes, with the aim of providing animals for scientifically based re-introduction projects: http://thebigcatsanctuary.org/
2. Wikipedia, 'Flehmen Response': https://en.wikipedia.org/wiki/Flehmen_response [accessed 3 September 2018].
3. Pica is the term for eating or chewing non-edible items. International Cat Care: https://icatcare.org/advice/pica-in-cats/ [accessed 3 September 2018].

Cat Chat: Wild At Heart: The Importance Of Play
1. Case, L.P. (2003), *The Cat: Its Behavior, Nutrition And Health*. Iowa State Press, pp.126–27.

Chapter Three: Do Cats Like Music?
1. Snowdon, T.C., Teie, D. and Savage, M. (2015), 'Cats Prefer Species-Appropriate Music', *Applied Animal Behaviour Science*, Vol. 166, pp.106–11: www.sciencedirect.com/science/article/abs/pii/S016815911500060X [accessed 19 January 2019].
2. Stanford, E. (2015) 'Music To Cats' Ears', 30 October: www.nytimes.com/2015/11/01/style/cat-music-for-cats-david-teie.html [accessed 15 June 2018].
3. McDermott, J. and Hauser, M. (2007), 'Nonhuman Primates Prefer Slow Tempos But Dislike Music Overall', *Cognition*, 104, pp.654–68: www.researchgate.net/publication/6853752_Nonhuman_primates_prefer_slow_tempos_but_dislike_music_overall [accessed 27 June 2018].

4. Hampton, A., Ford, A., Cox, R.E., Liu, C.C., Koh, R. (2019), 'Effects Of Music On Behavior And Physiological Stress Response Of Domestic Cats In A Veterinary Clinic', Pub Med, US National Library Of Medicine: www.ncbi.nlm.nih.gov/pubmed/30744475 [accessed 13 May 2019].

Cat Chat: Do Cats Absorb Human Energy?

1. Merola, I., Lazzaroni, M., Marshall-Pescini, S., Prato-Previde, E. (2019), 'Social Referencing And Cat–Human Communication', Pub Med, US National Library Of Medicine: www.ncbi.nlm.nih.gov/pubmed/25573289 [accessed 13 May 2019].
2. Finka, L.R., Ward, J., Farnworth, M.J. and Mills, D.S. (2019), 'Owner Personality And The Wellbeing Of Their Cats Share Parallels With The Parent-Child Relationship', PLOS ONE, 14(2), e0211862: https://doi.org/10.1371/journal.pone.0211862 [accessed 25 July 2020].
3. Dolan, E. (2019), 'Cats Tend To Be Less Healthy And More Anxious When Their Owners Are Neurotic', PsyPost: www.psypost.org/2019/02/cats-tend-to-be-less-healthy-and-more-anxious-when-their-owners-are-neurotic-53133 [accessed: 13 May 2019].

Chapter Four: Why Does My Cat Scratch Furniture?

1. Case, L.P. (2003), *The Cat: Its Behavior, Nutrition and Health.* Iowa State Press, pp.38–39.
2. Conrad, J., Wendelburg, K., Santinelli, S., Park, A. and American Association Of Zoo Veterinarians (2006), 'Deleterious Effects Of Onychectomy Declawing In Exotic Felids', TIB: www.tib.eu/en/search/id/BLCP%3ACN062985548/DELETERIOUS-EFFECTS-OF-ONYCHECTOMYDECLAWING-IN/ [accessed 13 February 2019].
3. Conrad, J., 'Declaw Surgery', The Paw Project: www.pawproject.org/declaw-surgery/ [accessed 13 February 2019].
4. American Veterinary Medical Association (AVMA), 'Declawing Of Domestic Cats': www.avma.org/KB/Policies/Pages/Declawing-of-Domestic-Cats.aspx [accessed 13 February 2019].
5. A list of declawing legislation around the world can be viewed here: https://en.wikipedia.org/wiki/Onychectomy
6. Hanson, H. (2019). Huffington Post. 'New York Becomes First State To Ban Cat Declawing'. https://www.huffingtonpost.co.uk/entry/cat-declawing-ban-new-york-state_n_5cf82ed0e4b0e3e3df14ab28?guccounter=1&guce_referrer=aHR0cHM6Ly93d3cuZ29vZ2xlLmNvbS8&guce_referrer_sig=AQAAAKRQEdonL3HYFtwhN0SWli8LaDBzjvlBOJceMCLDcR1lME1M6ubui_DtbS-NDS5ayq2rwIl-Xu6kdojQaI00kxIVMiQb76uBA8ruRO5hR5lHdZ_2Bn_wnImSyGGU2M60N8HAq82-txnF9P_QsDAKEhch6sJBSEAdmERb02uK-AB [accessed 8 August 2019]

Cat Chat: Cat Claw Covers And Other Alternatives

1. Kernot, H. (2017), 'Claw Covers Cause For Concern – Charity', *Vet Times*: www.vettimes.co.uk/news/claw-covers-cause-for-concern-charity/ [accessed 16 May 2019].

Chapter Five: I've Lost My Cat: What Should I Do?

Cat Chat. Letting Your Cat Out For The First Time.

1. Finka, L. (2019), *Your Cat* magazine, July, pp.42–44.
2. Cats Of Australia, 'Cat Enclosures': www.catsofaustralia.com/cat-enclosures.htm [accessed 25 May 2019].

3. *Your Cat* magazine, (2019), June, p.17.

4. Huang, L., Coradini, M., Rand, J., Morton, J., Albrecht, K., Wasson, B. and Robertson, D. (2017), 'Search Methods Used To Locate Missing Cats And Locations Where Missing Cats Are Found', US National Library Of Medicine: www.ncbi. nlm.nih.gov/pmc/articles/PMC5789300/ [accessed 19 January 2019].

5. Smith, L. (2019), 'Mum Claims Cat-napper Is Refusing To Return Beloved Family Pet': www.mirror.co.uk/news/uk-news/mum-claims-cat-napper-refusing-13925573 [accessed 16 May 2019].

Chapter Six: Can Our Cats Talk To Us?

1. David, N. (2019), 'Cats Can Recognise Their Own Names, Say Scientists', *The Guardian*: www.theguardian.com/science/2019/apr/04/cats-can-recognise-their-own-names-say-scientists [accessed 16 May 2019].

2. 'Melody In Human–Cat Communication (Meowsic)' (2016): http://vr.humlab. lu.se/projects/meowsic/ [accessed 13 February 2019].

Cat Chat: Interpreting Cat Language: How Else Do Cats Communicate?

1. Cat Time, 'Manx': https://cattime.com/cat-breeds/manx-cat#/slide/1 [accessed 25 May 2019].

2. Case, L.P. (2003), *The Cat: Its Behavior, Nutrition and Health.* Iowa State Press, pp.41–43.

3. Ibid, p.46.

4. Ibid, p.133.

Chapter Seven: Do Cats Grieve?

1. Brown, A.E. (1879), 'Grief In The Chimpanzee', *The American Naturalist*, 13(3), pp.173–75.

2. Silvestro, R. (2012), 'Are Other Animals Aware Of Death?', National Wildlife Federation: www.nwf.org/Magazines/National-Wildlife/2013/DecJan/Animals/ Animal-Mourning [accessed 3 July 2019].

3. Walker, J., McGrath, N., Handel, I., Waran, N., Phillips, C. (2014), 'Does Owning A Companion Animal Influence The Belief That Animals Experience Emotions Such As Grief?', *Animal Welfare*, 23, pp.71–79: https://doi. org/10.7120/09627286.23.1.071 [accessed 23 July 2020].

4. YouTube, 'Cat Tries To Revive Dead Friend': www.youtube.com/ watch?v=zaP7STV1aFs [accessed 2 July 2019].

5. YouTube, 'Two Cats React To Their Brother's Death': www.youtube.com/ watch?v=NAH2-JPfupE [accessed 2 July 2019].

6. YouTube, 'My Cat Tries To Revive His Dead Friend': www.youtube.com/ watch?v=DGvxZQI4yUc [accessed 2 July 2019].

Cat Chat: Toby And His Broken Heart: The Hidden World Of Cat Grief

1. Hartwell, S. (2004), 'When Cats Grieve': http://messybeast.com/cat-grief.htm [accessed 9 August 2016].

Chapter Eight: Can Cats Communicate Telepathically?

1. Sheldrake, R. (2012), 'Is Your Pet Psychic?', Mail Online: www.dailymail.co.uk/ femail/article-2084017/A-Cambridge-scientist-believes-seen-beginning-animals-telepathicpowers.html [accessed 19 May 2019].

2. Penelope Smith talks about the consultations of Peaches and Muffin in her book *Animal Talk: Interspecies Telepathic Communication*. Atria Books/Beyond Words (2008, reprint edition), pp.5–6, 84–86.

3. Wiktionary, 'Anima': https://en.wiktionary.org/wiki/anima [accessed 13 February 2019].

4. See Note 2 above.

Chapter Nine: Can Cats Be Trained?

1. Olmon, M. (2004), *Zeke* [video]: https://vimeo.com/8042668 [accessed 13 February 2019].

2. Bailey, M. and Bailey, B., 'Operant Conditioning And Behavior Analysis Workshop', Behavior1.com: www.behavior1.com/page10.html [accessed 13 February 2019].

Cat Chat: The History Of Clicker Training

1. Wikipedia, 'Operant Conditioning': https://en.wikipedia.org/wiki/Operant_conditioning [accessed 25 October 2012].

2. Wikipedia, 'Edward Thorndike': https://en.wikipedia.org/wiki/Edward_Thorndike [accessed 25 October 2012].

3. Skinner, B.F. (1951), 'How To Teach Animals', *Scientific American*, 185, pp.26–29.

4. Skinner, B.F. (1938), *The Behaviour Of Organisms: An Experimental Analysis*. New York: Appleton-Century-Crofts.

5. Pryor, K. (2013), 'History of Clicker Training I': www.clickertraining.com/node/153 [accessed 6 July 2016].

6. Pryor, K. (2001), *Getting Started: Clicker Training For Cats*. Karen Pryor Clicker Training.

7. Shelby Humane, 'Clicker Training Your Pet': https://shelbyhumane.org/wp-content/uploads/sites/10/2016/09/Clicker-Training-Your-Pet.pdf

8. Wilkes, G., 'Clicker Training: 'What It Isn't': www.clickandtreat.com/Clicker_Training/GG/GG001/ff001.htm [accessed 26 June 2016].

9. 'Pavlov's Dogs And Classical Conditioning', *Psychologist World*: www.psychologistworld.com/behavior/pavlov-dogs-classical-conditioning [accessed 25 July 2020].

10. Cherry, K. (2019), 'What Is Classical Conditioning?', Very Well Mind: www.verywellmind.com/classical-conditioning-2794859 [accessed 19 May 2019].

Chapter Ten: Why Do Cats Need To Be Groomed?

1. Engel, C. (2003), *Wild Health: Lessons In Natural Wellness From The Animal Kingdom*. Houghton Mifflin Harcourt.

2. Wikipedia, 'Lysozyme': https://en.wikipedia.org/wiki/Lysozyme [accessed 25 May 2019].

3. Bender, K. (2019), 'Kitty Cure: New Research Suggests An End To Severe Cat Allergies Could Be In Sight', *People*: https://people.com/pets/purina-research-end-cat-allergies/ [accessed 8 July 2019].

Chapter Eleven: What Should I Be Feeding My Cat?

1. International Cat Care (2019), 'TB In UK Cats Fed A Commercial Raw Food Diet': https://icatcare.org/tb-in-uk-cats-fed-a-commercial-raw-food-diet/ [accessed 25 May 2019].

Cat Chat: Cat Food Labelling: What Does It All Mean?

1. Cannon, M. and Forster-Van Hijfte, M. (2006), *Feline Medicine: A Practical Guide For*

Veterinary Nurses And Technicians. Elsevier Butterworth Heinemann, pp.39–53.

2. Case, L.P. (2003), *The Cat: Its Behavior, Nutrition and Health*. Iowa State Press, pp.289–314.

3. Wright, M. and Walters, S. (1980), *The Book Of The Cat*. Pan Books, pp.148–51.

4. Association Of American Feed Control Officials (AAFCO): https://petfood.aafco. org/Labeling-Labeling-Requirements [accessed 25 October 2012].

5. The Dog Food Project (2007), 'Identifying Better Products', Blog: www. dogfoodproject.com/index.php?page=betterproducts [accessed 13 August 2012].

6. FDA, US Food and Drug Administration: www.fda.gov/ICECI/ ComplianceManuals/CompliancePolicyGuidanceManual/ucm074712.htm [accessed 25 October 2012].

7. Food Gov UK: https://www.food.gov.uk/business-guidance/pet-food

8. Wikipedia, 'Meat and Bone Meal': http://en.wikipedia.org/wiki/Meat_meal [accessed 25 October 2012].

9. WikiVet, 'Bovine Spongiform Encephalopathy': http://en.wikivet.net/Bovine_ Spongiform_Encephalopathy [accessed 25 October 2012].

10. Chinyama, M.P.M. (2010), 'Alternative Fuels In Cement Manufacturing': www. intechopen.com/books/alternative-fuel/alternative-fuels-in-cement-manufacturing [accessed 25 July 2020].

11. Wikipedia, 'Fish Meal': https://en.wikipedia.org/wiki/Fish_meal [accessed 25 July 2020].

12. Wikipedia, 'Bycatch': https://en.wikipedia.org/wiki/Bycatch [accessed 25 July 2020].

13. Department For Agriculture, Environment and Rural Affairs (DAERA), 'Animal By-products General Guidance': https://www.daera-ni.gov.uk/articles/animal-products-general-guidance [accessed 25 July 2020].

14. Ibid.

15. DAERA (2017), 'Pet Food Manufacture': www.daera-ni.gov.uk/publications/pet-food-manufacture [accessed 27 July 2020].

16. Food Standards Agency, 'Pet Food': www.food.gov.uk/business-guidance/pet-food [accessed 25 July 2020].

17. Crude ash in dog food is described here: www.purepetfood.com/help/what-is-crude-ash-in-dog-food/ [accessed 27 July 2020].

18. Green Acres Kennel Shop, 'Understanding Pet Food Ingredients': www. greenacreskennel.com/products/pet-food/information/understanding-pet-food-ingredients.html [accessed 27 July 2020].

19. BBC News (2007), 'China Cracks Down On Food Safety': http://news.bbc. co.uk/1/hi/business/6638113.stm [accessed 25 July 2020].

20. Eckhouse, J., Pet food rendering article, *San Francisco Chronicle*. The series ran 19–20 February 1990. The 19 February article started on page C1, while the 20 February article began on page B1. The article is not available online but a copy was sent to me via the newspaper.

21. Pearson, L.A. 'Feeding Your Cat. Know The Basics Of Feline Nutrition': https:// catinfo.org/ [accessed 3 June 2020].

22. Rowe, E., Browne, W., Casey, R., Gruffydd-Jones, T. and Murray, J. (2015), 'Risk Factors Identified For Owner-Reported Feline Obesity At Around One Year Of

Age: Dry Diet And Indoor Lifestyle', Pub Med, US National Library Of Medicine: https://pubmed.ncbi.nlm.nih.gov/26265631/ [accessed 10 July 2019].

Chapter Twelve: How Can I Enrich My Cat's Living Space?

1. Ikea Hackers (Blog): www.ikeahackers.net/category/hacks/pet-furniture/cats [accessed 20 June 2020].

Cat Chat: How To Keep Your Indoor Cat Happy

1. Pet MD, 'Why Do Cats Eat Grass?': www.petmd.com/cat/wellness/evr_ct_eating_grass [accessed 24 May 2019].

Chapter Fourteen: Can Cats Be Therapy Pets?

1. Rosen, A. (1997), 'Obituary: Leslie Scott Ordish': www.independent.co.uk/news/people/obituary-lesley-scott-ordish-1267630.html [accessed 7 June 2019].

2. Qureshi, A., Zeeshan Memon, M., Vazquez, G. and Suri, M.F.K., 'Cat Ownership And The Risk Of Fatal Cardiovascular Diseases. Results From The Second National Health and Nutrition Examination Study Mortality Follow-up Study', *Journal Of Vascular and Interventional Neurology*: www.ncbi.nlm.nih.gov/pmc/articles/PMC3317329/ [accessed 7 June 2019].

3. O'Donnell, J. (2019) 'Talking To Your Pet Is Not So Wacky After All. It's Actually Good For You – And Your Health', *USA Today*: https://eu.usatoday.com/story/news/health/2019/05/07/mental-health-talking-your-adoring-pets-actually-goodyou/1128473001/ [accessed 7 June 2019].

Chapter Fifteen: How To Care For Elderly Cats

1. International Cat Care, 'How To Tell Your Cat's Age In Human Years': https://icatcare.org/advice/how-to-tell-your-cats-age-in-human-years/ [accessed 18 June 2019].

2. Hardie, E.M., Roe, S.C. and Martin, F.R. (2002), 'Radiographic Evidence Of Degenerative Joint Disease In Geriatric Cats', *Journal Of The American Veterinary Medical Association*, Vol. 220, 5, pp.628–32: www.ncbi.nlm.nih.gov/pubmed/12418522 [accessed 16 May 2020].

Cat Chat: Saying Goodbye

1. Wikipedia, 'Kübler Ross Model': https://en.wikipedia.org/wiki/K%C3%BCbler-Ross_model [accessed 27 May 2019].

2. Henry-Jones, E. (2016), 'The Grief Of Losing A Pet Is Traumatic And Universal. So Why Don't We Talk About It?', *The Guardian*: www.theguardian.com/lifeandstyle/2016/dec/22/the-grief-of-losing-a-pet-is-traumatic-and-universal-so-why-dont-we-talk-about-it [accessed 27 May 2019].

3. Winch, G. (2018), 'Why We Need To Take Pet Loss Seriously', *Scientific American*: www.scientificamerican.com/article/why-we-need-to-take-pet-loss-seriously/ [accessed 27 May 2019].

Chapter Sixteen: From Syria With Love

1. Ibraham, M.A., Mahran, M., Nelson, M., Demillo, K. (2016) 'A Crowd-Sourced Animal Sanctuary In East Aleppo Teaches Compassion: 'To Love The Small, Weak Cats Is To Love Everything', *Syria Direct*, 30 August: https://syriadirect.org/news/a-crowd-sourced-animal-sanctuary-in-east-aleppo-teaches-compassion-

%E2%80%98to-love-the-small-weak-cats-is-to-love-everything%E2%80%99/ [accessed 13 June 2018].

2. Wikipedia, 'White Helmets (Syrian Civil War)': https://en.wikipedia.org/wiki/ White_Helmets_(Syrian_Civil_War) [accessed 18 June 2018].

3. Guynup, S. (2017) 'How Syrian Zoo Animals Escaped A War Ravaged Zoo', *National Geographic*, 5 October: https://news.nationalgeographic.com/2017/10/ wildlife-watch-rescuing-animals-aleppo-syria-zoo/ [accessed 19 June 2018].

4. Asfar, R. (2017) 'The Lucrative Business Of Smuggling Supplies Into Syria's Besieged Eastern Ghouta', PRI, 27 April: www.pri.org/stories/2017-04-27/ lucrative-business-smuggling-supplies-syrias-besieged-eastern-ghouta [accessed 19 June 2018].

Recommended Books By Contributors

Total Cat Mojo: The Ultimate Guide To Life With Your Cat – Jackson Galaxy with Mikel Delgado – Tarcher Perigee

Cat Daddy: What The World's Most Incorrigible Cat Taught Me About Life, Love, And Coming Clean – Jackson Galaxy – Tarcher Perigee

Catify To Satisfy: Simple Solutions For Creating A Cat-Friendly Home – Jackson Galaxy and Kate Benjamin – Tarcher Perigee

Catification: Designing A Happy And Stylish Home For Your Cat (And You!) – Jackson Galaxy and Kate Benjamin – Tarcher Perigee

Animal Talk: Interspecies Telepathic Communication – Penelope Smith – Atria Books/Beyond Words

When Animals Speak: Techniques For Bonding With Animal Companions – Penelope Smith – Atria Books/Beyond Words

The Secret Language Of Cats – Susanne Schötz – HQ

How To Find Your Lost Cat: Advice From A Pet Detective – Kim Freeman

The Last Sanctuary In Aleppo: A Remarkable True Story Of Courage, Hope And Survival – Mohammed Alaa Al-Jaleel and Diana Dar – Headline

Contributor Websites

Kate Benjamin: www.hauspanther.com/about

Briony Smith, the Big Cat Sanctuary: http://thebigcatsanctuary.org

Dr. Jennifer Conrad: www.pawproject.org

Kim Freeman: www.LostCatFinder.com

Penelope Smith: www.animaltalk.net

Samantha Martin: https://rockcatsrescue.org

Dr. Susanne Schötz: http://vr.humlab.lu.se/projects/meowsic/about.html

Dr. Pete Coldshaw: https://jaffavets.com

Dr. Amy Bergs: https://thecatdoctor.co.uk

Sarah Fisher: www.ttouchtteam.org.uk

David Teie: www.musicforcats.com

Sheryl Woods: http://wetwhisker.com

Photo Credits

Kate Benjamin – John Burcham photography

Briony Smith – Alma Leaper

Penelope Smith – Art Rosch

Susanne Schötz – Lars Gustafsson

Jackson Galaxy – Dan Komoda

David Teie – Mona Sosa at Lady Dinah's Cat Emporium, London

Jennifer Conrad – Jim Jensvold

Lion suckling on arm

Samantha Martin – Sandra Rust

Tips For Teaching Your Cat To Enjoy Grooming – Cat: Ashabelle Hugo bred by Maria and Waldemar Tomo – owned by/photo credit Bettina Rupp

Sarah Fisher – Bob Atkins

Pete Coleshaw – Jaffa's Veterinary Practice

History of Clicker training. Kitten photo – Wendy Hackles

Mohammed Alaa Al-Jaleel – permission granted

All other cat photos – Anita Kelsey

Printed in Great Britain
by Amazon